The Episcopal Church in Crisis

**Recent Titles in
Religion, Politics, and Public Life**

The Faith Factor: How Religion Influences American Elections
John C. Green

The Episcopal Church in Crisis
How Sex, the Bible, and Authority
Are Dividing the Faithful

Frank G. Kirkpatrick

Religion, Politics, and Public Life

Under the auspices of the Leonard E. Greenberg Center for the Study of
Religion in Public Life, Trinity College, Hartford, CT

Mark Silk, Series Editor

Westport, Connecticut
London

Library of Congress Cataloging-in-Publication Data

Kirkpatrick, Frank G.
    The Episcopal Church in crisis : how sex, the Bible, and authority are dividing the faithful /
    Frank G. Kirkpatrick.
        p. cm. — (Religion, politics, and public life, ISSN 1934-290X)
    Includes bibliographical references and index.
    ISBN-13: 978-0-313-34662-0 (alk. paper)
1. Episcopal Church. 2. Anglican Communion—United States—Forecasting. 3. Twenty-first
century—Forecasts. I. Title.
BX5930.3.K57 2008
283'.7309049—dc22   2008008994

British Library Cataloguing in Publication Data is available.

Library of Congress Catalog Card Number: 2008008994
ISBN-13: 978-0-313-34662-0
ISSN: 1934-290X

First published in 2008

Praeger Publishers, 88 Post Road West, Westport, CT 06881
An imprint of Greenwood Publishing Group, Inc.
www.praeger.com

Printed in the United States of America

The paper used in this book complies with the
Permanent Paper Standard issued by the National
Information Standards Organization (Z39.48–1984).

10 9 8 7 6 5 4 3 2 1

To: My family: Liz, Amy, Dan, Jeff, and Penne.
May they find hope in the Church despite its discontents.

Contents

Series Foreword

In recent years, there has been no bigger story in American Protestantism than the civil war within the Episcopal Church. Brewing under the surface for some time, the conflict broke out in 2003, when the Church's General Convention ratified the election of Gene Robinson, an open and partnered gay priest, as Bishop of New Hampshire. The result was an uproar, both among Episcopalians and within the larger family of Anglicans around the world. Five years later, the Episcopal Church appears to be sliding into a species of schism, and its status in the Anglican Communion—the worldwide association of churches that derive from the Church of England—is anything but clear. What is clear is that the drama has captured worldwide attention.

The Episcopal Church has hardly been alone among American religious bodies in struggling with issues related to homosexuality. As the movement to secure equal rights for gays and lesbians (as well as recognition of the naturalness or "normalcy" of same sex orientation) has achieved considerable success in secular society, the country's faith communities have needed to determine what stance to take, and for most this has meant addressing traditional Judeo-Christian prohibitions, or what appear to be prohibitions, of sexual acts between men. Some bodies—including the Roman Catholic Church and conservative evangelical Protestant denominations—have simply reaffirmed condemnations of the sin even as they, to varying degrees, have expressed their love and understanding of the sinner. At the liberal end of the spectrum, Unitarians, Reform Jews, and the United Church of Christ, among others, have declared their full acceptance of gays and lesbians. But in the middle, and particularly in what is often called Mainline Protestantism, gay marriage is only the latest in a series of issues regarding gender and sexuality that have created prolonged and often bitter divisions. A generation ago, the role of women was front and center, and although that issue has largely been resolved in favor of equal rights, there is little question that, for many conservative mainliners, the question of the status of gays in the clergy has been more like a last straw than an isolated case.

As the preeminent mainline denomination in the country—if preeminence is to be judged by its historical wealth and social prestige—the Episcopal Church was bound to draw considerable attention when push came to shove. But it is the international context that has given this conflict its particular salience. By even the most generous estimates, the conservatives constitute a relatively small minority of the denomination. In a purely domestic religious body like the United Methodist Church or the Presbyterian Church USA, such a secessionist minority might cause some internal disarray, but would attract only limited attention outside the denominational walls. But in their secessionist effort, what the conservatives have in mind is to supplant the Episcopal Church within the Anglican Communion, and to that end they have enlisted conservative bishops from the Southern Hemisphere in their behalf. Those who were once missionized are now asked to oversee those who once sent out the missionaries, while the once lordly Archbishop of Canterbury, titular head of the Communion, forlornly seeks to keep the peace. The global ironies abound.

In these pages, Frank Kirkpatrick provides a blow-by-blow account of how all this has come to pass. The major episodes, from meetings of bishops in the United States, in England, and around the world to important pronouncements from left, right, and center, are carefully laid out and discussed. Anyone wishing to know the players and understand the plays will find *The Episcopal Church in Crisis* indispensable. To be sure, the story ends *in medias res*—in the midst of a series of events that has not come close to ending. But whether the end is with a bang, a whimper, or something in between, there is unlikely to be a more scrupulous detailing than what is on offer here. And even though the events will push the story beyond what is told in its pages, this book will remain essential reading for the historical and theological context and meaning that constitute its deepest concerns. How does the present conflict relate to the long-standing Anglican (and Episcopalian) tradition of inclusiveness? What is the nature of doctrinal and ecclesial authority in this tradition? Frank Kirkpatrick, himself an Episcopal priest and a liberal, here confronts his church with questions that cannot be avoided.

At the risk of speaking out of school, I should mention that I have been a colleague of Frank's for the past dozen years at Trinity College. I have worked with him in the Department of Religion, served under him when he served as interim dean of faculty, and edited articles of his on this subject for *Religion in the News,* the magazine of the center I direct. The fair-mindedness he brings to this most heated of subjects is remarkable only if you do not know him, for Frank is the most fair-minded member of the academic profession I have ever met, perhaps even to a fault. Conservatives will profit as much or more than liberals from their encounter with his acute theologian's mind, and will come away from this volume wiser than they went in, whatever answers they return to the questions that he poses.

Mark Silk
Hartford, Connecticut
February 2008

Acknowledgments

I would like to thank those who have helped me think through and understand more fully the issues, workings, and potential in the Episcopal Church: Bishops Mark Hollingsworth, Andrew Smith, and Arthur Walmsley. I also want to thank a number of lay and clergy for their insights into the issues the book takes up: Anne Brewer, Gerald Carroon, Leslie Desmangles, Abosede George, Donald Hamer, James Jones, Kathleen Jones, James Kowalski, Ian Markham, Richard Nolan, Borden Painter, Mary-Jane Rubenstein, Richard Tombaugh, and Alan Tull. I am also grateful to Ian Douglas and Randall Balmer for their critical and helpful comments during the final stages of bringing the book to completion. Finally, I want to offer a special thanks to Mark Silk who inspired the book in the first place and whose wisdom and insight into things religious brought a depth to the study that would not otherwise have been possible.

Abbreviations

AAC	American Anglican Council
ABC	Archbishop of Canterbury
AC	Anglican Communion
ACC	Anglican Consultative Council
BCP	Book of Common Prayer
ECUSA	The Episcopal Church in the United States of America
PB	Presiding Bishop
TEC	The Episcopal Church
ENS	Episcopal News Service
ELO	Episcopal Life Online
NYT	*New York Times*
RNS	Religious News Service

"The Second Coming" *

W. B. Yeats

Turning and turning in the widening gyre
The falcon cannot hear the falconer;
Things fall apart; the centre cannot hold;
Mere anarchy is loosed upon the world,
The blood-dimmed tide is loosed, and everywhere
The ceremony of innocence is drowned;
The best lack all conviction, while the worst
Are full of passionate intensity.
Surely some revelation is at hand;
Surely the Second Coming is at hand.
The Second Coming! Hardly are those words out
When a vast image out of Spiritus Mundi
Troubles my sight: somewhere in the sands of the desert.

A shape with lion body and the head of a man,
A gaze blank and pitiless as the sun,
Is moving its slow thighs, while all about it
Reel shadows of the indignant desert birds.
The darkness drops again; but now I know
That twenty centuries of stony sleep
were vexed to nightmare by a rocking cradle,
And what rough beast, its hour come round at last,
Slouches towards Bethlehem to be born?

* With apologies to Yeats, I will be using phrases from this poem as epigrams for the chapters of the book. The use of these phrases is not intended to be a commentary on or a reflection of the meaning of his poem.

Introduction

> The issue of whether gays and lesbians in committed relationships can have their unions blessed by their churches may be the single most divisive issue in U.S. Christianity today. Presbyterian, Methodist and Lutheran denominations all are torn over the issue. But it plays out dramatically on a global scale among Anglicans, who are the largest, most unified Protestant body in the world.

So wrote *San Francisco Chronicle* reporter Matthai Chakko Kuruvila on October 1, 2007.[1] There is a great deal of truth in his observation even though, as I hope to show, the divisions both within the Episcopal Church and between it and other churches in the global Anglican Communion of which it is a part also center around issues of Biblical interpretation, what Anglican tradition means, and the ambiguous nature of Anglican ecclesiastical authority.

It is ironic that the Episcopal Church in the United States of America (referred to as TEC or ECUSA) finds itself in this position. Its reputation (at least among non-Episcopalians) is that of a church primarily for the well-educated, well-bred, white middle and upper classes, many of whom have a particular fondness for all things English, or, as they like to say, Anglican. The Episcopal Church, once called the Republican party at prayer in the United States as its ecclesiastical predecessor in England was referred to as the Tory party at prayer, is not generally known for fiery evangelicalism, counterculturalism, radical prophetic action on behalf of the marginalized, or bold experiments in sexual ethics. But today its profile is quite different from this popular stereotype, even as its ability to attract and hold members continues to be challenged. It has garnered a disproportionate amount of publicity over the past five years and may well continue to do so as media rumors of major defections in its ranks continue to swirl, despite being greatly overblown.

Perhaps as a bellwether for other denominations, TEC is undergoing severe tension regarding its policies and practices with respect to homosexuality, at

least from a small if extremely vocal portion of its membership in the United
States but, more importantly, from a much larger number of Anglicans abroad.
This is because TEC is part of what is known as the Anglican Communion, a
body of churches around the world having historic links to the Church of England through its ecclesiastical head, the Archbishop of Canterbury.

The tension both within TEC and between it and the global communion
revolves around the following issues:

1. What is the authority of the Bible for proper moral practice?

2. What does the Bible say about human sexuality, and homosexuality in particular?

3. What are the appropriate principles for interpreting the Bible?

4. What protocols and authorities are in a position to adjudicate disputes within the
   Communion over these issues?

5. What does the history of Anglicanism contribute to an understanding of how the
   Communion should deal with these issues if it wants to be in continuity with its
   historical tradition?

There are also numerous subissues under these overarching ones that we shall
unpack in due course.

TEC is a denomination whose influence on American society is disproportionate to its size. Based on 2002–2004 data, it has lost nearly a third of its
membership since 1960, and presently claims roughly 2.3 million adherents.
Nevertheless, 10 percent of the members of the U.S. Senate identify themselves
as Episcopalians. And its "progressive" actions on women's ordination, civil
rights, and now homosexuality put it far ahead of many of its peer denominations. But as the *Chronicle* writer suggests, it is at the center of one of the most
divisive issues in the Christian churches today, and the way in which it is handling it has global implications because it belongs to a global organization
unlike any other Protestant or non–Roman Catholic denomination. Understanding how the Episcopal Church got itself into the present set of crises that challenge it and how it might be able to address those challenges without
disintegrating could provide a paradigm for other denominations. Most of them
will not have the global institutional issues of polity and governance that are
part of TEC's relation to other Anglicans around the world, but precisely
because we live in an increasingly interconnected world, the experiences of
TEC have wide-ranging significance for a form of Christianity that is, in principle, world-encompassing. How to be respectful to its global communion partners while remaining true to its interpretation of the authority of the Bible,
faithful to the experiences of many of its gay and lesbian members, and loyal
to its commitment to justice for the oppressed as that is experienced in the
context of American life and culture are the tasks that confront it. This book
intends to introduce this denomination to a non-Episcopal audience and, at the
same time, to illuminate for Episcopalians the historical background of the

development of Anglicanism to which all sides appeal, a history that may not be well known despite the claims by all sides that they are true to the Anglican "tradition."

This is a story that will be told in multiple parts. I will begin with the election and confirmation of an openly gay partnered man to the episcopate of the Diocese of New Hampshire. I will then set out the recent history of actions within and by the Church and the Communion leading up to that event, which shook the Anglican Communion to its core and which continues, in many ways, to define all the subsequent events that some predict may lead to irrevocable splits both within the Anglican Communion and between parts of the Episcopal Church in the United States.

Exploring briefly the origins of the Church of England in the sixteenth century from which all Anglicans claim descent and with which they assert continuing affiliation, I will then trace briefly the origins of the Episcopal Church in the United States. Since much of the current turmoil in the Church is based on what the opponents see to be the authority of the Bible on moral issues, I want to look at the way in which the Bible was used by Episcopalians to support slavery and initially to deny ordination to women. And since resolutions or pronouncements from the decennial meetings of all the bishops in the Anglican Communion (known as Lambeth Conferences) are generally appealed to by both sides in today's debates, I will trace the history of the Lambeth Conferences on issues of major contention within the Communion, looking at both the substance of those issues and at the way they were dealt with if not resolved.

I then want to trace the history of the struggles within TEC and between it and the Communion from the time of Bishop Gene Robinson's election to the present. Since the book is being written while events are still unfolding, I will have to conclude before all the effects of current events upon the Church are fully known. I want to tell the story of how TEC arrived at the place where it could confirm an openly gay man's election as bishop and how it has responded to the challenges both from within and without to its actions since that time. It is a story that has many players, including those from abroad. This marks the story as rather different from other denominations in the United States, which for the most part are not bound to transnational structures quite like TEC is.

The story I am about to tell is replete with both irony and ambiguity. Irony, in the sense that our best intentions often result in outcomes that are the opposite of what we intended and ambiguity in the sense that what might appear clear-cut on the surface is often clouded and uncertain deep down. Contemporary conservatives are deeply suspicious of ambiguity because it denotes a lack of clarity in the formulation of doctrine and moral practice, with all the messiness and experimentation that flow from ambiguity. Liberals tend to live more comfortably with it.

Three overarching issues will frame the narrative. First, I will give significant attention to the arguments for Biblical authority in matters of morality and how the Bible has been interpreted to that end. In many ways the issue of Biblical interpretation is at the heart of the crisis. Next, I want to look at the question of how ecclesiastical, moral, and doctrinal authority within and for the Communion has been understood and deployed. Finally, I will take up the question of homosexual acts and how they have been understood in the Bible. I will then summarize the central issues facing the Episcopal Church today and offer some observations and predictions about how the debate will continue and some possible ways to resolve it that are faithful to Anglican tradition and teaching.

My focus will be primarily on the *arguments* deployed by all sides in support of their positions. If this story were only about internecine power struggles, it would not be nearly as interesting as the one that it is really about: namely, what are the competing visions of the Church for this time and place, by what authorities does it live out that vision, and how do the visions get exemplified in the actual, and often quite diverse, communities that constitute the Church. That is what the debate is all about, and focusing on the arguments gets us far deeper into the fundamental issues at stake than does focusing on who is financing whom and to what end. If, at the end of the day, however, it seems clear that one side has more obviously than the other departed from the canons of rationality and Biblical scholarship, then the question of *what else is driving the contest* will need to be raised, if not fully answered.

A Note on Terms and References

Episcopalians are persons in the United States who belong to *The Episcopal Church* (TEC), also known as the *Episcopal Church in the United States of America* (ECUSA).

Anglicans are people and churches around the world who have historic and continuing ties to the *Church of England* from whose founding they trace their own roots, and they are linked to the tradition emanating from the Church of England through their ongoing ties to its ecclesiastical head, the *Archbishop of Canterbury* (ABC). The ABC is the senior bishop in the Anglican Communion by virtue of being the head of the Church of England. He is known as the *primum inter pares* or first among equals.

In today's conflict, some distraught Episcopalians are moving to call themselves Anglicans, not Episcopalians, as a way of identifying with what they take to be the majority view in the global fellowship of Anglican churches known as the *Anglican Communion* (AC). This Communion currently consists of 38 different provinces or regions (usually national churches). Each province selects an archbishop or *Primate* to serve as its head. In TEC the Primate is known as the Presiding Bishop. (The powers of these Primates differ from province to province.) The Primates meet regularly, under the chairmanship of the ABC, in what are called *Primates' Meetings.*

Every 10 years the ABC, at his discretion, invites the bishops of the AC to attend what is called the *Lambeth Conference* (named for the London residence of the ABC but more recently held on the grounds of Canterbury Cathedral in Kent, England). The Conferences have no legislative power and cannot dictate to any of the member provinces or dioceses how they should operate. The question of who the ABC chooses not to invite has become a highly contentious issue in preparation for the upcoming Lambeth Conference in the summer of 2008, as this book goes to press.

A more recently formed body, the *Anglican Consultative Council* (ACC), consisting of laypersons, priests, and bishops, meets once every three years to advise, facilitate, and coordinate the actions of the churches in the AC. It is the only Communion-wide body that includes laypeople among its members.

Together the Archbishop of Canterbury, the Lambeth Conference, the Primates' Meeting, and the Anglican Consultative Council comprise what are called the "instruments of unity" for the Anglican Communion as a whole. One of the most volatile issues at stake today in the Communion is what ought to constitute the individual and collective authority of these instruments.

Lying in the background are three traditional sources of authority for determining actions that are in conformity with Anglicanism. Articulated in the Chicago-Lambeth Quadrilateral, the authorities are denominated as:

a. The Holy Scriptures of the Old and New Testaments, as "containing all things necessary to salvation," and as being the rule and ultimate standard of faith.

b. The Apostles' Creed, as the Baptismal Symbol; and the Nicene Creed, as the sufficient statement of the Christian faith.

c. The two Sacraments ordained by Christ Himself—Baptism and the Supper of the Lord—ministered with unfailing use of Christ's Words of Institution, and of the elements ordained by Him.

d. The Historic Episcopate, locally adapted in the methods of its administration to the varying needs of the nations and peoples called of God into the Unity of His Church.

Acceptance of these principles was given by the Lambeth Conference in 1888 after having first been approved by the U.S. House of Bishops in 1886.

Another formula, which captures some of the essential elements in Anglicanism and is known as the three-legged stool, acknowledges the authority of Scripture, tradition, and reason in determining actions that are in keeping with historic Anglican teaching. Some would add a fourth element, that of experience, and this addition will become one of the most important points of contention in the current debate, especially when it refers to the experience of gay and lesbian persons.

On "Conservative" vs. "Liberal"

These are loaded and, for some, pejorative terms. They also tend, in their stark use, to conceal rather than reveal important nuances and qualifications in the thoughts of individuals who are often lumped for the sake of convenience into one or the other category. But there is simply no way one term can capture all the meanings both implicit and explicit in ideas about the authority of Scripture, received doctrine, and the historic practices of the Church. Alternatives to "conservative" are "orthodox" or "traditionalist," but since the press tends to use "conservative" I will also, however, but only with the understanding of that term that I am developing here. Even trying to divide the arguments into simple polar opposites is too crass since such a division does not do justice to all the nuances involved in thinking through these contested issues. So, in the interests of keeping the arguments as clearly articulated as possible, I will use polar terms but with the understanding that they are crude and broad and a more fine-grained analysis will reveal in particular instances some interesting combinations of what on the surface might appear to be hard divisions.

Ironically, the word "conservative" can be applied to both "sides" or "camps" in the current debate because both want to conserve something very important. They simply disagree about what is to be conserved.

Nevertheless, there is something in the terms "conservative" and "liberal" that is appropriate in representing the views of those who are customarily placed under those rubrics. I will use the term "conservative" to refer to those in the Church who want to conserve, from what they believe to be the corrosion of secular, individualistic, and relativist thought, absolute truths that they take to be the clear meaning of Scriptural passages regarding sexuality and human sin, without qualifying or contextualizing that meaning by appeals to ancient cultural conditions or the evolution of human thinking. Conservatives are suspicious of secular human-centered tendencies to question and subvert what has been conserved over centuries as the right-thinking (i.e., orthodox) wisdom of the human race as revealed by God and preserved in the natural law, the earliest creeds, and the teachings of the historic Christian churches, all of which they believe are faithful to the clear message of the Bible. Conservatives are not necessarily Biblical fundamentalists. They do not have to believe that every word of the Bible accurately conveys truth. But they are Biblical absolutists or literalists with respect to some moral positions. They believe that the Biblical references to homosexual acts are absolutely and eternally binding. Conservatives also tend to value the unity and continuity of the Church's teachings when they reflect these absolutist moral positions in contrast to what they see as the innovation and imposition of narrowly drawn, fashionable, secular-driven justice agendas typically advanced by "liberals." They are suspicious of the unjustified and naïve optimism and overly generous view of human nature found in liberal thinking. They understand human sin to be a constant, not a variable, in the human condition and are wary of any claims that sin can be eradicated solely by social programs or justice agendas, as important as the latter may be for other reasons.

I will use the term "liberal" to refer to those in the Church who want to conserve what they take to be the underlying or overarching intent of Scripture (its "essential" message). But in the process of that conservation they are ready, under the tutelage of Biblical scholarship, to contextualize some of the Bible's references to practices that, in their opinion, are culturally and morally outdated. Liberals emphasize the virtues of social justice for the oppressed and marginalized and are willing in the name of liberation to challenge status quo conditions that they believe demean the flourishing of persons, including gays and lesbians, and that in the process frustrate God's intention for the fulfillment of humankind. (Most liberals would also include transgendered persons in their list of those currently being treated unjustly by the Church.) They tend to have a more positive view of human nature and its progressive development over time (without thereby denying the reality of human sin or believing that social progress will inevitably eradicate it). They are more ready than conservatives to challenge structures and institutions that, in their opinion, have perpetuated social injustices. What they are conserving is the comprehensiveness of the Anglican tradition that has lived with different views simultaneously without splitting the fundamental unity of the Church.

On "Homosexual" and "Homosexuality"

Throughout much of the literature on the debates in the Episcopal Church and Anglican Communion on matters sexual, the terms "homosexual" and "homosexuality" are often used. Although the context often makes it clear what is being referred to, I think it would be more precise to refer to *sexual acts or feelings* of sexual/genital attraction between persons of the same gender. (There may, of course, be sexual acts between persons of the same gender without any mutual attraction, such as in rape or violence as a way of exercising dominance. But I will not use "homosexuality" to cover these acts simply because it would require far too many qualifications and distract us from the main topic, which is the sexual expression of attraction, intimacy, love, mutuality, and commitment by persons of the same sex.) By putting it this way, we do not begin by presuming that homosexuality existed as a category for understanding some forms of personal relationship in the ancient Biblical cultures. In fact, as we shall see, homosexuality as such was probably not known to the Biblical writers. (One well-known exception might be the special friendship between David and Jonathan.)

Finally, all readers of this text deserve a word about the views of the author. I am squarely in the "liberal" camp though I believe that my brand of liberalism seeks to conserve some of the most important traits of Anglicanism: a tolerance for diversity, a commitment to comprehensiveness, a tolerance for a degree of ambiguity in the articulation of doctrine and polity, an acceptance of the

development of doctrine, a suspicion of doctrinal, Biblical, and moral absolut-
ism, respect for the findings of contemporary Biblical scholarship, a willingness
to accept the living experience of the members of the Church as an "authority"
for belief and practice, a suspicion of hierarchialized authority, and a willingness
to live with disagreement as long as it does not damage the fundamental integrity
of the human beings who comprise the Church. I do intend to present the
arguments and points of view of both sides with scrupulous honesty, but my
critical comments on many of the positions taken by conservatives will reflect
a more liberal orientation, and the reader needs to be forewarned that that is
the case.

Section One

The Beginnings of the Crisis

— 1 —

The Resolution that Shaped the Debate and the Election that Shook the Communion

"Mere anarchy is loosed upon the world"

The Election of Gene Robinson: There Is a Gay Gene

On June 7, 2003, the small Episcopal Diocese of New Hampshire elected an openly gay, partnered man, Vicki Gene Robinson, to be its next bishop. That act, coupled with a resolution passed overwhelmingly by the Lambeth Conference just five years previously that condemned homosexuality as incompatible with Scripture, brought to public visibility a drama that is still playing itself out both in the Episcopal Church and in the larger global Anglican Communion (AC), which comprises 38 different regional churches or provinces. It is a drama structured around conflicting views among members of the Communion on sexuality, Biblical interpretation, and the appropriate authorities for determining policy and practice for the churches within the Communion.

Before we join the story of Robinson's election and the events that followed it, and in order to understand how all this turmoil came into being, it is necessary to step back to the other, earlier event that set the stage for the debate over Robinson's election. It was the passage of a resolution at the 1998 Lambeth Conference regarding homosexuality and Biblical authority, known simply as 1.10.

The Lambeth Resolution 1.10 of 1998

The centrality of the sex issue at Lambeth 1998 is, in some ways, surprising since none of the nine regional conferences that met to identify issues for the

Conference had given it the highest priority.[1] But actions throughout the Communion, especially in the United States and Canada between Lambeth '88 and '98 dealing with the sexuality issue (see pp. 45–50) should have been enough to anticipate some kind of decisive debate on the topic at Lambeth '98. In its final form resolution 1.10 said, among other things, that the Conference, "in view of the teaching of Scripture, upholds faithfulness in marriage between a man and a woman in lifelong union, and believes that abstinence is right for those who are not called to marriage." [2] It recognized the existence of persons in the Church having a "homosexual orientation" and the need to listen to their experience. Nevertheless, it felt compelled to reject homosexual practice as "incompatible with Scripture" and for that reason could not "advise legitimizing or blessing same sex unions nor ordaining those involved in same gender unions." The resolution passed 526–70 with 45 bishops abstaining, including, ironically, the next Archbishop of Canterbury Rowan Williams, who would inherit all the problems emerging from Lambeth '98.

The resolution was a profound disappointment to many moderate and liberal bishops from the North but was strongly supported by conservative bishops and especially by bishops in the Global South and East (Africa, Asia, and South America). For the first time in Lambeth history the African, Asian, and other Southern bishops were able to control the debate and succeed in getting a resolution passed to their liking on this issue. It was as much a coming out party for bishops historically marginalized by British and American bishops as it was a closing of the door on gay and lesbian persons seeking a coming out party of their own within the corridors of power and privilege in the Communion. It was probably the most divisive and contentious issue ever debated at Lambeth Conferences and, for many, further widened the gap between conservatives and liberals.

The Conference was attended by almost 750 bishops from 37 provinces and 164 countries, including 11 women bishops (who received "tepid" applause when introduced). The women bishops were mainly from Canada and the United States (at a time when still half the Communion did not recognize women as eligible even for ordination to the priesthood). There were 224 bishops from Africa and 95 from Asia, comprising a little under half of the entire body of bishops at the Conference.

The debate over sexuality was kept at a high boil because Bishop John Spong, of the Diocese of Newark and as someone known within the Communion for highly publicized extremely liberal views, had introduced at the General Convention in 1994 what he called a "Koinonia Statement" (signed by 55 bishops) asserting that sexual orientation was "morally neutral" and that "faithful, monogamous, committed" relationships of gays and lesbians deserved moral respect.[3] As soon as Lambeth '98 opened, the Bishop of Rwanda called for all signers of the Koinonia Statement to be declared out of the Communion. (This did not happen, in part because Lambeth has no power to expel anyone. Only the Archbishop of Canterbury [ABC] can invite or decline to invite participating bishops.) Spong had also infuriated the African bishops and their American supporters by asserting that African Christians were "superstitious, fundamentalist Christians" who are a short step from animism and embrace a "very superstitious kind of Christianity . . . [and have] yet to face the intellectual revolution of Copernicus and Einstein." Another American, Martin Smith, called the Southern churches "appallingly repressive authoritarian societies . . . which do not allow even the concept of gay and lesbian people, patriarchies that have no way of admitting into consciousness the realities we know here." And he claimed that "literally hundreds of bishops in the newly expanded churches [in Africa and Asia] have had no more theological education than a few months of bible school, and the only form of discourse they know is a very simple form of biblical literalism." [4] One African bishop replied that he and his counterparts had gone to the same schools as American church leaders and have had the same training. "But they are saying we have not gone very far, we are still primitive, untrained, because we have supported an orthodox teaching." [5] Spong later apologized for his remarks but left himself an easy target for conservatives who saw him as personifying the arrogance and cultural captivity of the American liberals. The cross of Spong has weighed heavy on the backs of other liberals seeking a less confrontational approach on these issues.

The African and Asian bishops were in no mood to compromise on the issue of homosexuality. Some participants reported that some African bishops refused to talk about homosexuality and even denied that there were homosexuals in their dioceses.[6] Bishop Bolanle Gbonigi of Nigeria is reported to have said that he would not listen to homosexuals because "it would be a sheer waste of time . . . it is against the word of God. Nothing can make us [African bishops] budge because we view what God says as firm." [7] Bishop Emmanuel Chukwuma, also of Nigeria, said that Leviticus was clear in calling for the death penalty for anyone engaging in homosexual acts (presumably believing that it should be instituted as law today). Bishop Chukwuma was probably best know at Lambeth for his attempt to "exorcise" the demon of homosexuality from one Richard Kirker, a member of the Lesbian and Gay Christian Movement in the United Kingdom, who claimed to have had his first homosexual experience in Nigeria.[8] The Bishop said to Kirker, "you are killing the Church. This is the voice of God talking." [9] Kirker responded to the attempted exorcism by saying to Bishop Chukwuma, "May God bless you, sir, and deliver you from your prejudice against homosexuality." [10]

There was much speculation about the role American conservatives were playing in preparing the African bishops for their presentations in support of the resolution. As one writer put it,

> it was the conservatives' canny marriage of US-style political organization with the scriptural fundamentalism of many of the African and Asian bishops that enabled the conservatives to dominate. . . . [T]he conference deliberations revealed an

ideological colonization of Anglicanism driven by the politics of the Episcopal Church USA.[11]

Charges were thrown around that a lot of American conservative money was financing the preparation and entertainment of the African and Asian bishops. Certainly the influence of the conservative American Anglican Council (AAC) was present. James Solheim reports one observer's claim that it spent nearly $450,000 at Lambeth, but an American bishop associated with AAC, James Stanton of Dallas, said it had spent only $27,000. One spokesperson for the American conservatives denied maneuvering the African/Asian bishops at Lambeth. Rather, he said, unintentionally perhaps evoking the violent repercussions called for by Leviticus against homosexuals, "our philosophy was, if we stacked up the rocks next to the pit, the Africans would be more than happy to throw them." [12] While it is certainly true that the American conservatives were heartened by the vote at Lambeth, it cannot be said that they manipulated the African or Global South bishops. The latter had come to Lambeth already firmly committed to pushing a strong Biblically based opposition to any recognition of homosexuals as deserving of ordination or the Church's blessing of their relationships. They urged a decision on what they called "first order moral issues" because failure to do so would further threaten the unity of the Communion (following what they thought was the corrosive impact of decisions on women's ordination).[13]

Not all African bishops were on board with the majority's views on homosexuality. Former Archbishop Desmond Tutu and his successor in Capetown, Archbishop Njongonkulu Ndungane, were much more tolerant of homosexuality than their counterparts in the rest of Africa. Tutu said,

it is a matter of justice. We struggled against apartheid in South Africa because we were blamed and made to suffer for something we could do nothing about. It is the same with homosexuality. The orientation is a given, not a matter of choice.[14]

Ndungane, after affirming the right of the American church to exercise its provincial autonomy to do what it did, went on to say that the

issue of [sexual] orientation knows no culture and my fellow bishops are in denial, they have an ostrich mentality on this subject. Our church must learn how to live together as a diverse community. That's what should be on the agenda, not seeking to cast stones or talking about schisms.[15]

(Archbishop Peter Akinola responded to Ndungane's remarks by saying that "where the autonomy of any part of our communion becomes a scandal in the entire Christian world, then we must be humble enough to accept rebuke and correction." [16]) Bishop Chukwuma also said of Tutu that he was "spiritually dead." British journalist Stephen Bates speculated that with Tutu's retirement the leadership of the Council of Anglican Provinces of Africa (CAPA) was up for grabs. Ndungane was considered too liberal because of his views on sexuality, and this prepared the way for Peter Akinola, Archbishop of Nigeria, to assume the leadership position in Africa.[17] Akinola would soon become a major voice of opposition to the Episcopal Church's actions on issues of sexuality.

The resolution on sexuality underwent revisions introduced by the African bishops before it was finally passed. The original resolution, the product of three weeks deliberation by a drafting group, had said only that the traditional understanding of marriage was affirmed and that those not called to the married life should remain celibate. Chastity was then considered as an option for those not in monogamous heterosexual relationships, but this was rejected and replaced with the imperative of "abstinence." (It was believed that the notion of chastity might implicitly condone faithful committed relationships between persons of the same sex.) The original version of the resolution also did not contain any reference to a Biblical condemnation of homosexuality. But, even though it had technically missed the deadline for consideration, an amendment to declare homosexuality as incompatible with Scripture was accepted (in part for fear that had it not been the African bishops would have bolted). The debate was characterized by some bishops present as one of judgment and condemnation and filled with "moral ugliness." [18] *Tolerating* homosexuality, one conservative participant claimed, would be "evangelical suicide" to which New York Bishop Catherine Roskam (one of the few women bishops present) said *condemning* homosexuality would be evangelical suicide in her region.[19] Barbara Harris, an African American bishop from Massachusetts, reflecting later on the debate at Lambeth, said that the "vitriolic, fundamentalist rhetoric" of some of her African and Asian fellow bishops was reflective of the missionary influence imposed upon those regions.[20] She also quipped that "at times it was difficult to fathom what holds the Communion together beyond our love of the Lord Jesus Christ and Wippell's [a favorite clerical clothing supplier]." A Canadian bishop sadly noted that the debate was "full of a kind of passion and homophobia." Gays and lesbians, another lamented, "must be feeling just totally as if they've been written off, totally rejected." Yet racist comments, akin to those ascribed to Spong and Smith, were also heard, according to eyewitness James Solheim. One was heard to say in reference to the African bishops, "we need to educate those people." [21] But in the end even those from the North and West most opposed to the resolution either abstained or voted for it, according to some observers, because it kept getting harsher as amendments were added and accepted, and they concluded it was better to get it passed and move on. There was also, of course, an undercurrent of concern on the part of many white bishops that to defeat the resolution of their black colleagues would be seen as racist and patronizing. Moderate and liberal American bishops, according to anthropologist Miranda Hassett, showed "weak participation" in the debate. Their lack of participation may also have been due to the hissing and booing whenever comments were made critical of the resolution.[22] Perhaps many white bishops were afraid of being on the wrong end of one African bishop's observation that nearly all the "no" votes were white. "Those supporting [homosexuality], all of them, we saw their white hands up!" [23]

Given all that preceded Lambeth '98 it was not surprising that, aside from the issue of homosexuality, the two dominant themes were those of Biblical authority and the unity of the Communion. As if it were not already clear, Lambeth '98 felt the need to pass a number of resolutions reaffirming the "primary" authority of the Bible as containing all things necessary for salvation and serving as the ultimate standard of faith and practice. But perhaps realizing that this begged multiple questions about its interpretation, some bishops urged another resolution that Christians should build upon the best in scholarship so that the Bible could continue to "illuminate, challenge and transform cultures, structures, and ways of thinking, especially those that predominate today." It was not clear whether this was intended to support the more literalist reading of Scripture underlying the resolution on sexuality (homosexuality being declared as incompatible with Scripture) or to support a more liberal, contextual, cultural interpretation of the Bible's references to sexual acts between persons of the same gender. The specific question of how to interpret the Bible in light of that scholarship was never openly debated. If Archbishop George Carey is any guide, the conservative interpretation was dominant. He said, following the vote on sexuality, that he saw "no room in Holy Scripture or the entire Christian tradition for any sexual activity outside matrimony." [24] (For this comment Carey received a letter from the Reverend Albert Ogle, saying that the resolution was "an act of aggression towards a defenseless people and will probably haunt you and your leadership for the rest of your life." Ogle went on to say, "we have compromised in Anglicanism on everything from polygamy for Africans to divorce for westerners, and is there no room on the rickety old three-legged stool for gay Christians?" [25])

A group known as "Affirming Catholicism," which began in 1990 (and to which Archbishop Rowan Williams belonged), spoke to the issue of Biblical interpretation in a letter to Archbishop Carey immediately after the vote. Affirming Anglicanism describes itself as "a movement in the Episcopal Church and the Anglican Communion called to witness to the generosity of the Reign of God being made present in our midst through the riches of the catholic tradition in our Church." It argues that

> discerning the Spirit involves being attentive to difference as we seek to respond to the same gospel in very different cultures. Such a dynamic understanding of God's revelation in Jesus Christ implies development and change. Affirming Catholics profess that the church is being called to demonstrate a more progressive approach in relation to issues of social justice, the environment, gender and sexuality. But new approaches must stand in the light of gospel truth and the catholic tradition as we have received it. [26]

In its statement to Carey, Affirming Catholicism said that rejecting all homosexual practice as incompatible with Scripture "lacks the customary reflective balance of Scripture, tradition, sound scholarship and pastoral discernment found in classical Anglican approaches to controversy." It also noted that the Church's treatment of women or those who remarry after divorce is not treated in "this lit-eralist fashion." [27] To remain silent on this issue "would effectively be collusion in an apparent attempt to undermine the church's celebration of the insights of the critical study of the Bible" (the celebration Lambeth's resolution on the Bible already recognized). Other critics of the conservative position on the Bible also weighed in. Bishop Frank Allan of Atlanta said, "a new biblical fundamentalism has taken hold in the Anglican Communion, and this concerns me because it is idolatrous. The issue is not the authority of Scripture, but the interpretation of Scripture." [28] And Bishop Michael Ingham of New Westminster added that with respect to the Bible's use at Lambeth, "it was as if the last 150 years of biblical theology and academic research had never happened for many participants." [29] Some lamented the fact that the experience of gays and lesbians had received short shrift, despite the words in the resolution, and that this failure limited a deeper reflection on the Biblical material.[30] But in the end it might well be that Bishop Paul Barnett of Australia captured the reality of Lambeth '98 on Biblical interpretation correctly: "There are two integrities in the church. They are both reading biblical texts differently. The two views cannot be held together in one church." [31]

The question of what can be held together was the third underlying theme (along with sexuality and Biblical authority) at Lambeth. What ought to consti-tute the unity of the Communion in the face of such radically different interpre-tations of Scripture? Did Lambeth, as Pittsburgh Bishop Robert Duncan, a leader of the American Anglican Council and Network of Confessing Dioceses and Churches, asked, reestablish the appropriate balance between the autonomy of national churches and their interdependence? Or, as others would ask, did it fracture that interdependence by the harsh stand it took toward homosexuals as candidates for ordination and as worthy of having their relationships blessed? Should any bishop supporting equal rights for homosexuals either repent or leave the Communion? Should tolerance of different cultural practices (including those that include gays and lesbians in all the privileges of the Church) be affirmed even when it seems, to some, to fly in the face of the plain sense of Scripture? Was the individualism (read relativism) of some liberal churches leading to the "autonomous rejections of legitimate authority"?[32] Should the Communion heed the words of Bishop Chiwanga of Tanzania that "forcing your point of view by excluding from your circle those who disagree with you, or by compelling acceptance, is to usurp the place of God"?[33] Should the traditional respect for diocesan and provincial boundaries be overturned "when the central unity in Jesus is damaged" by tolerance for homosexuality? "If," as one bishop put it, "liberalism becomes tyrannical, it is the duty of orthodox bishops to pro-tect the faith." [34] The summary question, at the end of the day at Lambeth '98 was whether to act on the desire of some "that the Anglican Communion . . . had a stronger center, one that could free the church from the paralyzing effect of endless speculation, lobbying, maneuvering, and debate, [and] also bring into line any dioceses or provinces that stray from orthodox practice." [35] That question would be answered in the affirmative many times over when the Diocese of New Hampshire would a few years later elect an openly gay partnered man, Vicki Gene Robinson, to be its next bishop.

From Lambeth '98 to Minneapolis '03

There were a number of events that transpired between the Lambeth Conference of 1998 and the election of Gene Robinson in 2003 that helped to shape what happened following his election.

About a year after the Lambeth Conference of 1998 a group of Primates met in Kampala, Uganda (November 1999) with a number of conservative American leaders. The question before them, as one African put it, was "whether the bishops in American Anglican Council confirm the pleas and demands of [a number of conservative groups in America]. . . . We wanted to make sure that when we intervene, we intervene with enough information from different [groups] before the Primates." [36] On the part of the Americans present, one, the Reverend Geoffrey Chapman of First Promise (the author of the infamous 2003 Chapman memo), broached the issue of submitting U.S. churches to African control. He said,

> We believe that it is essential that much of the Episcopal Church be rebuked by the international communion and called to repentance. . . . [Therefore,] we ask for a new jurisdiction on American soil, under the temporary oversight of an overseas province. We believe that such a jurisdiction would provide the best hope for supporting those who are being persecuted [*sic*] for biblical faith and values . . . Such a jurisdiction would also provide a visible restraint and warning to those who oppose the Gospel. [37]

First Promise began shortly after the 1997 General Convention. By 1998 it comprised about 200 clergy. [38] Its declaration of intent said simply that

> when the Church itself departs from the faith it has received, [faithful Christians'] first loyalty must be to apostolic faith rather than the authority of canons, institutions, and bishops. . . . We will not be bound, in the exercise of our priestly or diaconal ministries, by the legal or geographical boundaries of any parish or diocese.

They insisted that they would remain under the jurisdiction of "faithful bishops," and they appealed to the bishops of the AC to support "theologically orthodox Anglicans in America, and to discipline those members who have departed from it." [39] Three years later First Promise would become the Anglican Mission in the Americas also known as Anglican Mission in America (AMiA). Its stated intention was to provide missionary outreach to the United States "sanctioned" by some Anglican Archbishops. It would provide a way for American congregations "to be fully Anglican" and also "free from the crises of faith, leadership and mission" in the Episcopal Church in the United States of America (ECUSA). [40] It intended to plant Anglican congregations across the country.

One action that created an uproar was the attempt by First Promise to establish a parish in Arkansas that would ally itself to First Promise. The Bishop of Arkansas refused to recognize the parish as an Episcopal Church. The rector of the parish was transferred by his bishop, Ed Salmon of South Carolina, to the authority of Bishop John Rucyahana of Rwanda. Even the conservative ABC at the time, George Carey, was concerned at this potential unsettling of the polity of Anglicanism and wrote to Bishop Rucyahana in July 1998: "It is my clear view that what you are doing is completely illegal and I hope you will quickly disentangle yourself from something that is quite unconstitutional." [41] But the transfer worked and the parish in Arkansas slipped out from under the authority of the Episcopal Church.

In March 2000 the Primates held an important meeting in Porto, Portugal. While other things were on their agenda, one item of concern was the issue of Biblical authority and homosexuality. The Primates acknowledged "deep problems arising from conflicting teaching and practice in relation to sexual ethics" across the AC.[42] They went on to say that they have the freedom to "call one another to account" on divisive issues, and that this clearly poses the question "of what would be sufficient grounds for a complete and definitive rupture of communion between Provinces in the Anglican family." However, they stated that the divisions over Lambeth Resolution 1.10 do not "necessarily amount to a complete and definitive rupture of communion." Nevertheless, the "rejection" of the resolution in some provinces has "come to threaten the unity of the communion in a profound way." They urged those provinces contemplating such actions to listen to the "pain, anger and perplexity" from other parts of the Communion.

The 2000 General Convention also addressed the issue of sexuality. It said, in a way that did not focus exclusively on heterosexual relationships, that

> we acknowledge that while the issues of human sexuality are not yet resolved, there are currently couples in the Body of Christ and in this Church who are living in marriage and couples in the Body of Christ and in this Church who are living in other life-long committed relationships; and that we expect such relationships will be characterized by fidelity, monogamy, mutual affection and respect, careful, honest communication, and the holy love which enables those in such relationships to see in each other the image of God; That we acknowledge that some, acting in good conscience, who disagree with the traditional teaching of the Church on human sexuality, will act in contradiction to that position; and [that] in continuity with previous actions of the General Convention of this Church, and in response to the call for dialogue by the Lambeth Conference, we affirm that those on various sides of controversial issues have a place in the Church, and we reaffirm the imperative to promote conversation between persons of differing experiences and perspectives, while acknowledging the Church's teaching on the sanctity of marriage.[43]

For some people these words would be interpreted as applying equally to gay and to heterosexual couples, though this was not, apparently, what was intended by those who proposed the resolution.

Nevertheless, there was a sense of inclusiveness and a refusal to draw hard and fast lines in the areas of sexuality that characterized these resolutions from the 2000 Convention. That inclusiveness and tolerance, at least among a vocal minority at the next General Convention in 2003, seemed to have been lost somewhere along the way.

At its 2002 meeting in Hong Kong, the Anglican Consultative Council called upon the dioceses and bishops of the Communion

> not to undertake unilateral actions or adopt policies which would strain our communion with one another without reference to their provincial authorities; and for provincial authorities to have in mind the impact of their decisions within the wider Communion; and [for] all members of the Communion, even in our disagreements to have in mind the "need for courtesy, tolerance, mutual respect and prayer for one another." [44]

It would be the failure of the Church in the United States at its 2003 General Convention not to undertake unilateral actions that would "strain our communion with one another without reference to their provincial authorities" that would prove to be one of the most serious threats to the unity of the Communion, perhaps even more so than the actual confirmation of the election of Gene Robinson itself. The U.S. Church would be criticized as much for its disregard of the effects of its actions as it would be for the substance of what it did. This suggests that preserving the unity of the Communion is even more important in some respects to most members of the Communion than what views one holds on the morality of homosexuality.

One step ahead of the Church in the United States, however, in June 2002, the western Canadian Diocese of New Westminster took the dramatic step of approving a motion (by 215–129) asking its bishop to authorize a rite of blessing of same sex unions in parishes that wanted to do so.[45] This was not a precipitous action. The House of Bishops of the Anglican Church of Canada had begun thinking about the issue of homosexuality as far back as 1976 by creating a national task force to consider it. In 1979 the Canadian House of Bishops approved a resolution that said, in part, "homosexual persons, as children of God, have a full and equal claim with all other persons, upon the love, acceptance, concern and pastoral care of the church." However, the bishops declined to accept the blessing of same sex unions. In 1987 congregations were encouraged to study the role social attitudes and faith had on their understanding of sexuality. Another task force on human sexuality was created in 1992. That same year the Westminster Diocesan Synod moved to ask the House of Bishops to make its requirements for ordination the same for both homosexual and heterosexual candidates. In 1993 a further study of sexuality was encouraged. In 1998, just prior to the Lambeth Conference, the Diocese of New Westminster voted 179–170 to permit the bishop to authorize clergy to bless covenanted same sex unions. The bishop declined because of the closeness of the vote. Nevertheless, following Lambeth 1998 Bishop Michael Ingham agreed to authorize the blessing of same sex unions if it was found that there were no canonical or civil impediments to doing so. The Diocesan Synod in 2001 asked Bishop Ingham a second time, but by a much larger majority, to approve same sex blessings. Over the next few years a number of parishes engaged in a "dialogue" process discussing the issue of sexuality.

In April 2001 the Legal and Canonical Commission ruled that the bishop has the authority to authorize a rite for blessing same sex unions. Two months later the Diocesan Synod again asked the Bishop to authorize the blessing of same sex unions. The vote was 226–174 and the bishop again said the margin was not sufficient to convince him to do so. Finally, in June 2002, Bishop Ingham agreed to authorize the blessings but established a conscience clause ensuring that no clergy will be required to participate in such a ceremony. Finally, on June 15, 2002, a sufficient majority (215–129) approved the authorization of same sex unions and the bishop consented. It is clear from this chronology that no matter what his own views on the subject were (very liberal) Bishop Ingham wanted his decisions to be as consonant as possible both with the canons of the Church and with the views of the vast majority of the people in his diocese. Contrary to implied charges that the liberals were charging ahead with an agenda far in advance of their congregations, Ingham's actions reveal just the opposite.

In May of the following year, 2003, Bishop Ingham allowed six parishes that have voted to be venues for same sex blessings to proceed to do so. The first such blessing took place on May 23. This immediately evoked a negative response from the ABC, Rowan Williams, who said that the diocese had "gone significantly further than the teaching of the Church or pastoral concern can justify and I very much regret the inevitable tension and division that will result from this development." [46] Despite the Archbishop's words, and ironically just across the far eastern Canadian border, the Diocese of New Hampshire, less than a month later, would elect Gene Robinson as its new bishop. The stage was now set for a major crisis in the Anglican Communion, provoking the very "tension and division" the Archbishop had feared would arise from the actions of the Diocese of New Westminster.

In Canada Bishop Michael Ingham was a pivotal figure in all this. As the chronology shows, he would not act until he had the support of the majority of his diocese even though his personal convictions were strongly in favor of same sex blessings. A few months after Robinson's election and confirmation, in September 2003, Ingham delivered a very forceful address entitled "Reclaiming Christian Orthodoxy" at a conference called Halfway to Lambeth (2008).[47] Speaking of the experience of the Diocese of New Westminster, Ingham said that in the past several years the Church has become aware "that gay and lesbian Christians have been starved and denied the spiritual food of acceptance and love they have a right to expect as baptized members of the Body of Christ." In his diocese and in the province of ECUSA decisions were made to do something about this. "We believe," he said, "that the continued exclusion of people through the misuse of Scripture, and the repetition of inherited and unexamined prejudices against minorities, is a sin against the love of God."

Ingham went on to say that the actions taken by Canada and the United States were in response to changes in the sciences and social sciences that "affect our understanding of human sexuality." And, significantly in light of the charge that these actions were un-Biblical, Ingham said that in a classic expression of liberal thought "they were taken not in rebellion against Scripture, but in faithfulness to its constant and greater witness that God does not deny his own children the bread of compassion and justice." As to the charge that these actions were unilateral, he countered by noting that the Church of England came into existence through unilateral actions against the universal consensus or common mind of the Church of Rome. He also challenged the assumption that "orthodoxy' is dogmatically uniform and unambiguous in matters of sexuality. Instead, from what he called a "broader orthodoxy," "God condemns no one who has been made in God's image" and that "no doctrine of creation which ignores homosexual persons is an adequate doctrine of creation." Indeed, "moral standards do in fact vary in different parts of the Christian world, and that is a cause for deeper discussion rather than separation." (This claim about the variety of moral standards was, according to its conservative critics, precisely the problem with the liberal position.) The Quadrilateral, he pointed out, has "no fixed and immutable conception of sexuality or Christian sexual ethics." Ethics is a derivative from the foundational belief in God. Those obsessed with the issue of sexuality have, in effect, elevated a secondary issue to a first order issue "on the same level as the very existence of God." He accused the conservatives of having committed "intellectual theft" of the word "orthodoxy." Once "cherished and fiercely held doctrines" have now been abandoned throughout the Communion, such as the divine right of kings, slavery, prohibition against usury, contempt for the Jews, and prohibition of divorce and remarriage. What has been held constant is the Church's "universal moral commitment to love and compassion for the despised and the rejected, to justice for the suffering and the poor, to bread for the hungry." Today, unfortunately, homophobia "has replaced anti-semitism [*sic*] as the last acceptable prejudice in some parts of the church." Returning to the theme of Biblical authority, Bishop Ingham denied any attempt to reject the authority of Scripture. Indeed, he said, "the same Spirit that inspired the writers of the Bible inspires the church in its reading of the Bible." But reading Scripture requires prayer and study, discernment and reason. Through this process we have learned, according to Ingham, that parts of Scripture have been used to sanction male superiority over women. These "texts of terror" (in the words of Biblical scholar Phyllis Trible) are ones "in which humiliation, subjugation, rape and murder seem to be justified by biblical authority." But in the light of Christ, love should be the guiding principle for interpreting Scripture. Therefore, the

hatred, contempt and vilification of God's gay and lesbian children that claims the name of orthodoxy today is not condoned nor blessed by Jesus Christ. It has more to do with those forces of religious fearfulness that crucified Jesus than with the love for which he gave up his life.[48]

Ironically, at the same time that the two North American provinces were initiating actions that would roil the Communion, the Church of England and the newly elected and consecrated Archbishop of Canterbury, Rowan Williams, were facing their own internal scandal. Rowan Williams had been appointed by the Crown as the 104th Archbishop of Canterbury in July 2002 and enthroned on February 27, 2003, a few short months before events in Canada and the United States would challenge his episcopacy more than one could possibly have imagined and must have led him, in some private moments, to ask "why me, why now?"

One of the first issues in which he became embroiled had to do with Dr. Jeffrey John who had been chosen by the Bishop of Oxford, Richard Harries, to be the next suffragan bishop of the Diocese of Reading. Dr. John was an openly gay man living in a 27 year relationship with another man and had spoken publicly, frequently, and positively about homosexuality.[49] Williams was well aware of John's thinking and personal background, having collaborated with him in founding "Affirming Catholicism." [50] Williams initially had consented to Harries's choice of Dr. John and agreed to consecrate him. But Williams came under fierce attack by the conservatives in the Church when they became aware of his intended action, and eventually Williams asked for John's resignation to which John, "in view of the damage my consecration might cause to the unity of the Church," acceded. But this "victory" did not endear Williams to the very conservatives who had demanded it because they were convinced that he had been aligned with John's views and had caved in only under pressure, not out of conviction.

Just a few weeks before the 2003 General Convention of ECUSA a "pastoral letter" [51] was issued by the Primates' Meeting in Brazil at the end of May. The letter is significant in that it both rejected any support for authorizing the blessing of same sex relationships and, in language that would be exploited in late 2007 by the U.S. House of Bishops, seemed to permit such blessings (at least by implication). "It is necessary," the Primates say, "to maintain a breadth of private response to situations of individual pastoral care." Under the rubric of pastoral care and without the sanction of official rites, a "private response" might include blessing a same sex relationship, though this implication was not explicitly articulated. It would be quoted back to the Primates by the Episcopal Church's House of Bishops at the end of September 2007.

The Election and the Turmoil It Created

Robinson's election by the Diocese of New Hampshire was entirely in keeping with the way dioceses in the Episcopal Church select their bishops. The delegates to the diocesan convention chose a man who had for many years served both the diocese and the regional body of Episcopal churches and was well-known to the delegates. His being both gay and partnered was not a canonical obstacle to their belief that he was the best man to lead them as bishop. But because of the peculiarities of Episcopal polity his election had to be ratified by the General Convention of the Episcopal Church meeting later that summer in Minneapolis. The General Convention (GC), which meets every three years, is the only authoritative body that can establish policy, canon, and constitution for TEC. The actions of that 2003 convention in confirming Robinson's election proved to be a magnet for media attention and the catalyst for crisis in the whole Anglican Communion from that moment until the present.

Despite vicious rumors to the contrary at the time, Robinson and his former wife had amicably divorced a number of years before he met Mark Andrew, his partner. Robinson's daughter, Ella, a strong supporter of her father throughout the ordeal, read a letter from her mother to the General Convention in which she said that "our lives together both married and divorced have been examples of how to deal with difficult decisions with grace, love, integrity and honour." [52]

As the convention in Minneapolis approached, some began claiming that if Robinson's election was confirmed people would die in Africa because of the hostility there to homosexuals.[53] The assumption, apparently, was that the confirmation of Robinson's election by the Church in the United States would so outrage African Muslims in Africa that they would kill Christians in Africa and Asia. Moral theologian Ian Markham has claimed that one Pakistani Anglican told him, "Christians in Pakistan died because of the progressive decision of the American Church." [54]

The vote in favor of Robinson's election was 2–1 in the House of Deputies. The House of Bishops, the other legislative body, went for Robinson 62–43 (two abstentions were counted as "no" votes). Many deputies voted to confirm Robinson not because they believed that homosexuals ought to be bishops but because they could see no reason for denying his election since it had not violated any of the canons or protocols for the election of persons to the episcopate. In acceding to his election they were acknowledging the right of the people in a diocese to make their own choice of bishop unless there were canonical irregularities.

The Response

Some dissenting bishops immediately declared that this was a "pastoral emergency" and that they would call on the Primates of the other provinces to intervene in the affairs of ECUSA to invalidate the election.[55] One man, whose actions and words would become central to the ensuing conflict, Archbishop (or Primate) of Nigeria, Peter Akinola, exclaimed that with Robinson's election Satan had entered the Church.[56] Kendall Harmon, canon theologian for the Diocese of South Carolina and a major voice in the conservative camp, said the confirmation of Robinson's election "is a watershed. It is a crossing of the line." [57]

More than a dozen conservatives walked out after the vote. Bishop of Pittsburgh Robert Duncan, who would play an increasingly important role in challenging the Episcopal Church's leadership, said his grief was too deep for words[58] (though later he found his voice returning since he has issued multiple statements in increasingly hyperbolic language on the future of the Church and the impending martyrdom of those who are defending the orthodox position). A key lay leader on the conservative side, Diane Knippers, said in response to the actions of the Convention that the current leaders in ECUSA are middle class elites who came of age in the 1960s. They listen to National Public Radio (NPR) and do not watch Fox TV, thus rendering them, apparently, unable to understand or sympathize with the views of "real" Americans.[59]

Despite the anguish over Robinson's election, it is significant that the Convention refused to authorize a process for creating liturgies for the blessing of same sex unions. If its action in confirming Robinson's election was "liberal," it displayed a traditional conservatism in not moving forward in other areas of sexuality.

With the specter of a major split in the Communion hanging over the convention, Robinson was urged by some to follow the route of Jeffrey John in England and resign his episcopate.[60] He refused to do so.

Despite the near hysterical and apocalyptic language of some of Robinson's detractors, the issue of his election was serious enough that the new Archbishop of Canterbury, Rowan Williams, felt compelled to respond, especially after some conservatives pointedly asked him if he wanted to remain in communion with liberal provinces such as ECUSA.[61] Williams acknowledged that the decision of the convention "will inevitably have significant impact on the AC" and said he hoped that ECUSA and the AC "will have the opportunity to consider this development before significant and irrevocable decisions are made in response." [62]

Not surprisingly the question of who would retain the property of churches that might seek to disaffiliate from ECUSA was soon on the table. At the 1979 General Convention a church law had been added to the canons asserting that "all assets of a congregation are 'held in trust for this church and the diocese thereof' by the diocese." This would prove an important but still controversial canon as threatened litigation evolved in the months to come.[63] Some churches also began talking about cutting off funding to the national church.[64]

Shortly after the Convention, Presiding Bishop Frank Griswold sent a letter to all clergy in ECUSA. He tried to frame the issue as one of tolerance for people living within a wide variety of webs of relationship constituting the fullness of the Church: congregations, dioceses, provinces, national self-governing churches, and the Anglican Communion as a whole. Giving the best spin he could to the events, he referred to the different points of view as "forcefields of energy" constantly interacting, challenging, and enlarging one another. Conservatives were not particularly swayed by Griswold's argument, if they took it seriously at all. Nevertheless, in early September Griswold met with a group of ten bishops from across the theological spectrum to discuss how they could live together given their divergent points of view.

The Repudiation of the Election and the Reaction of the Mainstream

Some dioceses were not interested in waiting for such a way to emerge. The dioceses of Central Florida and Albany (New York) voted to disassociate themselves from the actions of the General Convention, and the Diocese of Florida said it would seek the intervention of the Primates of the Anglican Communion. The dioceses of Fort Worth, Pittsburgh, and South Carolina voted in special conventions to "repudiate" the actions of the Convention. (It was not clear what "repudiation" and "disassociation" from its actions would mean in practice for these dioceses.) The issue of intervention was soon to become one of the major bones of contention within the Church since it is an action not provided for by the canons. Bishop Duncan, while passionately opposed to the actions of the Convention, nevertheless claimed that the resolutions of the conservative dioceses ought not to be construed as tantamount to leaving the Church. "We will always be Episcopalians," he asserted, though by the end of 2007 he had begun moves to take his diocese out of the Episcopal Church. Bishop Ed Salmon of South Carolina said that the Convention "has endorsed a new religion" and that the Church needed intervention from outside.[65] It is ironic that South Carolina became one of the first and most vociferous opponents of what had taken place in Minneapolis. As one reporter observed, the follow-up convention in South Carolina had an atmosphere "eerily reminiscent of the mood in Charleston on the eve of the firing upon Fort Sumter" in 1861. Some conservatives even called themselves secessionists, and their arguments for Biblical authority on sexuality echoed earlier arguments for slavery having Biblical sanction.[66]

Outside the Communion other eyes were looking hard at the actions of the General Convention. On October 4, 2003, Pope John Paul II, in a meeting with the ABC, said acceptance of openly gay clergy will present "new and serious difficulties" in the relation between the two churches. He indicated, as the conservatives would continue to do, that the issue of gay clergy is not just a matter of polity but extends to essential matters of faith and morals,[67] a position on which they would be challenged by more liberal commentators.

Also in early October under the auspices of the American Anglican Council,[68] a meeting of conservatives took place in Dallas, Texas, near Plano, the place from which much of the planning for the conservative response has emanated. The 2,674 attendees, including 46 current and retired bishops, 799 priests, and 103 seminarians, called for a "new alignment for Anglicanism in North America." More particularly, they called on the Primates to erase traditional church boundaries and to "encourage faithful bishops to extend episcopal care, oversight and mission to across [sic] current diocesan boundaries." This would become the most important part of the conservative response, directly challenging the notion of the inviolability of provincial and diocesan boundaries and the authority of the bishops within them. Significantly, the meeting received a greeting from then Cardinal Joseph Ratzinger of the Roman Catholic Church and head of the Congregation for the Doctrine of the Faith (formerly the Inquisition or Holy Office) and now Pope Benedict XVI, who expressed his "heartfelt prayers" for the gathering and said Christians share a "unity of truth" with one another.[69] Ratzinger, in 1986, was also the author of one of the most forceful rejections of homosexuality while he served as head of the Congregation.

One attendee was a clergyman from Connecticut, Christopher Leighton, who said, "A new American Anglicanism is emerging in North America. Whatever happens, it will not look like the old Episcopal Church, that's for sure." His comparison of the event to Gettysburg or D-Day[70] became part of the list of world-shattering events the conservatives would tend to identify with in their struggles. Leighton would soon become one of the leaders of a concerted attempt in the Diocese of Connecticut to challenge the authority of its bishop, Andrew Smith. That story will be told later.

Other parts of the Anglican Communion were also watching closely what had happened in Minneapolis. On September 26, Archbishop Robin Eames of Armagh, Northern Ireland, a major voice in the Anglican Communion, wrote in the Church of Ireland *Gazette* that the vote in the General Convention raises questions about the unity and relationships of diverse provinces that constitute the AC. For him the fundamental issue was how members of the Communion can live together with differing opinions. Anglicanism has always jealously upheld a principle guarding the autonomy of local provinces. But, warned Eames, if there are no rules for membership, then "there are no rules for expulsion of a member church."

A diversity of culture, practice and lifestyles have been and will most likely continue to be the experience of a world family such as the Anglican Communion.[71]

Shortly following Eames document, the Primates of the Communion met at Lambeth Palace in London. They issued a statement on October 16 directly addressing the issue of primatial oversight of provinces other than their own. They said that they were "seeking to exercise the 'enhanced responsibility' entrusted to us by successive Lambeth Conferences." ("Entrusted" does not mean that they were granted this enhanced responsibility by the Lambeth Conference since it has no power to determine the actions of the Primates, let alone provinces and dioceses.) While acknowledging a "legitimate diversity of interpretation" within the Communion, they warn that "each province needs to be aware of the possible effects of its interpretation of Scripture on the life of other provinces in the Communion." They reaffirmed the Lambeth 1998 resolutions, especially 1.10[72] as "having moral force and commanding the respect of the Communion." And they remind the provinces that they have no authority to "substitute an alternative teaching as if it were the teaching of the entire"

Communion (apparently including their own, but they do not acknowledge that). And they "call on the provinces concerned to make adequate provision for episcopal oversight of dissenting minorities within their own area of pastoral care in consultation with the ABC on behalf of the Primates." As a final shot, they observe that in most provinces Robinson's homosexuality would have been a "canonical impediment to his consecration." They even repeat a warning first heard in Minneapolis that if the ABC relaxes the Church's teaching on homosexuality, if a gay person is elected, confirmed, and consecrated a bishop in the Episcopal Church, some people will die.[73] The ABC added his hope that Robinson would not be consecrated.[74] Griswold returned from the meeting and reassured Robinson of his continuing support.

For the immediate future, however, the most important result of the meeting of the Primates was their request to the ABC to create a commission to look into the issues. Williams accepted the request and created a commission charged to look at life in the Anglican Communion in the light of recent events with specific reference to the Canadian Diocese of New Westminster's authorization of same sex blessings and Robinson's election. Archbishop Eames is asked to chair the commission. Its report would be released the following October under the title *The Windsor Report* and for many would become the litmus test for "orthodoxy" in the Communion.

The response of the conservatives to the Primates' statement was generally very positive. The Reverend David Roseberry of Plano, TX said it represents a "substantial intervention" and makes possible a mechanism "by which sanctions and discipline are, for the first time, possible in the AC." Conservative Bishop Jack Iker of the Diocese of Fort Worth said he will try to hold ECUSA together by promoting "alternative episcopal oversight." Former ABC George Carey, while at a clergy retreat in South Carolina, called Robinson's confirmation "an ecumenical scandal." [75]

Although increasingly eclipsed by the events his election provoked, the man at the center of the storm, Gene Robinson, replied to all the charges swirling around him by saying that he feels that God wants him to proceed to consecration. "God and I have been about this for quite a while now and I would be really surprised if God were to want me to stop now." [76]

Upon his return from the Primates' Meeting at Lambeth, Presiding Bishop Frank Griswold wrote to his fellow Primates on October 23:[77]

> though we affirm our allegiance to the Scriptures and the Creeds, our unity in the body of Christ does not mean we have only one way of reading the Bible, nor do we need to be in agreement about all of the contemporary issues with which we are called to struggle.

Griswold remained steadfast in the view that contexts do matter. "Concerns of sexuality present themselves differently in our various contexts." He said to the Primates that the consecration of Robinson will proceed.

Following the Primates' meeting, Truro Church in Fairfax, Virginia, the eastern states' counterpart to Plano, Texas, hosted another meeting of conservatives on October 23, 2003. Canon Theologian Harmon claimed seven American dioceses will join the new network of "confessing dioceses and parishes," which he claimed the ABC has suggested.

In a denomination known for its many conferences, meetings, reports, letters, and statements, and not to be outdone by the conservatives, a conference of the Lesbian and Gay Christian Movement in Great Britain met at virtually the same time on October 24–26 with 250 people in attendance. Robinson spoke to the group via satellite link. Rowan Williams did not attend.

Attempting to keep open lines of communication in the Church, the Executive Council of ECUSA, which conducts the business of the Church between General Conventions, met from October 24 to 27, 2003, and committed itself to "listen carefully to the perspectives of all the members of the church. . . . We believe there is room in our church for a wide spectrum of opinion and perspectives . . . addressing divisive issues with civility, openness and charity." [78]

Meanwhile, undeterred by the controversy surrounding him, Gene Robinson was consecrated as the Bishop of New Hampshire on November 2, 2003, by 55 bishops,[79] including PB Griswold and Nevada Bishop Katharine Jefferts Schori who, in 2006, would be elected as Griswold's successor as Presiding Bishop (PB). At least 4,000 people were in attendance. The ceremony was briefly treated to a vivid description of gay sex by an Episcopal clergyman, Earle Fox, during the period when individuals are invited to speak. Bishop David Bena of Albany read a letter saying that 36 U.S. bishops will not recognize Robinson as a bishop.[80] One layperson said during the ceremony: "We must not proceed with this terrible and unbiblical mistake, which will not only rupture the Anglican Communion; it will break God's heart." [81] Archbishop Akinola chimed in from Nigeria that the Global South churches will not recognize Robinson. He also declared a state of "impaired communion" now exists between America and the rest of the AC. (Though no one could explain exactly what impaired communion meant.) But Archbishop Eames reminded everyone that Anglicans had conquered divisions over women priests and could also do so over gays.[82]

Two days after the consecration, on November 4, the *Times* of London ran a piece by Ruth Gledhill saying, in rather hyperinflated language, that "Anglicanism began a rapid descent into global chaos as dioceses and churches representing more than 50 million of its 77 million members issued threats of heresy and schism" as they broke off communion with Robinson and the Diocese of New Westminster. Her description of the present state of Anglicanism has not, to date, proven to be accurate.

In early December Pittsburgh Bishop Robert Duncan was selected to lead the newly formed Network of Confessing Dioceses and Congregations (which self-reports on its Web site[83] that it includes 13 active Episcopal bishops and 384,935 laity). At the same time, the AAC was collecting applications for parishes wanting "alternative oversight." The identities of those parishes were not disclosed. The president of the AAC, the Reverend David Anderson, was quoted as saying that if a local bishop does not agree to provide such alternative oversight "it might have to be jammed down his throat." [84] Duncan also went out of his way to claim that the Network parishes are not separating themselves from the Episcopal Church. This reluctance to adopt separation would gradually diminish on Duncan's part as he moves by the fall of 2007 to form an entirely new province that would seek recognition as an independent part of the Anglican Communion. However, of the original 13 dioceses listed as members of the Network, two (Southwest Florida and Central Florida) denied that they are allied with it despite Duncan's assertion that they were.

As 2003 drew to a close, reports began to circulate[85] about the emergence of "via media" groups in a number of dioceses, which are based on the recognition "that the truth of one generation might be understood differently in the next . . . one ideology's devil is another movement's martyr." Via media groups were beginning to spring up in the generally conservative dioceses of Albany, Pittsburgh, Central Florida, Fort Worth, Springfield (Illinois), and San Joaquin. While not associated or organized as a single group, each recognizes the General Convention as the highest legislative body in ECUSA. Some of them claim that the conservative effort to get the support of foreign Primates is a

> betrayal of our most treasured Anglican principles. It's religious terrorism of the worst kind, by a group of American bishops who lost a vote on sexual morality and would rather blow us all up than have to learn to live with the diversity of the church.[86]

Moderator Donna Bott of the Diocese of Central Florida was reported as saying: "We are mainstream Episcopalians who represent the middle ground—the place where everyone is welcome and we can find unity despite our differences." In Fort Worth, the via media group reported that Bishop Iker's claims to have signed up 18,000 members of the diocese for membership in the Network are bogus. The diocese, via media pointed out, has only 19,000 people total. In Pittsburgh, Joan R. Gundersen of Progressive Episcopalians of Pittsburgh (PEP) said, "the Episcopal Church we know and love is a place open to multiple Biblical interpretations, united through Creeds and worship." Another member of PEP said she thought the issue was money and power, not sex. The growing influence of many of the via media groups is indicated by the fact that despite urgent attempts on the part of conservatives, many dioceses, through their diocesan conventions, have so far refused to approve resolutions condemning the vote on Robinson at the General Convention.

The story of what happened in TEC and the Communion from the end of 2003 to the present cannot be told, however, without providing some crucial historical background, including the emergence of Anglicanism during the Protestant Reformation, the history of the Episcopal Church in the United States, the history of the Lambeth Conferences, and in particular the struggle for women's ordination.

Section Two

The Way We Were: Historical Background

—— 2 ——

From Rome to Post-Establishment America by Way of Canterbury

"Things fall apart"

The Church of England

People who consider themselves part of the Anglican Communion are always a little put off when they hear that their "branch" of the wider Christian Church came into being because an English king wanted a divorce and could not get papal permission for it. While not denying the role King Henry VIII had in establishing what came to be called the Church of England, Anglicans like to point out that they have always been in historical continuity with the "primitive" Christian Church and are both "reformed" and "catholic" at the same time, i.e., reforming what had become corrupted over 1,500 years while retaining the essence of the faith found universally throughout the Church's history. What Henry did was mess with the ecclesiastical structure of the Church, especially its relation to the sovereign of the state, but he did not interrupt the continuity of faith and practice that had marked the Church from its earliest days. Nevertheless, part of the multiple crises that face the Episcopal Church in relation to the Anglican Communion today is rooted in Anglicanism's place in the particular history of the English church and, later, its expansion through the spread of the British empire around the world.

England was not, of course, spared the effects of the Protestant Reformation that historians conventionally date from Martin Luther's posting of the 95 Theses on a church door in Wittenberg Germany in 1517. Luther had wanted a *reform* of the Church, not the creation of a new church. English Christians, including Henry VIII, wanted the same thing. As is now generally well known, Henry's attempts to nullify his marriage to Catherine of Aragon because their union had not produced a male heir led to a dispute with Pope Clement VII over whether he would be granted such a nullification, not, as popular forms of telling the story sometimes say, a divorce. Technically Henry had married the widow of his elder brother Arthur and had required a papal dispensation to do so since, according to Leviticus 20:21, he had committed an "abomination." ("If a man takes his brother's wife, it is an impurity.") In light of the current appeal by many conservatives in the Anglican Communion to the purity codes in Leviticus, which treat homosexuality as an impurity and an abomination, it is ironic that the man who is credited with freeing the Church in England from papal tyranny may be seen to have acted (with papal permission) in an impure, abominable way in marrying Catherine. Granting a nullification of marriage was not unprecedented, of course, in Rome's dealings with monarchs in European history. But in Henry's case, providing the nullification would have offended Emperor Charles V, who was Catherine's nephew and someone the pope believed he could not afford to displease. It is reported[1] that Clement was willing to consider permitting Henry to commit bigamy rather than nullify his marriage to Catherine. But Henry wanted a legitimate marriage with Anne Boleyn to ensure the legitimate succession of any male heir that union might produce. There was no quick resolution to Henry's request, and he was eventually advised by Thomas Cromwell that in civil matters no court outside England ought to have any legitimate jurisdiction, including Rome. Why should a foreign bishop (and the pope was the bishop of Rome) have any power over a matter internal to the Kingdom of England? (This ironically foreshadows some of the current debate over the intervention of foreign bishops into the affairs of provinces other than their own.) Cromwell's reasoning convinced Henry, and in 1532 he issued an "Act of Restraint of Appeals" in which he proclaimed, in a rather prolix way, that

> this realm of England is an *empire* . . . governed by one supreme head and king . . .
> instituted and furnished by the goodness and sufferance of Almighty God, with
> plenary whole and entire power pre-eminence authority prerogative and jurisdiction
> to render and yield justice and final determination to all manner of folk . . . in all
> causes . . . without restraint or provocation to any foreign princes or potentates.[2]

In 1533 Thomas Cranmer, who had just been appointed Archbishop of Canterbury, declared that the marriage to Catherine was null and void, thus freeing Henry to marry Anne. Shortly thereafter Pope Clement excommunicated Henry and declared his marriage to Anne invalid. Henry responded to this papal action by getting Parliament to pass the Act of Supremacy in which the King of England and his successors were declared to be "the only supreme head in earth of the Church of England, called *Anglicana Ecclesia*." After a short suspension of this act under Queen Mary, it was restored by Queen Elizabeth in 1559 and has remained in effect, with some modifications, ever since.

And so began the establishment of the Church of England and with it a multiplicity of challenges, opportunities, and problems that haunt the Anglican Communion down to the present. Not least of these problems is that what had been the Church *in* England now became an established church, the Church *of* England, dependent upon the authorization of both royal and parliamentary power for much of its life. Parliament, for example, still must approve any revisions in the *Book of Common Prayer,* or give authorization for the priesting of women. The establishment of the Church meant that the American Episcopal Church would have great difficulty in getting its first bishops ordained and consecrated in England because any English bishop must take the Oath of Supremacy to a potentate whom the Americans had just defeated in their Revolution and from whom they now claimed absolute independence. The English Church still retains a strong flavor of these Erastian arrangements (ones that give the State power over Church affairs), while most of the Anglican provinces around the world have no established churches. This suggests for many today that the Church of England should be no model for how other provinces in the Communion order their ecclesiastical structures, especially those that observe strict separation of Church and State. Even the role of the Archbishop of Canterbury is, for many, compromised by its continuing dependency on the Crown since the ABC's appointment is at least officially a matter for the State alone to decide.

Henry's actions, no matter how much they were predicated upon a power struggle with the papacy, did find resonance among much of the English population. Luther's works had been read in England since at least the early 1520s, and people were ready for some kind of reformation of the Church that had been part of English history since Augustine's missionary work in the late sixth century. As Church historian Roland Bainton has put it, "Henry well calculated that he would meet no serious popular opposition so long as he toppled merely the papal tiara and not the holy Trinity or the established dogma." [3] Henry himself was not enamored of most of the ideas of the reformers and tried to keep intact much of Catholic liturgy and doctrine. He even enacted the Six Articles in 1539, which punished with death any denial of transubstantiation and upheld communion in one kind, clerical celibacy, monastic vows, private masses, and auricular confession to a priest. He was more concerned with establishing his authority as a sovereign than he was with the internal theological, liturgical, and ecclesiological debates of the Church itself, though he claimed the right to appoint new bishops for it. But under Henry, the Church of England adopted most of the main principles of the Protestant Reformation: a reliance upon Scripture accessible to the laity in the vernacular, its supreme authority for belief and practice, the formulation of worship in accord with the language of ordinary folk, acceptance of the doctrine of justification through divine grace alone as appropriated by faith, and a refusal to accept the supremacy of the Pope in matters of faith and practice. These Reformation principles, however, in no way were regarded as deviating from the faith "once delivered to the Saints" (Jude 1:3) at the beginning of the Christian Church. The Church of England was believed to be a continuation of the earliest faith of the Christian Church but in a slightly altered ecclesiastical structure adapted to the history and customs of England, in relation to the national sovereign, and without some of the polity and corrupt practices that had accreted to the Church between the fourth and sixteenth centuries.

Out of all this, the Church of England created what was eventually to become perhaps the single most important unifying factor among all those around the world who claimed some historic connection with the Church of England, namely the *Book of Common Prayer* (BCP). It was first introduced under Henry's son, Edward, in 1549, and reflected in its underlying theological assumptions a strong Lutheran influence. It became the required form of worship in England and all other forms were prohibited. Its liturgy (and its order for the ordination of deacons, priests, and bishops) can be found today, slightly altered in some cases, in every Anglican or Episcopal Church throughout the whole Anglican Communion. Its underlying theology reflects both Catholic and Protestant sentiments: reliance upon Scripture as sufficient for salvation and a notion that Christ is still really present in the Lord's Supper; reception of both elements by the laity and the reservation of the consecrated elements.

Supplementing the BCP, the Church of England in 1563 added what was in effect the first attempt at systematizing doctrine for the Church in the Protestant-leaning "Thirty-Nine Articles" (whittled down from 42 articles in 1552). The Articles are not altogether consistent with each other, and their status as authoritative for belief was and remains unclear. For a time priests could not be ordained without subscribing to them, but in 1865 this requirement was modified to demand only that clergy affirm that the doctrine of the Church as found in the BCP and the Articles "is agreeable to the Word of God, and to undertake not to teach in contradiction of them." [4] Central to the Articles as far as current events are concerned is the clear statement that

> Holy Scripture containeth all things necessary to salvation: so that whatsoever is not read therein, nor may be proved thereby, is not to be required of any man, that it should be believed as an article of the Faith, or be thought requisite or necessary to Salvation.

In addition, the Creeds are authoritative only to the extent that they may be "proved" by Scripture (it also goes on to state that the Church has no power to "expound one place of Scripture, that it be repugnant to another"); that General Councils of the Church are not of themselves infallible (though the faith of the primitive Church on which Anglicanism is supposed to rest accepts the authority of the first four ecumenical councils of the Church); and that, while neither transubstantiation nor a mere memorial of Christ's death are sufficient to explain the Eucharist, Christ is still somehow present in the sacrament. The Articles were adopted by the American Church in 1801 and reaffirmed in 1928 during a debate over the revision of the prayer book. In practice, however, a person's disagreement with any of the Articles is not sufficient to bar his or her ordination or standing within the Church since assent to them is not required. Nevertheless, the Articles continue to be invoked by some in the debate over homosexuality. But while they may summarize what have historically been the key doctrines of Anglicanism (which Anglicans claim are the key doctrines of Christianity itself), they lack the authority of the creeds, of Scripture, and even of synods or General Conventions in establishing the contours of acceptable affirmations of faith and belief. In fact, it is not clear whether Anglicanism, as such, has any clear and explicit doctrines that all Anglicans must assent to. Some today deplore the lack of precision in the formulation of Anglican doctrine while others applaud the flexibility and capaciousness (the favorite term today is comprehensiveness) of Anglican doctrine. Anglicanism has always been reluctant to go beyond the creeds (primarily the Nicene but also the Apostle's and the Athanasian creeds' "Quicunque Vult") and the councils of the Church from Nicaea to Chalcedon, which defined the nature of Christ in relation to God.

Of course, one of the distinguishing features of Anglicanism is its acceptance of the historic episcopate as useful (some would argue essential) to the well-being (some would say very being) of the Church. An *episcopus* is a bishop, which means superintendent or overseer. Anglicans recognize three orders of ordained ministry: deacons, priests (or presbyters), and bishops. There has been much debate, as we shall see, over the exact role of bishops but the "Outline of the Faith," also known as the Catechism in the Episcopal Church's *Book of Common Prayer,* says that the ministry of a bishop is to

represent Christ and his Church, particularly as apostle, chief priest, and pastor of a diocese; to guard the faith, unity, and discipline of the whole Church; to proclaim the Word of God; to act in Christ's name for the reconciliation of the world and the building up of the Church; and to ordain others to continue Christ's ministry.

(On this last point it is important to remember that only bishops can ordain or consecrate other bishops.)

This description, of course, begs many questions. Acting for reconciliation, for example, might mean for some bishops accepting gay persons as priests and as deserving of a blessing for their committed relationships; but guarding the unity of the Church might mean denying both of these things. Nevertheless, bishops are understood to have jurisdiction (within limits) over dioceses, which consist of individual congregations normally situated within a single geographical area. Whether bishops can intervene in dioceses other than the ones to which they have been elected is a point of great contention in the current debates within the Anglican Communion.

No discussion of the Church (of which Anglicanism considers itself a part) would be complete without reference to a principle sometimes called the Vincentian Canon. It comes from a fifth century church thinker Vincent of Lerins. His canonical principle would be appealed to throughout Church history, especially in the Roman Church, and is still in play in the current debates within the Anglican Communion. Briefly put, Vincent was concerned about *who* was to determine orthodox Christian belief. He was profoundly aware of the different interpretations that sincere Christians could place upon Scripture. Since no one interpretation could, by itself, claim superiority to all the others, there had to be an authoritative principle for determining what would count as legitimate belief and interpretation. As Vincent recognized, "the statements of the same writer are explained by different men in different ways, so much so that it seems almost possible to extract from it as many opinions as there are men." There is, therefore, "great need for the laying down of a rule for the exposition of Prophets and Apostles in accordance with the standard of the interpretation of the Church Catholic." [5] The Church must serve as the interpreter of last resort because only through its collective judgment can the subjectivity (and potential destabilization) ingredient in private interpretations be checked. Thus, Vincent comes to his well-known (but deceptively simple) formula for determining true belief as *that which has been believed everywhere, always, and by all*. This means what has been believed universally, in antiquity, and by the consent of the faithful. It will be better therefore to prefer the whole over the parts. The true believer will "prefer the healthiness of the whole body to the morbid and corrupt limb." If a new idea is proposed for belief, the believer should take care to "cleave to antiquity, which cannot now be led astray by any deceit of novelty." With this understanding of what counts as true belief in the Church, the scales are weighed against innovation and what contemporary American church historian Bruce Mullin calls the "myth of the pure [i.e., primitive] church," [6] and its beliefs become the cleaver by which to strike off any ideas that either have no support in the early church or cannot be reconciled with the teachings of that church. In the hands of today's conservatives, that cleaver is being employed to suggest that contemporary "liberals" have abandoned the faith "once delivered to the saints" in order to go whoring after the whims of the mothers, sisters, and gay and lesbian cousins who are being driven by the winds of the secular culture into areas that have nothing to do with the true faith.

ECUSA: A Post-Establishment Denomination

The planting of the Church of England in the colonies was not simple or uniform. It was first established in Virginia where it held on to the prerogatives of establishment down to the American Revolution. A bill "For Establishing a Provision for Teachers of the Christian Religion" in Virginia introduced by Patrick Henry in 1784 would have stipulated that the members of all churches would have to affirm that they believe in God, that there is a future state of rewards and punishments, that the Christian religion is the true Religion, and that the Bible in its entirety was divinely inspired. [7]

In response, James Madison argued that the fruits of legal establishment have been "pride and indolence in the Clergy; ignorance and servility in the laity; in both, superstition, bigotry and persecution." [8] This suggests that Anglicans were for the most part on the wrong side of the religious freedom and anti-establishment debate because they had located authority in an alliance between monarchy and church that simply could not prevail in the national experiment in religious liberty into which the Episcopal Church would have to fit following the success of the "glorious cause."

No matter what the arguments for and against establishment were at the time, the one thing all the Anglican established churches in the colonies lacked were resident bishops. The one thing the Puritan establishment in New England did not want was bishops imposed on them by the Church of England. A strong argument for sending bishops to the colonies had been made by numerous Anglicans on this side of the Atlantic (though the plea for bishops was not unanimous even among Anglicans). The Reverend Thomas Chandler, a New Jersey priest, makes the most spirited case for bishops in the colonies. In "An Appeal to the Public," [9] Chandler explicitly links the Church of England with the monarchy.

> The Church of England, in its external Polity, is so happily connected and interwoven with the Civil Constitution, that each mutually supports and is supported by the other. . . . Episcopacy and Monarchy are, in their Frame and Constitution, best suited to each other.

And, in what some Anglicans who would embrace the Revolution in America might have seen as completely unhelpful, Chandler concludes by asserting that "Episcopacy can never thrive in a Republican Government, nor Republican Principles in an Episcopal Church. . . . He that prefers Monarchy in the State, is more likely to approve of Episcopacy in the Church, than a rigid Republican." While Chandler is clearly rowing against the tide of emerging republicanism and is, in effect, ironically offering to republican-minded Americans precisely the reasons why they should continue to keep English bishops away from American soil, he is nonetheless pointing to a difficulty (the lack of indigenous or resident bishops) that would continue to imperil the Anglican Church in America until it could sever its ties with Great Britain and create a nonestablished Episcopal Church of its own. In short, it was by a defiance of authority (in this case the royal authority to appoint bishops for an established church) that permitted Episcopalians, as they came to be called, to create a Church in the newly formed United States. Had Erastian principles prevailed in the new republic there would likely have been a Methodist, Baptist, or Congregationalist establishment given the supremacy of their numbers, not one favorable to the Episcopalians. In one more of the many ironies of our history, the man who would be credited with beginning the attempt to create a denomination legally and in many ways ecclesiastically independent of the Church of England was someone who had resisted the move to republicanism in the State and, for a time, in the Church as well.

Samuel Seabury had been elected by the Anglicans in Connecticut as the man they hoped would eventually secure ordination to the episcopate in England and return as the first resident bishop in the colonies. However, Seabury's path to episcopal ordination was not a smooth one, but was filled with dissents, disagreements, irregularities, and diversity of opinion among his fellow Anglicans, the very things many of today's defenders of Anglican unity at all costs seem to have forgotten in their eagerness to quell dissent and difference. But it was out of such controversy, sometimes vociferously expressed, that the Episcopal Church in the United States was born and, to a large extent, given its vitality.

As Church historian Paul Marshall has pointed out, there was a variety of points of view on religious and political issues among the Christian colonists in America in the late eighteenth century.[10] Samuel Seabury of Connecticut, for example, had thrown in his political lot with the Tories. This was not surprising given his highly monarchial and hierarchical view of political authority. He believed that societies are best understood as organic wholes in which each part ought to be in interdependent relation with all the other parts organized under a head that directed and controlled the whole organism.[11] The Whigs drew the boundaries of the republican community much more narrowly than the Tories such as Seabury. They wanted small communities, approximating face to face relationships in which the common good would transcend and not simply reconcile conflicting interests. They had come to conclude that maintaining community with Great Britain was both logistically and politically impossible. But Seabury enlarged the notion of community to include both the colonies and Great Britain in one organic whole. If the organic community requires due subservience to the whole, then there was no reason why it should not obligate the colonies to obey their mother, Great Britain, by whom they had been "nursed with the greatest parental Tenderness, and protected and defended with her choicest Blood and Treasure—They had grown up under her fostering Care and they had securely flourished under the Shadow of Her Wings." To seek independence from that to which one was organically bound would produce "Anarchy and Confusion, Violence and Oppression." [12] The debate, in other words, between Seabury and his Whig Republican opponents was not over the organic nature of government, but over who would occupy the role of political authority for it.

It is significant that today's conservatives adopt a generally Seaburian line on ecclesiastical unity. They tend to argue that the Anglican Communion, especially as represented by her bishops and archbishops, is the mother who embraces all her constituent parts. The unity she provides by her motherly inclusion of all her children should temper and control their individual actions, especially those rebellious ones that threaten to damage the harmony of the whole. Today's liberals, on the other hand, seem to be more like the Whigs and rebels who lean toward the virtues of the smaller, more local, communities whose interests may not be the same as those of the body as a whole.

Conservatives such as Seabury could point out that the rebels were in effect challenging the clear Biblical injunction in Peter 2:17 to fear God and honor the Emperor (which Seabury utilized in his critique of the rebellion and for which he substituted the word "King" for "Emperor"). Had that particular Biblical teaching, along with Romans 13:1–2 ("Let every person be subject to the governing authorities; for there is no authority except from God, and those authorities that exist have been instituted by God"), been strictly adhered to no faithful Christian could have taken up arms against his rightful political superiors in Great Britain. In the same section of the Bible from which many current opponents of homosexuality take their Biblical authority, it clearly says in 1 Samuel 15:23 that "rebellion is no less a sin than divination" (which is tantamount to putting oneself in the place of God). But one assumes that most conservatives today are not so tied to a literal reading of the text that they would in retrospect deny the right of the colonists to seek independence from Great Britain in the latter part of the eighteenth century.

It is ironic as well that Seabury's own struggle to get ordained to the episcopate would eventually take him outside the very mother country to whom he was counseling total political allegiance. By ultimately receiving consecration at the hands of nonjuroring bishops in Scotland, he wound up receiving what many of his own colleagues in the newly formed United States would regard as an irregular ordination that only later would be recognized as valid by English-ordained bishops for the American Church.

As early as 1780 Dr. William Smith, educator and Anglican priest, began to convene meetings of Anglicans (both clergy and lay) in the colony of Maryland to discuss the situation created by the actions of the revolutionaries.[13] At a meeting in 1783 they agreed to change their name from the Church of England to the Protestant Episcopal Church. They also elected Smith to be their candidate for ordination to the episcopate. Smith was keeping a former student of his, the Reverend William White of Philadelphia (who had been ordained in England) informed of what was going on in Maryland. In 1782 White published an article, "The Case of the Episcopal Churches in the United States Considered," which was to be seminal in the founding of the American Episcopal Church. In the article White urged the calling of colonial conventions to elect clergymen who would function as overseers until such time as the new church in the States could have its own bishops. His plan of organization gave "presiding clergy" (the name he gave to the overseers in lieu of there being no "official" bishops in the interim), other clergy, and laypersons roles to play in the governance of the Church. This plan would bring him into direct conflict with Seabury's antirepublican political philosophy. For White, democracy ought to characterize church government and its basic unit ought to be the local parish or congregation, not the diocese or the bishop. White concluded that

> one natural consequence of this distinction [between parish and diocese] would be to retain in each church every power that need not be delegated for the good of the whole. Another, will be an equality of the churches; and not, as in England, the subjection of all parish churches to their respective cathedrals.[14]

White was clearly coming down hard on the side of a more local understanding of community, eschewing the Seaburian notion that the larger the social unit under hierarchical authority, the better.

White's notion of ecclesiastical polity guided by a devolutionary understanding of authority would be an important factor in the development of the Episcopal Church in the United States. It stands in stark contrast to contemporary efforts to elevate the authority of provinces, Primates, and a foreign bishop (of

Canterbury) in order to solve problems caused by ecclesial units further down the chain of devolved authority. White was not, as Marshall notes, particularly concerned with doctrine nor with the "Thirty-Nine Articles," which, in his opinion, "designedly left room for a considerable latitude of sentiment."[15] White's view reflects the reality of the early Episcopal Church in America in which congregations were a great deal stronger than their bishops.[16]

White's tract was a major impetus in getting a number of Episcopal delegates from New York, New Jersey, and Pennsylvania to a meeting in New Jersey in 1784 to plan for a general convention later that year. But the New England delegation soon withdrew from the idea of a General Convention and proceeded to pursue their ideas on a different track. In replying to White they said "Really, sir, we think an Episcopal Church without Episcopacy, if it be not a contradiction in terms, would, however, be a new thing under the sun."[17] And the one thing conservative Anglicans do not like is "a new thing under the sun," though in time they often get used to what was at one time considered radical and even potentially heretical, including the role of the laity and women in the upper levels of governance and priesthood of the Church. (The Episcopal Church was rather late in recognizing the role of the laity, however. It was not until the twentieth century, for example, that laypersons could serve on the Standing Committee in the Diocese of Connecticut.)

Seabury and his colleagues refused to join the organizing meeting in 1784 claiming, in words that anticipate the contemporary conservative charge that the liberals have been hijacked by secular forces, that "the Christian Church is not a mere piece of secular manufacture, indifferently wrought into any shape or mould, as the Political Colour fancies."[18] In March 1783 ten Anglican clergy in Connecticut decided that Seabury should seek episcopal consecration in England. The difficulty he, as well as other American candidates for the episcopate, would face was the requirement, due to the legal establishment of the Church of England, that any bishop ordained in England by English bishops had to swear allegiance to the Crown. By itself this would not have troubled the monarchial oriented Seabury, but in a country that was removing all official governmental ties with England such allegiance would be impossible. But it was not clear to the English bishops whether they could on their own remove the obligation of allegiance to the Crown or whether they had to seek the Crown's consent to such a radical move.

Once in England, Seabury waited for many months to get interviews with the Archbishop of York and the Bishops of London and Oxford.[19] Ironically, one of the obstacles to a positive reception by the Archbishop of Canterbury was Seabury's failure to get official support from the laity in his proposed Diocese of Connecticut. Following further frustrations, Seabury concluded that he would have no hope of getting his consecration at the hands of English bishops and turned instead to Scotland. There clearly were bishops in Scotland whose episcopacies were in the apostolic succession. The problem was that they were nonjuroring bishops; that is, they had refused to swear allegiance to William of

Orange, the new ruler of England, in 1688. One advantage to Scotland was that it could not be suspected of wanting supremacy over the Church in the United States. There were strains between the Scottish Church, of which Robert Kilgour was the Primus, and the Church of England *in* Scotland. Seabury eventually received approval from the bishops of that diminished church to be consecrated by them despite the entreaty from William Smith that they not proceed with the consecration because it was premature and might interfere with current efforts in the States to create a Protestant Episcopal Church.[20] Smith's argument was not persuasive, and on November 14, 1784, Seabury was consecrated by three bishops as a bishop in what he and the consecrating bishops considered to be the line of apostolic succession. The consecrating bishops made it clear that their action in no way was implicated in or supported by the secular powers of the State, thus giving Seabury the right to say that his consecration would be fully consistent with the First Amendment that officially separated church and state in America (but which was not ratified until 1791).

It is significant that Seabury and the consecrating bishops also agreed to maintain between their two communions a state of "brotherly fellowship."[21] One might argue that the Anglican Communion began at this precise moment since two different countries, each with its own Episcopal Church, had agreed to a communion of a kind but without recognizing any foreign ecclesiastical, let alone civil, authority over them.

In 1786 the English Parliament eventually passed a bill allowing the consecration in England of three bishops for the American Church: two of them, William White and Samuel Provoost (of New York), were consecrated by English bishops in 1787. Their consecration, however, did not end the debate in the new country over the appropriate plan for the union or constitution of the Episcopal Church in America. The Seabury faction continued to object to what it regarded as the White faction's refusal to acknowledge sufficiently the difference between bishops, clergy, and laity in the governance of the Church. An English objection to the validity of Seabury's consecration was voiced by the Archbishop of York who said, while acknowledging that the original nonjuroring bishops in Scotland in 1688 were in the line of apostolic succession, it was nonetheless "very doubtful how a succession of their authority could be continued for a number of years after their death, amongst persons who have no real Congregation or Charge, but only a nominal or mere titular appointment over an invisible Church. . . ."[22]

Despite these doubts, Seabury did return to America as a bishop, at least in his opinion and, later, but after much controversy, in the opinion of the three bishops officially consecrated in England. At that point America had, in effect, three forms of Episcopal polity: the hierarchical one advocated by Seabury, the republican one advocated by White and Smith, popular in the middle Atlantic and Southern states, and the Methodist alternative, the latter of which had, as it turned out, no future within the Episcopal Church as such.

At one point, ironically, John Skinner, bishop co-adjutor of Aberdeen, Scotland, wrote to Seabury suggesting something like the present notion of delegated episcopal oversight for those who had problems of conscience recognizing the validity of the consecration of a bishop co-adjutor for Seabury. In the case of such a consecration, the bishops of the South, Skinner suggested, would not "refuse their brotherly assistance." Only if the other bishops "required a violation of the consciences of Connecticut's bishop and clergy would they [the Scottish bishops] proceed to consecrate another bishop for them." [23] In the meantime Seabury was ordaining priests from some of the middle states. His action was greeted by the General Convention of that year with an instruction to the dioceses not to recognize the validity of Seabury's "nonjuroring orders." [24] Out of these arguments came one important provision recommended by White to the convention in June 1786, namely that the Church in the United States must not receive any clergymen "professing canonical subjection to any Bishop, in any State or country, other than those Bishops who may be duly settled in the States represented in this Convention." [25] Thus was established early on the principle that there cannot be more than one bishop with authority in any diocese and those bishops must receive authorization from the General Convention. That ruling seems not to be given serious attention by contemporary conservatives who look to African bishops for episcopal leadership in the United States within dioceses that are part of the Episcopal Church.

There were also debates over how much latitude the new Church ought to permit in the way of doctrine. At one point an Episcopal layperson by the name of Miller had written to William White asking whether his congregation in New York, which was inclined toward Unitarianism, might remain within the Episcopal Church. As Miller put it,

> the object of our society in our new liturgy was to leave out all such expressions as wound the conscience of a Unitarian, without introducing any which would displease a Trinitarian. . . . A multitude of different opinions may be entertained by Christians who conscientiously use the same liturgy.[26]

Miller was arguing that the pursuit of truth demanded such an accommodation to different points of view. White was not sympathetic and insisted that any changes in doctrine or liturgy must not be "contrary to what appears, from the institutions and the conduct of the Church of England, to be her sense of the essential doctrines of the Gospel" and must be only "in what the same Church has declared to be matters subject to change." [27] In this correspondence we see a glimpse of the kind of argument that has continued to the present day without clear resolution: how wide should doctrinal accommodation or comprehensiveness be; does the Prayer Book contain a clear, single, and consistent theology; if it does, must it be officially adhered to by all who use it in worship; what are the "essential doctrines" of the Gospel, and who determines them?

The completion of this story, with its convolutions, questions of improper actions, irregularities, suspicion of validity of orders and consecration, uncertainty over the authority of bishops, the power of individual congregations and all the rest finally came in 1789. Before that event, however, Seabury continued his opposition to White's federal plan for the constitution of the new Church, calling it perhaps "episcopal in its orders, but Presbyterian in its government." Instead, he argued, using language that foreshadows that of contemporary conservatives, that the Church must be built on the model of the primitive church, "always remembering that the government, and doctrines, and sacraments of the Church are settled by divine authority, and are not subjected to our amendment, or alteration." And this divine authority, for Seabury, had spoken clearly and unambiguously in God's word in Scripture, and we must be "content to submit our ignorance to his knowledge, and to think of him, and believe in him, as he has represented himself to us."[28]

Finally, in 1789 the Protestant Episcopal Church in the United States of America officially came into being. An earlier proposal to require lay delegates at all diocesan conventions was removed (thus satisfying Seabury's concerns). Also to satisfy him, two governing bodies were created: a House of Bishops and a House of Lay and Clerical Deputies. The House of Bishops would have, in effect, veto power over the House of Deputies (unless that House overrode the veto by a four-fifths vote), thus preserving, in part, the power of episcopal authority so dear to Seabury.

The Convention went on to say that it was "seeking to keep the happy mean between too much stiffness in refusing, and too much easiness in admitting variations in things once advisedly established. . . ." It also assured the delegates that the convention was "far from intending to depart from the Church of England in any essential point of doctrine, discipline, or worship; or further than local circumstances require." These lines from the Preface to the new *Book of Common Prayer* stress continuity with the earliest churches in Christendom and with the Church of England, especially with respect to the continuation of the episcopate. There was also a strong sense of the need for unity, avoiding schism at all costs. (This would later be exemplified in the refusal of the churches in the North to cut off relations with Southern churches during the Civil War.) Finally, there was acknowledgement of diversity in the Church.[29]

And thus the American church began its journey with a kind of flexibility and latitude in liturgical practice, and a pragmatism in ecclesiastical governance that would characterize it down to the present day. Compromises had to be made between various factions simply in order to bring the Church into being in this country. Insistence on absolutes, precisely defined and obligatory for all, was greatly diminished, if not extinguished entirely. That refusal to absolutize practice or belief is now what is under attack from those in the Church who think too much pragmatism and concession to the reigning culture threatens the very meaning of what it means to be an Episcopalian and a member of the Anglican Communion. How this came about is the story we still need to tell.

— 3 —

The Bishops Assembled: The Lambeth Conferences from 1867 to the Present

"Surely some revelation is at hand"

A central part of the Anglican Communion has been the Lambeth Conferences, convened roughly every 10 years by the Archbishop of Canterbury. It might be argued that the Communion really began when there were three geographically and jurisdictionally separate Episcopal Churches in Scotland, Canada, and the United States, all of whom claimed descent from the Church of England.[1] But until the middle of the nineteenth century there were no formal meetings between the diocesan bishops or the Primates of these churches.

As early as 1851 Bishop John Henry Hopkins of Vermont, the Presiding Bishop of ECUSA wrote to the Archbishop of Canterbury, Charles Thomas Longley suggesting a meeting of the heads of the Anglican churches outside England who were in communion with the Archbishop. Shortly after that the Archbishop received a similar but an even more urgent request for a meeting from the Canadian Provincial Synod, which was disturbed by the possibility of revisions in the canons of the Church of England that would, if passed, affect the Canadian Church's polity, especially around the question of lay representation in the highest councils of the Church. Canada was concerned that it not "drift into the status of the Episcopal Churches of Scotland and America."[2] Longley accepted the request and called a meeting for February 1867 for all bishops (not just the Primates) of the existing provinces, 76 of whom attended. Longley was clear that the meeting "was not a general synod capable of enacting canons, but a conference to discuss practical questions, on which they could pass resolutions which would be a guide for future action."[3] In the more than 140 years since that first meeting no attempt has succeeded to give the Lambeth Conferences any greater authority than that envisioned by Longley.[4]

The Colenso Affair

One of the first issues that the first conference took up was what has come to be known as the Colenso affair. John Colenso had been consecrated bishop for the Diocese of Natal at the request of the Bishop of Capetown Robert Gray.[5] Someone inclined toward liberalism in theology, Colenso was dedicated to bringing the Gospel to the Zulus. But his liberalism led him to deny the traditional doctrine of the Atonement and the belief that there would be eternal torment for unbelievers.[6] Colenso, already studying the new scholarship on Scripture coming out of Germany, also asked hard questions about the literal accuracy of some parts of the Bible, such as the story of the flood. He advocated the acceptance of many tribal customs, including polygamy.[7] When summoned to Capetown by Bishop Gray to answer charges that he was deviating from the true faith, he refused to accept Gray's authority over him, arguing in effect for his own local episcopal autonomy. Gray nevertheless convinced a synod to permit him to depose Colenso. When the case was brought before the first Lambeth Conference, the American bishops, ironically, were the strongest in seeking to condemn this deviant from the faith (ironic because today they stand accused by African bishops of themselves deviating from the truth faith). Gray was able to return to South Africa with a signed declaration accepting Gray's sentence of excommunication, even though the gathering at Lambeth had no ecclesiastical authority to impose or ratify such a sentence.

The Chicago-Lambeth Quadrilateral

The next Lambeth Conference occurred in 1878, and from that point on they have been held with some exceptions every ten years. The Conference of 1888 is significant because it was there that the so-called Chicago-Lambeth Quadrilateral, initiated in the House of Bishops in ECUSA in 1886, was adopted. The Lambeth resolution reads as follows:

> That, in the opinion of this Conference, the following Articles supply a basis on which approach may be by God's blessing made towards Home Reunion:
>
> a. The Holy Scriptures of the Old and New Testaments, as "containing all things necessary to salvation," and as being the rule and ultimate standard of faith.
> b. The Apostles' Creed, as the Baptismal Symbol; and the Nicene Creed, as the sufficient statement of the Christian faith.
> c. The two Sacraments ordained by Christ Himself—Baptism and the Supper of the Lord—ministered with unfailing use of Christ's Words of Institution and of the elements ordained by Him.
> d. The Historic Episcopate, locally adapted in the methods of its administration to the varying needs of the nations and peoples called of God into the Unity of His Church.

No significant changes have been made to this foundational document of the Episcopal Church since that time.

At the 1920 Lambeth Conference (its sixth meeting), women were affirmed as lay members of synods and General Conventions. The Conference also took the opportunity to address the issue of marriage, declaring that its main purpose is "the continuation of the race through the gift and heritage of children." (Later many of the Churches in the Communion would add to and reorder the priority of the purposes of marriage to include mutual affection and sex within marriage as a means to the enjoyment and manifestation of that affection. This is significant because there are many gay and lesbian persons today who would argue that while they technically cannot produce children through sexual acts of their own, they can manifest all the virtues of committed, loving, and mutually affectionate relationships, i.e., of marriage.)

The 1920 Lambeth Meeting also took up the issue of a divided Christianity. While extolling the virtues of a united Christian community, it stressed the importance of diversity. "It is through a rich diversity of life and devotion that the unity of the whole fellowship will be fulfilled." [8] Twenty-eight years later at the 1948 Lambeth Conference, the contemplated ordination of a woman, Florence Li Tim-Oi (see Chapter 4 on women's ordination), was taken up and the Conference concluded that it "would be against the tradition and order . . . of the Anglican Communion" to accept the ordination of a woman and rejected any need for further discussion of the matter of women's ordination.

More significantly, however, coming out of the 1948 Meeting was a reflection on the nature of Anglicanism itself, compared to which Church historian H. R. McAdoo has said no Lambeth Conference has ever produced "anything better on the nature and instruments of authority as understood by Anglicans." [9] Calling the Communion of Anglicans around the world a "fellowship," the gathering issued a committee report discussing the nature of the Anglican Communion. The Communion rests, it said, on a territorial principle and does not require (nor has there been) a "single pattern or mould to standardize Church policy, nor do the churches that comprise the Communion recognize any peculiar authority as being vested in the Archbishop of Canterbury; but he is given . . . a position of leadership." [10] The provinces are recognized to be "each autonomous in its own sphere, and each in full communion with the Anglican Communion." However, the Lambeth bishops were deeply concerned about finding a basis for order in the Church, and they asked the crucial question: "is Anglicanism based on a sufficiently coherent form of authority to form the nucleus of a worldwide fellowship of Churches, or does its comprehensiveness conceal internal divisions which may cause its disruption?" This prescient question still haunts the Communion 60 years after it was first posed. The bishops did go on to note that the authority that binds the Communion is "moral and spiritual, resting on the truth of the Gospel, and on a charity which is patient and willing to defer to the common mind." And this is precisely what is being challenged today: some claiming that the moral practices of some members of the Communion have gone too far. This claim cuts both ways, however: the conservatives claiming that granting gay persons and lesbians the right to be ordained and have their relationships blessed is moral blasphemy and the liberals claiming that to deny them that right is moral injustice. At the same time, it is not clear who today is asking whom to be patient, who is exercising charity toward the other, and, above all, what would count as "the common mind" of the Communion given that there is no authoritative body delegated to determine and enforce the common mind. Even consensus among the bishops (who comprise over 75 percent of the "instruments of communion") does not equal consensus among all the faithful where laity far outnumber the ordained.

Also given that the ultimate authority for many conservatives today is Scripture, it is significant that the 1948 Conference, while affirming that Scripture is the "ultimate standard of faith," nevertheless advised that it "should be continually interpreted in the context of the Church's life." The liberals today would argue that the context of interpretation, at least for many provinces, the United States and Canada chief among them, is the open and inclusive embrace of the experience of gay and lesbian persons living in committed and loving relationships. The conservatives would argue that the context of interpretation should be nothing narrower than the opinion of the entire Communion, the majority of whose members, they claim, are radically opposed to ordaining gay persons and lesbians or blessing their relationships.

The authority of Scripture was one of the chief items of concern at the following Lambeth Meeting in 1958. Its first eight resolutions all had to do with the centrality of Scripture for the Christian faith. It affirmed that the Bible "discloses the truths about the relation of God and which are the key to the world's predicament." The Church is the guardian and interpreter of Holy Scripture; and the Conference also repeated the traditional Anglican premise that the Church may teach nothing as "necessary for eternal salvation but what may be concluded and proved by Scripture." So far this was all standard Anglican teaching. What is significant is what Lambeth '58 did not say. It did not say that everything in Scripture is necessary for eternal salvation, nor did it endorse any one particular school of Biblical interpretation. In fact, it "gratefully" acknowledged its debt to "devoted scholars who, worshipping the God of Truth, have enriched and deepened our understanding of the Bible, not least by facing with intellectual integrity the questions raised by modern knowledge and modern criticism." [11] The significance of this embrace of modern scholarship would not become fully evident until the 1990s when many Biblical scholars would reject a noncontextual (and to them simplistic, absolutist, and literal) reading of parts of the Bible regarding sexuality, a reading that would nevertheless be held up by conservatives not only as the clear teaching of Scripture but as morally binding today as it had been for ancient Israel.

The 1968 Lambeth Meeting was the first to take up in detail the issue of women's ordination. [12] It said simply that it believed that the arguments for and against the ordination of women were "inconclusive" and therefore asked every Province to study the question of the ordination of women to the priesthood and to make these studies available to the whole Communion. The doors to women's ordination were almost, but not quite, all the way open in the minds of the bishops at Lambeth in 1968.

Less momentous at that gathering was the official internment of the prevailing status of the Thirty-Nine Articles, assent to which, Lambeth suggested, ought no longer to be required of ordinands, and even where it might still be required that it be done "only in the context of a statement which gives the full range of our inheritance and sets the Articles in their historical context." Another sign of what many conservatives saw as an opening wedge toward relativism in the abandonment of ancient authoritative texts was the odd pronouncement by Lambeth 1968 on polygamy. While not explicitly permitting polygamy and while clearly reaffirming the traditional view that "monogamous life-long marriage [is] God's will for mankind," Lambeth '68 nevertheless recognized that polygamy "poses one of the sharpest conflicts between the faith and particular cultures" and also recognized that "in every place many problems concerning marriage confront the Church." [13] This position on polygamy was actually urged by African bishops trying to get the "North" or "Western" world to accept the unique cultural conditions in Africa that they as bishops must struggle with daily. Ironically, the chief opponents of treating homosexuality in its cultural setting today are some African bishops who had pleaded for a sympathetic understanding of polygamy at the Lambeth Conference of 1968.

Finally Lambeth '68 resolved that a new body be created known as the Anglican Consultative Council (ACC), which would "facilitate the co-operative work of the churches" of the AC and help to coordinate common action. It came into existence primarily to provide a body for the Communion that would meet more often than once a decade (in this case every three years or so). What is most significant about the ACC, however, is the fact that it includes both laypersons as well as priests (one of each from each Province), thus giving voice to people historically excluded from the other "instruments of communion," which are exclusively episcopal.

By the time of the next Lambeth Conference in 1978, the issue of authority in the Communion was still unresolved and issues, such as women's ordination to the priesthood and the episcopate, were beginning to divide many of the Provinces in the Communion. Lambeth '78 "advised" the member Churches

> not to take action regarding issues which are of concern to the whole Anglican Communion without consultation with a Lambeth Conference or with the episcopate through the Primates Committee, and requests the Primates to initiate a study of the nature of authority within the Anglican Communion,

now some 30 years after the issue of authority had been so concisely and trenchantly raised at Lambeth 1948.

However, Lambeth '78 did recognize (it is interesting how often Lambeth resolutions take the form of acknowledgements and recognitions: meaning that they are in some sense *ex post facto,* following decisions, actions, and changes of mind that have already taken place within one or more of the provinces that comprise the Communion as a whole) that some member churches might wish to consecrate a woman to the episcopate. It also "accepted" that each such member church "must act in accordance with its own constitution" (in keeping with the principle of local autonomy and dispersed authority that had long been part of the Anglican tradition). Nevertheless, the Conference "recommended" that

> no decision to consecrate be taken without consultation with the episcopate through the primates and overwhelming support in any member Church and in the diocese concerned, lest the bishop's office should become a cause of disunity instead of a focus of unity.

Note the ambiguity in this resolution (e.g., there is no clarity about what constitutes "overwhelming support" and how it is to be determined) and its almost exclusive reliance upon the wisdom of bishops. Priests and laypersons are not mentioned at all as constituting the voices that ought to be consulted before proceeding to any provincial action on women in the episcopate.

What seems to matter most to Lambeth '78 is the preservation of unity in the Communion. At least it seems to matter more than whether the ordination of women to the priesthood and consecration to the episcopate is just and right and must be done no matter how distressed and pained some members of the Communion might feel.

It is now clear that Lambeth will continue to caution member churches to go slow in doing anything that might upset other member churches. The default position has now become one in which actions that even Lambeth admits are canonically legal in individual member provinces should be prohibited if there is the possibility that they might cause distress in other provinces. The issue for the twenty-first century is whether demands for justice should trump the inherent conservatism of the ecclesiastical fellowship as a whole. The more inclusive of diverse views the Communion becomes, the more hesitant it is to upset those constituent members who are the most reluctant to accept changes. Rather unlike Roman Catholic polity in which a centralized authority can make decisions without inclusive consultation with all the members of the Church, the polity of the Anglican Communion (assuming one can call the actions of the Lambeth Conference, the ABC, the Primates Meetings, and the ACC a polity) is to engage in such inclusive consultation (admittedly restricted almost exclusively to bishops) and to act only when there is virtually unanimity among all the provinces. The Roman Catholic approach can result in clear and unqualified positions on controversial moral topics such as abortion, contraception, and the death penalty, which are not subject to modification despite their lack of acceptance, in many instances, by a majority of Catholics on the ground. The Anglican approach is to wait until there is an emerging consensus among all the members before endorsing the actions of a few. Thus, women's ordination did eventually come about but only with a conscience clause for bishops who continue to oppose it. The struggle for the ordination of gay persons and lesbians and the blessing of their relationships is facing the same obstacles. But in this case the willingness of some dioceses and provinces to accept the ordination of gays and lesbians has not been stymied by the concern that such willingness is perceived as a threat to the unity of the larger Communion.

Slouching Toward Lambeth 1998

Lambeth 1988 once again took up the issue of the ordination or consecration of women to the episcopate (significantly it was the first resolution coming out of the meeting). It asked that each decision on the issue by particular provinces be respected without the principles behind the decision necessarily being "accepted," while maintaining "the highest possible degree of communion with the provinces which differ." Consistent with the Anglican appeal to "reception," it also asked the Archbishop of Canterbury in consultation with the Primates (again apparently no laity or priests were to be involved) to appoint a commission that would "ensure that the process of reception includes continuing consultation with the other Churches as well." The conscience clause was again affirmed when it resolved that any diocesan bishop ought to make "pastoral provision for, those clergy and congregations whose opinions differ from those of the bishop, in order to maintain the unity of the diocese." And it concluded that when hurt is experienced both by those who were subjected to questioning the validity of the episcopal acts of a woman and by those "whose conscience would be offended by the ordination of a woman to the episcopate," the Church needs to exercise sensitivity, patience, and pastoral care.

In addition to sensitivity and care needed over the issue of women in the episcopate, however, Lambeth 1988 reaffirmed the "historical position of respect for diocesan boundaries and the authority of bishops within these boundaries." This notion of diocesan boundaries would become one of the flash points of the current debate in ECUSA as bishops from outside the Province of ECUSA are seeking to cross diocesan boundaries in order to exercise episcopal authority over parishes that have taken positions of opposition to the actions of ECUSA. Lambeth 1988 was quite clear that it "is deemed inappropriate behaviour for any bishop or priest of this Communion to exercise episcopal or pastoral ministry within another diocese without first obtaining the permission and invitation of the ecclesial authority thereof." Lambeth 1988 also reaffirmed the earlier position on polygamy, allowing it to continue as long as the local context was permissive and because the putting away of multiple wives would cause them a social deprivation.

Lambeth 1988 was only a warm-up, however, to the fireworks and significance of Lambeth 1998, the meeting from which decisions that would rock the whole Communion, beginning in 2003, would emanate. The lead-up to Lambeth 1998 really began four years after Lambeth 1988 when a study document, released by the Inter-Anglican Theological and Doctrinal Consultation (1992) entitled "Belonging Together," noted that the AC was embracing "an increasing variety of cultures." [14] This variety has led some in the Communion to "claim to offer certainty in the midst of cultural dislocation, ways of construing reality which offer clarity, certainty and an escape from conflict." This even applies, according to the authors of the document, to the Bible, which is often used "in a way that takes little notice of the context in which they [the Bible and other resources] were written and the rich and diverse layers of meaning they contain." The problem with refusing to consider context, they warned, was that it "can lead to . . . uncritical commitment to one authority." [15] This assertion would by and large be ignored six years later when Lambeth '98 gathered to deal with the issue of sexuality in the Bible. "Belonging Together" also warned that issues of sexuality needed to be "comprehended in a wider framework [than just a narrow reading of the Bible] which includes justice and human rights," and it noted, presciently, that all the contentious issues are "complicated by differences in the interpretation of the Bible." [16] The document observed that Scripture has always been read in a "variety of competing ways." A more critical reading would enable people to

> overturn uncritical readings which have been used as tools of oppressive ideology. Interdependence [among the provinces and cultures making up the Communion] allows us to listen to each other's readings, and to criticize our own and each other's as we do so.[17]

Nevertheless, while acknowledging the difficulty of formulating the exact meaning of Scripture, the means of interpretation must always be "subjected to the touchstone of the church's ongoing reading of scripture" [18] (though the authors do not formulate that touchstone). The document did emphasize the place of human experience in interpreting Scripture and, in language that many would think had been ignored at Lambeth '98, especially with respect to the experience of gay and lesbian persons, that

> sometimes the dissonance between scriptural precedents and the desire in the community for change provokes [a] major crisis, . . . the absoluteness of scriptural authority and the integrity of lived experience seem to clash.[19]

Thankfully, the authors contend, "we are blessed with a community of interpretation that can bring to bear on Scripture and tradition experience from a diverse and inclusive community." [20] The minority at Lambeth '98 would argue that insufficient attention was given to the diversity and inclusivity of the experience of gay persons and lesbians in the Communion when the issue of sexuality was being considered. The document also reminded the Communion that reaching a common mind (which subsequent meetings within the Communion denied had been achieved around the issue of homosexuality) would take time.

The following year, 1993, a joint meeting of the Primates and the Anglican Consultative Council met in Cape Town and produced a document entitled *A Transforming Vision: Suffering and Glory in God's World,* which reaffirmed the Lambeth '88 resolution calling for "respect for diocesan boundaries and the authority of bishops within these boundaries" and which also said it would be inappropriate to any bishop to exercise episcopal authority within a diocese without first securing permission from the resident bishop.

The action of some bishops did continue to roil the waters on which the AC was sailing, however. In May 1996 an ecclesiastical court was convened to consider charges by 10 bishops of ECUSA against a retired American bishop, Walter C. Righter, for improperly ordaining a noncelibate gay man living in a partnered relationship. The court eventually dismissed the charges, saying that it was not giving a judgment on the morality of same sex relationships but that what Righter had done was not contrary to the core doctrine of the Church. The accusers had rested their case on what they believed was Righter's violation of doctrine. The Court found that "this is overreaching the Anglican understanding of doctrine. We are not a confessional church which has carefully articulated and identified the entire scope of its teaching and the disciplinary consequences for the violation of its teaching." [21] Core doctrine, in the Court's opinion, does not include any beliefs regarding homosexuality or "prohibiting the ordination of a non-celibate, homosexual person living in a faithful and committed sexual relationship with a person of the same sex." The Court noted that the teaching of the Church on such issues as slavery changed over time. But today the Court could not find any "full and clear authority of the Church" or "full and clear expression at this time and in this case" on the moral teaching regarding homosexuals. A 1979 General Convention resolution stating that *"it is not appropriate for this Church to ordain a practicing homosexual, or any person who is engaged in heterosexual relations outside of marriage"* was "recommendatory only" and not binding on its own terms.

The Court, in its conclusion, in effect opened the door to further attempts to more narrowly define the kind of actions that would merit ecclesiastical discipline. It said that at the present time the Church

> is in a period of indecision with respect to its moral doctrine concerning same gender relationships and we do not find sufficient clarity in the Church's teaching at the present time concerning the morality of same sex relationships to hold that ordination of a non-celibate homosexual person violates a bishop's ordination vow to uphold the "discipline" of the Church.

This would be a red flag for the conservatives who now felt the time was ripe for greater clarity on the Church's teaching on sexuality. It would be one goal of the majority at Lambeth '98 to move from indecision to decisiveness and from lack of clarity to absolute clarity regarding homosexuals in the priesthood.

The 10 bishops who brought the presentment against Righter said immediately after the Court's verdict that its decision "has swept away two millennia of Christian teaching regarding God's purposes in creation, the nature and meaning of marriage and family." [22] Their statement would become the majority position of the bishops at Lambeth '98.

Two other documents in the year before Lambeth '98 are crucial for setting the stage for that meeting. One was the statement on human sexuality issued by

80 bishops and archbishops of Africa and Asia meeting in February 1997 as the Second Anglican Encounter in the South.[23] Known as the Kuala Lumpur Statement, it expressed concern about the moral teaching on the ordination of gay persons and lesbians and the blessing of their relationships going on in some provinces of the North (meaning primarily Canada and the United States). For the signers of the statement, God's will was crystal clear on these topics because it could be found in the "clear and unambiguous teaching of the Holy Scriptures." To ordain gay persons would "call into question the authority of the Holy Scriptures" and the statement declared that this is "totally unacceptable." To remedy the false teaching and practice of the northern churches would require "mutual accountability and interdependence within our Anglican Communion" and the reaching of a "common mind before embarking on radical changes to Church discipline and moral teaching." [24]

In the United States ECUSA in the summer of 1997 held its triennial General Convention and came within a vote of approving a request that the Commission on Liturgy and Music develop a ritual for the blessing of same sex unions.

The Virginia Report

Finally, in the same year the Kuala Lumpur Statement was issued, another report from the Inter-Anglican Theological and Doctrinal Commission (which came to be known as the Virginia Report) was published.[25] Chaired by Archbishop of Armagh Robin Eames, the Commission's report was a response emanating from the decision of ECUSA to ordain a woman to the episcopate before securing the consent of all the provinces in the Communion.

The Virginia Report is well aware that the Communion is riven by disagreement and conflict over serious issues, but it asserts the traditional Anglican "tolerance for deeply held differences of conviction and practice," including different forms of Biblical interpretation. And it reminds Anglicans to "listen to the experience of other ecclesial communities." (It is not clear whether it had in mind liberals listening to the experience of conservatives around issues of sexuality, of conservatives listening to liberals, or of both. But Lambeth '98, now only a year away, would be seen by many as listening only to the voices of the conservatives.)

On the tricky question of Biblical authority, the Report, while acknowledging Scripture as the "primary norm for Christian life and faith," insists that the writings of the Bible must be "translated, read, and understood, and their meaning grasped through a continuous process of interpretation . . . afforded by the contexts of 'tradition' and 'reason.' " Reason can be understood, in part, as "the mind of a particular culture" and no one culture has a "monopoly of insight into the truth of the Gospel."

On authority within and for the AC, the Report seeks to balance provincial autonomy with the interdependence of all the members of the Communion.

"In practice," it declares, "autonomy has never been the sole criterion for understanding the relation of the Provinces to one another. There has generally been an implicit understanding of belonging together and interdependence. The life of the Communion is held together in the creative tension of Provincial autonomy and interdependence."

The Report recognizes that there are some local practices that are incompatible with the Christian faith (they mention apartheid). And it admits that "local churches can make mistakes." The question at Lambeth '98 would be whether the tension mentioned by the Report would lead to division or whether it could remain "creative." Division seemed the more likely and appropriate course, at least for some.

Primates are warned by the Report that they should not "seek uniformity where diversity is legitimate, or centralize administration to the detriment of local churches." These warnings seem to have been ignored by most conservatives in the present climate. But Lambeth 1988 had begun to give greater weight to the opinions of the Primates, urging them "to exercise an enhanced responsibility in offering guidance on doctrinal, moral and pastoral matters." But even as the AC was moving slowly toward a greater centralization of authority (albeit so far in theory, if not in fact), the Report wonders "whether the bonds of interdependence are strong enough to hold them together embracing tension and conflict while answers are sought to seemingly intractable problems." The strength of those bonds would be sorely tested by Lambeth '98's resolution on sexuality.

The Virginia Report includes a reference to the principle known as "subsidiarity." It means that if a local body can handle an issue satisfactorily, it need not be handled at a higher level. "As much space as possible should be given to personal initiative and responsibility." But the Report urges consultation prior to action on matters "which touch the life of the whole Communion." Discernment and reception are an important part of the Church's life and cannot be "hurried" and, the Report confesses, there is no one way of establishing what constitutes consent of the Communion. This "problem" has still not been resolved as defections mount. "Truth is gradually discerned" the Report claims and is "never an uncomplicated and straightforward matter." At the same time, the Report argues, a Province needs to guard against "becoming bound by its culture." And cultures are inevitably filled with ambiguities that do not yield easily to moral absolutes. "The corrosive effects of particular environments are often not perceptible to those who are immersed in them." This is phrased ambiguously enough that conservatives can lament the cultural immersion of liberals in the Western tradition and liberals can decry the cultural blindness of those in more traditional cultures, especially regarding issues of sexual morality. The Report hedges how to handle this ambiguity by requesting that provinces should "respect" the decisions of others without conceding any acceptance of the principles by which the others are making their decisions.

In one particularly telling sentence, the Report states that "the Church is effective when it is embedded [in] a local place, challenging wrongs, healing relationships, standing with the vulnerable and marginalized, and opening up new possibilities for mutual service, respect and love." Liberals from many of the Northern provinces would argue that this is precisely what places like the Diocese of New Westminster and ECUSA are doing with respect to gay and lesbian Episcopalians. They are challenging the wrongs done to homosexuals, healing the relationships that have divided gays and straights in the Church, standing with those gay persons and lesbians who have been the victims of marginalization and discrimination, and bringing their relationships under the blessing of the Church, thereby opening up new possibilities for respect and love.

In the end, the Virginia Report weaves uneasily between twin commitments: one to the unity of the Communion, the other to a diversity of ideas and practices within it. It accepts, at least by implication, the principle of dispersed authority in the Communion while at the same time expressing a willingness to consider more centralization of authority, especially that of the Primates and the Lambeth Conference. It is less of a coherent position statement than a collection of insights, principles, and wisdom gleaned from the history of Anglicanism, which have not been brought together systematically into a single doctrine of ecclesial authority. At the very least the Report does not give clear instruction as to how the Communion should deal with the contentious issues ahead of it. It gives advice on what to avoid and what to hold in tension, but it does not resolve the tension and, in this sense, would prove to be less than fully satisfactory to either side in the upcoming debate on homosexuality at Lambeth 1998.

—— 4 ——

The Uncompleted Struggle for Women's Ordination: From Defective Men to the "Conscience Clause"

"The blood-dimmed tide is loosed"

Probably the most significant parallel to the debate over the ordination of gay and lesbian persons is the struggle over the ordination of women, both to the priesthood and to the episcopate. Both issues, not surprisingly, involve sexuality. Today there are many women priests and a number of women bishops in the Anglican Communion (though most are found in the province of the United States). How the Communion handled the issue is instructive for how it might be able to handle the issue of homosexuality.

In the nineteenth century the Episcopal Church recognized an office for women known as deaconesses. Deaconesses were not nuns, but they did take vows and were inducted into an ecclesiastical order. A report on the appropriateness of ordaining women as deaconesses was issued in 1919 by a commission appointed by the Archbishop of Canterbury.[1] Lambeth 1920 stated that "the Ordination of a Deaconess confers on her Holy Orders."[2] But the 1930 Lambeth Conference made it clear that this order was the only one to which women could be admitted. In 1964 the General Convention of ECUSA added the order of deaconess to the orders of ministry in the Church. This action would lead Bishop James Pike to *admit* to the diaconate (an order to which men were admitted prior to their ordination to the priesthood) a woman who was already a deaconess, believing that in ordering her to be a deaconess, the Church had already ordained her to a recognizable ministry so that she did not need "re-ordination" to be admitted to the diaconate.[3] In 1970 the General Convention declared that deaconesses are within the order of deacons and thus no longer a Holy Order separate from the diaconate. By this declaration Pike's action was, in effect, ratified retroactively, thus continuing the precedent that something done before being officially approved by the standing authoritative bodies can be brought within such approval after a period of time. Remember that Seabury's consecration in 1784 was not officially accepted by the Church in the United States until after the fact, once the General Convention in 1789 affirmed it. What was once prohibited now becomes sanctioned retroactively. This would prove to be a vital precedent for the women who would be ordained "irregularly" in 1974.

Women as Defective Men

The history of women's ordination and the arguments that swirled around it are important in understanding similar issues that have arisen around the question of ordaining gay persons. Not even the most conservative Christian would deny that women are "natural" creatures (in a way that many maintain homosexuals are not). But even this self-evident fact about women has not always been the prevailing view among Christians. Probably the greatest theologian in the Church's history, St. Thomas Aquinas, could refer to the individual nature of women as "defective and misbegotten, for the active power in the male seed tends to the production of a perfect likeness according to the masculine sex; while the production of woman comes from defect in the active power," though nature did intend the creation of women "as directed to the work of generation" [4] and as a helper to man. As a result of her ontological subordination to and derivation from man, women were considered to lack traditional male faculties, such as rationality, physical strength, and the ability to control their emotions. It was not, of course, coincidental that women became particularly vulnerable to charges of witchcraft, because their "weakness" could so easily be exploited by the power of the Devil and their sexual seductiveness (their compensation, apparently, for lacking the rational faculties of men) made them particularly dangerous to holy men, thus undermining the latter's authority and that of the political and ecclesiastical structures committed to their charge.

This "obvious" superiority of the male person is the ontological basis for the view that only men could represent God sacramentally in the tabernacle. Thus, it was argued, Christ had to be male and by that fact the perfect representative of God on Earth. This argument for the supremacy and primordiality of men is, according to the conservative reading of that time, built into the very nature of things and thus into Scripture. Any mention of the cultural and social conditions of the time in which women were regarded as the property of men and any mention of changed social and cultural conditions are beside the point once one has built a view of the inferiority of women as bearers of authority into the very foundations of nature itself. In this respect it is difficult to see how the opponents of women's ordination could ever give ground on the issue since, presumably, nature does not change. But many original opponents did eventually give ground and are now shifting their attention to the legitimacy of ordaining gay persons.

Why did they give ground? Clearly the cultural stereotype of women as less than fully human had eroded. There must have been something in the way in which both the secular and religious voices had come to assert the equality of women in all things that truly mattered that led to a change of mind about women's eligibility for ordination.

Nevertheless, the struggle for women's ordination did have to face the challenge of the argument, which seemed obvious to many Christians throughout the centuries, that women could not represent Christ in the role of priest, let alone bishop. Defenders of the restriction of the priesthood to men point out that while Jesus had many followers, both male and female, he chose only men to be his immediate disciples and apostles. And the longer the Church restricted ordination to men alone, the more such restriction took on the authority of tradition.

But a close look at Scripture reveals that women played very prominent roles in the ministry of Jesus and in the earliest Christian communities. Priscilla, the wife of Aquila, is referred to by Paul on more than one occasion as a clear leader in one of the early churches. Phoebe is referred to as a deacon of the Church. In Galatians Paul says that in Christ there is neither male nor female. The first witnesses to and proclaimers of the resurrection of Jesus were women. One can only conclude that the role of women, at least in Paul's eyes, as equal to men as leaders, disciples, and apostles was studiously ignored as women were increasingly written out of Church history. The struggle for women's ordination is not, therefore, a struggle to gain a privilege they never had but instead to reclaim a standing they once enjoyed and from which they were systematically removed.

Women and the Lambeth Conference

In 1968 in a report entitled "Women and the Priesthood" given to the Lambeth Conference of that year, Alan Richardson, then Dean of York, distinguished between logical arguments against their ordination (conceding, in effect, that there were none) and theological arguments. It was the latter that, in his opinion, had to be given weight by the Church. If a branch of the Church (by which he meant the Church universal) took a decision on the matter, it would be

> making an innovation for which there was no ancient or ecumenical precedent. This is the crucial question which underlies the debate whether the Anglican Communion [a branch of the universal Church] should proceed to the ordination of women to the priesthood now. It is a profoundly theological question, since it raises the issue of authority in the separated branches of the universal Church of Christ.[5]

Despite Richardson's caution, Lambeth 1968 resolved that "theological arguments as at present for and against the ordination of women to the priesthood are inconclusive" and ordered every national and regional Church "to give careful study to the question of the ordination of women to the priesthood."[6] Other authors of "Women and the Priesthood" acknowledged the importance of Scriptural testimony and of tradition on the issue, but concluded that "the data of

Scripture appear divided on this issue." Tradition, they acknowledge, is also less than absolute on the subject. They note, foreshadowing arguments made today in defense of homosexual persons, that the medieval church

> reflects biological assumptions about the nature of woman and her relation to men which are considered unacceptable in the light of modern knowledge and biblical study and have been generally discarded today.

Given that this is the case, they go on to say,

> if the ancient and medieval assumptions about the social role and inferior status of women are no longer accepted, the appeal to tradition is virtually reduced to the observation that there happens to be no precedent for ordaining women to be priests. [But they add] The New Testament does not encourage Christians to think that nothing should be done for the first time.

Having staked their argument for the validity, in principle, of women's ordination, the Lambeth Conference did recommend that no Church proceed to ordain women until the "advice of the Anglican Consultative Council be sought and carefully considered." [7] In the meantime, Lambeth 1968 also recommended that Churches and Provinces should be encouraged to make "canonical provision" for

> duly qualified women to share in the conduct of liturgical worship, to preach, to baptize, to read the epistle and gospel at the Holy Communion, and to help in the distribution of the sacraments,

in short to do everything but consecrate the elements, the one remaining privilege reserved for male priests.[8] At its first meeting in 1971 at Limuru, Kenya, the newly formed Anglican Consultative Council narrowly passed a resolution advising the bishop of Hong Kong that should he proceed to ordain women to the priesthood, it will "be acceptable to this Council." The resolution also encouraged all the Provinces of the AC "to continue in communion with these dioceses" that were contemplating ordaining women.[9] Hong Kong did proceed to ordain two women, Jane Hwang and Joyce Bennett, on Advent Sunday of 1971.

Two years later, in 1973, when the ACC met in Dublin it "recognized," almost unanimously, that ordination of women would have "important ecumenical repercussions" that needed to be taken into account, but, significantly added that "this consideration should not be decision. The Churches of the Anglican Communion must make their own decision." [10]

By 1958 nearly 50 churches belonging to the World Council of Churches were ordaining women. By 1970 this number had risen to 72. In 1972, at a diocesan convention in New York, Professor of Church History at General Theological Seminary Robert Wright observed that the issue of women's ordination was not one of "whether we shall swim with the current or not, but of speaking the truth we believe when we are called to do so." Referring to the ACC's resolution referring the matter to the Provinces, he argued that[11] to claim to be waiting for the mirage of some future ecumenical council to deal with this relatively minor matter is . . . only to stall, to deny our own process of authority, and to call into question our ability as a part of the Catholic Church to make a decision on a matter of church *order* which we have always claimed (as when we abolished celibacy) was in our province to be dealt with, and which our own highest possible authorities have already declared is a regional or provincial matter.

Wright's view clearly indicates that the issue can be handled at the provincial level without running afoul of Anglican tradition and polity.

Women and General Convention

In 1973, the following year, the General Convention of TEC barely defeated a motion to affirm the ordination of women. Position papers, such as one coming from Concerned Laywomen of the Episcopal Church supporting the motion, utilized the argument that by denying women the priesthood the Church was denying their full participation within the body of Christ and their ability to "express their humanity sacramentally." [12] (This is an argument that anticipates one being made today by gays and lesbians: that their humanity as such should be able to be expressed sacramentally. If, as Bishop Paul Moore argued, Jesus took on *all* humanity in his incarnation [a theological concept deeply embedded in the Anglican tradition], then "any human being can be the celebrant of the eucharist." [13])

The issue of women's ordination in the ECUSA came to a head in 1974 when, on June 29, 11 women who had already been ordained to the diaconate, were ordained as priests by four bishops. All the participants seem to agree that this was an "irregular" ordination because it had not yet been sanctioned by the General Convention. But, they argued, it was valid since they were being ordained by bishops who were in full communion with the Church. (The parallels to Seabury's consecration to the Episcopate are remarkably similar.) In defense of their action the participating bishops said in an open letter to the Church,[14]

we are painfully conscious of the diversity of thinking in our church on this issue and have been deeply sobered by that fact . . . [but] there is a ruling factor which does require action on our part. It is our obedience to the Lordship of Christ, our response to the sovereignty of His Spirit for the Church.

The 11 women priests added to the bishops' letter their affirmation that

our primary motivation is to begin to free priesthood from the bondage it suffers as long as it is characterized by the categorical exclusion of persons on the basis of sex.[15]

Nevertheless, less than two weeks later the House of Bishops, meeting in a special session, denounced the irregular ordinations, saying that "the wrong means to reach a desired end may expose the Church to serious consequences unforeseen and undesired by anyone." [16] In response, Bishop J. Antonio Ramos of Costa Rica, one of the participating bishops, appealed to the actions of St. Paul who had chosen to "disobey the old dispensations to extend the promises of God to the world." He added that "in our own days others, including members of this house and this church, had to disobey the law of this land and of secular and religious institutions, to abolish color of skin as a new circumcision." [17] Ironically, in defense of the actions in Philadelphia, the bishops involved were appealing directly to Scripture, not in opposition to it.

Two years later, in 1975, the ACC met again and, in effect, told the Communion that it now ought to "work from" the reality of the ordination of women. Thus, when the Episcopal Church met at its next General Convention in Minneapolis in September 1976, the ground was prepared to authorize retroactively the ordinations of 1974. And the Convention did so. In a letter the Convention sent to the Church, it said, in part, that in its struggle over this issue everyone "dug more deeply into the issues and found that changes could be made in our tradition." [18] The Convention then concluded its work by resolving that the canons for the admission of candidates for ordination as bishops, priests, and deacons "shall be equally applicable to men and women." [19]

On the following day the House voted to allow the status of the 11 women to be "regularized" without a second ordination. David Sumner notes in his summary of these events that three years after ECUSA officially approved the ordination of women to the priesthood nearly 300 women had been ordained and by 1985 more than 600 had entered into Holy Orders.[20]

In response to the commonly heard criticism that proceeding to approve the ordination of women before consensus had been reached by the Church universal was improper, a Canadian Archbishop, Edward Scott, replied

> I wonder . . . if waiting for a universal consensus does not in fact rule out any action. If we are prepared to act, but also to recognize that our action must be tested by experience . . . then we may be helping the whole church reflect at a deeper level.[21]

This same argument is presently being deployed by the supporters of the ordination of gay persons today. Sometimes performing an action when it is reflective of the experience of a particular branch of the Church universal might well help the larger body to rethink its own opposition, especially if the action arises out of and expresses the deepest sentiments of those within the branch.

The Conscience Clause

Objections to the vote soon began to pour in, and dissent led to attempts on the part of some parishes to leave the Church. Others resorted to what some have called a "conscience clause." It was introduced a year after the 1976 General Convention at the House of Bishops meeting at Port St. Lucie, Florida. Presiding Bishop John Allin told the bishops that he was "unable to accept women in the role of priest" and that he would resign as Presiding Bishop if it was decided by the House that his refusal to accept women priests disqualified him from serving in that role. Buffaloed by his threat, the House decided that it would respect his right "to hold a personal conviction on this issue" and to retain his ecclesiastical position. It went on to adopt a policy of "conscience" that said that "no bishop, priest, or lay person should be coerced or penalized in any manner" for either endorsing or rejecting the ordination of women.

This conscience clause raises a host of issues, not least of which is why an individual's conscience is to be respected when it comes to refusing to recognize women's ordination (as approved by the only authoritative body in the Episcopal Church, the General Convention) but apparently not for refusing to recognize the legitimacy of the ordination of divorced, multiply married, polygamous, Black, or Hispanic clergy, the first three of which conditions seem to be condemned by Jesus and the latter two being ones that were greatly resisted by many White Episcopalians over the years. Was there something about women that could justify permitting a bishop to refuse to accept them as priests? However, one might wonder if something like a conscience clause, once having gained a foothold in Episcopal polity, might be invoked by some parts of the Church to sanction a refusal to recognize the legitimacy of the ordination of gay and lesbian persons even while other parts of the Church (through their various provincial synods or conventions) do affirm such ordinations.

The conscience clause is also, on its face, demeaning to women. Once General Convention had authorized their ordination, why should anyone be permitted to ignore the force of that action? It seems to many to be a way of maintaining communion without having to face the full moral implications of allowing conscience to trump the authoritative actions of the Church.

At the first Lambeth meeting (1978) following the actions of the '76 General Convention it was acknowledged that any particular province had the autonomy "to make its own decision about the appropriateness of admitting women to Holy Orders." It also urged, by an overwhelming majority, all the members of the AC to "respect the convictions of those provinces and dioceses" that have either accepted women's ordination or refused to do so.[22] Lambeth 1978 did caution against legally ordained women exercising their ministry in Provinces that have not ordained women and even where appropriate "syndodical authority be given to enable them to exercise" their priesthood, it should be exercised only "where such a ministry is agreeable to the bishops, clergy, and people where the ministry is to be exercised."[23] Clearly what was at stake for the Church here was finding a way to retain some degree of unity within the Communion while recognizing the legitimacy of actions on the part of some Provinces not acceptable to other provinces. It even went on to caution that no decision be made by any Province about ordaining women to the episcopate without due consultation with the Primates and only with "overwhelming support in any member Church and in the diocese concerned, lest the bishop's office should become a cause of disunity instead of a focus of unity."[24]

Women and the Episcopate

It is not clear why, having been ordained to the priesthood, women being elected to the episcopate would become such a contentious issue. The question of the legitimacy of women receiving holy orders had been settled for those provinces affirming ordination to the priesthood. What additional principle or concern would be brought into play if women were elected to the episcopate? Lambeth 1978 hints at this additional concern by expressing a fear that women in the bishop's office might become a cause of disunity within the Communion. The concern for unity, almost at any cost, seems to trump all other considerations in this area and continues today into the area of gay ordinations.

The 1988 Lambeth Conference resolved that each province "respect the decision and attitudes of other Provinces in the ordination or consecration of women to the episcopate, without such respect necessarily indicating acceptance of the principles involved, maintaining the highest degree of communion with the Provinces which differ." It also recognized

> the serious hurt which would result from the questioning by some of the validity of the episcopal acts of a woman bishop, and likewise the hurt experienced by those whose conscience would be offended by the ordination of a woman to the episcopate.[25]

In 1990 the Diocese of Massachusetts elected and consecrated the first woman bishop in ECUSA, Barbara Harris (and thereby the first woman bishop in the Anglican Communion).

ECUSA's House of Bishops in 1995 accepted an opinion from its Constitution and Canons Committee that the 1976 resolution permitting women's ordination was, in fact, binding and mandatory. It submitted this finding to the 1997 General Convention, which declared that the canon on women's ordination was applicable to all dioceses. It resolved to change the canons of ECUSA to the effect that "no-one shall be denied access to the ordination process nor postulancy, candidacy or ordination in any parish or diocese of this church on account of his or her sex." However, it hedged a little by stating that the canon does not *require* a bishop who dissents from this rule to ordain or institute a woman priest (even though he cannot inhibit her from going to a parish that requests her). He must even make arrangements for her ordination at the hands of another bishop if he will not do it himself.

Although ECUSA was now formally committed to the ordination of women, the "mother" Church of England had yet to make a final decision on the matter. In 1987 the General Synod of the Church of England (its counterpart to the General Convention of ECUSA) voted by a large majority to open the way toward women's ordination. Its House of Bishops, in a 1987 report entitled "The Ordination of Women to the Priesthood" called upon those who were opposed to such ordination "at the very least to respect the Church's order and decision to act within the safeguards provided." Here, interestingly enough, the default position was that of the legitimacy of women priests (though the formal vote approving would not happen until 1992) because, as the bishops went on to say, it would be difficult to see how a parish priest could "refuse the ministrations of a diocesan bishop without straining the communion and order of the Church." [26] In 1992 women's ordination became canonically legitimate in the Church of England. The first woman was ordained in 1994. Within four years there were more than 1,700 women priests in the Church of England.[27] It has been reported that initially almost 500 male priests left the Church but almost 60 eventually returned. By 2005 a total of 720 priests had left (though it is not clear whether these defections were caused exclusively, primarily, or only in part by the fact of women's ordination).[28]

A year after the final approval of women's ordination in the Church of England its Synod passed a crucial resolution known as the "Episcopal Ministry Act of Synod 1993." Although the report of 1987 on women's ordination put the burden of proof for disrupting the unity of the Church upon those opposed to women's ordination, the Episcopal Ministry Act seemed to reverse course and, as had their cousins in ECUSA, began to provide for conscientious objection to women as priests (and eventually bishops). While claiming to "make provision for the continuing diversity of opinion" and to mutually recognize and respect "the integrity of differing beliefs and positions" with respect to women's ordination, it said somewhat ambiguously that one's views on women's ordination (presumably negative) must not be the basis for excluding persons holding those views from ordination themselves. Provision was to be made for "provincial episcopal visitors" (PEVs) for those parishes still in opposition to women's ordination. Each such "visitor," however, was under the authority of the diocesan bishop, not a replacement for him. Lambeth 1988 had reaffirmed a long-standing Anglican position of "respect for diocesan boundaries and the authority of bishops within these boundaries." It was therefore "inappropriate behaviour for any bishop or priest of this Communion to exercise episcopal or pastoral ministry within another diocese without first obtaining the permission and invitation of the ecclesial authority thereof." [29] Once again we see attempts to hold together a number of possibly incompatible principles that seem today, in light of the issues surrounding homosexuality and ordination, to be disintegrating: the autonomy of provinces and dioceses to make their own determination of what is right and proper for them; the authority of diocesan bishops to determine what takes place within the parishes of their dioceses; respect for diocesan boundaries by those not resident or having authority therein; and, most importantly, an attempt to maintain unity and avoid division by permitting conscientious objection even to formally approved positions taken by the Churches according to due process, especially when they have to do with women and gay and lesbian persons. Anglican Church historian Paul Avis correctly picks up what he terms a "crucial ambiguity" in the way in which the Church of England attempted, through the Episcopal Ministry Act of 1993, to maintain unity. This was an ambiguity, he claims, that was "the price that had to be paid to secure the priesting of women without producing a schism." [30] In Avis's view, however, if the intention of the Act was to extend the ministry of the diocesan bishop, then the "visitor" should not be a visitor at all but a full member of the diocesan family.

> "I cannot see," Avis claimed, "how the idea of a separate college of presbyters, in communion with a PEV, but in a merely impaired state of communion with the diocesan [bishop], can avoid being in effect schismatical." [31]

Avis puts this into an even larger context by observing, correctly and presciently, that

> the notion of designated dioceses for special constituencies leads logically to manifold parallel jurisdictions, rampant private judgement as individuals choose their own bishop, and portends a postmodernistic dissolution of community, tradition, authority and order. [32]

Avis is right that the provision of conscientious objection to women priests is tantamount to rejection of the episcopate. Why those opposed to women's ordination (and now to the ordination of gay persons) should be able to trump the long-established Anglican recognition of episcopal authority at the local (diocesan) level in the name of an alleged moral principle that has not been universally endorsed by the Church universal, nor found in its doctrines and creeds, nor articulated by Jesus, is not clear, and one would assume the burden of proof is on the opponents to show why their opposition is more consistent with Anglican tradition than that of their opponents. The conscience clause, in other words, while seeming to be generous and inclusive, actually permits the very exclusion of women priests in this instance that synodical and General Convention actions (the final authoritative bodies for the provinces) have authorized as canonically legitimate.

Following Lambeth 1988 (one year after the first vote of Synod in the Church of England in favor of women's ordination but before its conclusive vote in 1992), a commission was established by ABC Robert Runcie, which came to be known as the Eames Commission after its chair, Robin Eames, the Archbishop of Armagh (Northern Ireland), to monitor how women's ordination to the priesthood and the episcopate was being dealt with by the various provinces in the AC. Its primary mission was to determine how the member churches were "striving to maintain the highest possible degree of communion" and "to live together in diversity during an open period of reception." [33] It was committed to working within the Lambeth resolution that called on each Province to "respect the decision and attitudes of other Provinces in the ordination or consecration of women to the episcopate, without such respect necessarily indicating acceptance of the principles involved." [34] (It is not clear how people who differ on principles, presumably of great importance to them, are to respect people who hold conflicting principles. But figuring out how to do that was one of the tasks the Eames Commission had set itself.)

The 1997 report noted the role that culture plays in the acceptance or refusal (what it called "cultural hesitancy") of women's ordination. The Monitoring Group invited "reflection upon the inherent tension between the need for the inculturation of the Gospel, and the encouragement of a development which is contrary to a particular culture." It asks whether there might be places where it would be inappropriate "to expect the ordination of women by reason of respect for that particular culture?" By the same token it asks, "are there some cultures where the role of women supports the ordination of women" to the priesthood and episcopate? (A similar argument is being made today that there are cultures that support the ordination of gay and lesbian persons, and should, by the same logic, be accorded respect for their practice given their particular cultural practices.)

The Commission also observed that tolerance for the conscience clause in some provinces was waning. In ECUSA, for example, there was a "build up of opinion in favour of making the principle of women's ordination 'binding' " while opponents of such a view were leaning toward some form of "parallel jurisdiction." [35] Not surprisingly, the Eames report approved of the Church of England's Act of Synod's prescriptions for the use of provincial episcopal visitors, which, in its opinion, clearly affirm that "to dissent to the ordination of women is not to be a disloyal Anglican. And that there will be no coercion, penalization, or canonical disability for those objecting." [36]

Drawing on what was called the Grindrod Report, the Eames Commission noted the role reception played in the early church on such matters as circumcision and the formation of the creeds. Some actions taken by one part of the Church were "in advance of the decision of the whole Church." [37] As applied to the ordination of a woman to the episcopate (which had become the next issue women had to face after the approval in many provinces of their ordination to the priesthood), the Grindrod Report argued that should a Province ordain a woman to the episcopate, that action should be given over to the process of reception and could not be "expressed as the mind of the Church until it were accepted by the whole Communion." [38] The Eames Commission essentially accepted the Grindrod Report's assessment and support for the process of reception as applied to women's ordination, especially to the episcopate. It stressed the need for the various Provinces to listen to each other with courtesy and respect and to be willing to offer to their fellow Provinces their thinking and insights. It cautioned that reception is a process that cannot be hurried. (This indicates the dominance of the view that maintaining unity in the face of different opinions ought to override demands that justice be done *now* rather than wait for the long run.) It characterizes ECUSA's position as suggesting that "it is difficult to sustain an adequate level of tolerance throughout a long period of reception. Patience frays, opposition hardens and temptations to malice proliferate." But ECUSA so far had shown no enthusiasm for creating an extraterritorial Province containing all those who remain opposed to women's ordination. Similar reluctance to accept such a Province had also been expressed, at least in 1997, by the

Archbishop of Canterbury, the Primates, the Anglican Consultative Council, and an earlier Eames Commission.[39]

At the end of its monitoring report the Eames Commission suggests that the process used in dealing with women's ordination be followed in future cases when issues threaten the unity of the Communion. Once a Province has decided its own mind on an issue that will affect the whole Communion, it should request the Archbishop of Canterbury, the Primates, and/or the Anglican Consultative Council

> to consider whether it be appropriate to bring such a matter to the next Lambeth Conference. . . . It would then be for the Lambeth Conference itself to resolve whether the issue were one to be put to an open process of reception in the Communion.[40]

It is not entirely clear whether it is being recommended that the Province should proceed to act on its decision or whether it should refrain from acting until the Communion has made up its mind. In one sense, unless there is an action (such as ordination of women by one or more Provinces), there is nothing to be received. What the Report probably intended was that a Province's decision should be submitted to the Communion before it is acted upon. But there is ambiguity in the Eames Commission recommendation on this point.

The Report of the Monitoring Group did not explicitly mention the emerging issue of ordination of gay persons and lesbians, but it must have had it in mind in making its final recommendations to the Communion. In fact, the issue came to a furious boil in the 1998 Lambeth Meeting to which the Group submitted its report. We have already explored that extremely contentious and seminal gathering, as well as the election of Gene Robinson, and we are now ready to pick up the story.

Section Three

From Robinson's Election
to the Present

—— 5 ——

From the Chapman Memo to the Windsor Report: The Tension Between Unity, Uniformity, and Episcopal Authority

"The centre cannot hold"

As 2004 opened, the first effects of the anger against ECUSA's actions in 2003 began to be more fully felt. In mid-January Alan Cooperman of the *Washington Post*[1] released information revealing a secret scenario allegedly informing the actions of many conservative priests and parishes against bishops they consider not sufficiently orthodox on the issue of sexuality. Cooperman had discovered what came to be called the "Chapman Memo." Written on December 28, 2003, on behalf of the AAC and their Bishops' Committee on Adequate Episcopal Oversight (AEO—their alternative to DEPO [Delegated Episcopal Pastoral Oversight]) by the Reverend Geoff Chapman, a priest in Sewickley, PA, the confidential letter was addressed to Episcopalians who had contacted the AAC opposing the consecration of Gene Robinson. At the heart of the memo is the decision to challenge the authority of sitting allegedly liberal bishops with the expectation that civil lawsuits and ecclesiastical charges against them would follow, thus draining the financial resources of these "nonorthodox" dioceses. Chapman says that, given the "rejection of the historic Christian faith and the rejection of biblical and Communion authority by the leadership of ECUSA," his group's ultimate goal is "a realignment of Anglicanism on North American soil committed to biblical faith and values." They want a "replacement" jurisdiction with confessional standards. Denouncing Bishop Griswold's "extended episcopal care" as unacceptable, fundamentally flawed, and disingenuous, the dissenters will offer AEO instead. The group will seek to transfer parish oversight across geographic diocesan boundaries to an orthodox bishop, the right of pastoral succession to be determined by the parish itself, liberty of conscience in financial stewardship, and negotiated property settlements affirming retention of ownership in the local congregation. The issue of property will be revisited many times in the coming months.

In the scenario Chapman outlines, Stage 1 would involve parishes publicly announcing that their relationship with their diocesan bishop is "severely damaged" but not committing any unnecessary canonical violations. During Stage 1 the participating parishes will build a Network of Anglican Communion Dioceses and Parishes in the diocese under attack. Stage 2 will seek negotiated settlements in matters of property, jurisdiction, pastoral succession, and communion. In this stage a faithful disobedience of canon law may become necessary. Chapman reminds the parishes that they already have nongeographical oversight available from "offshore" bishops. "We" will have a "cluster strategy" of 3–30 churches per cluster in 15–30 dioceses, he suggests. The stronger clusters will go first. "Congregations moving in clusters have the advantage of leveraging their combined strength."

Chapman warns participating parishes and rectors not to inform the bishop of their intention to apply for AEO. "We will inform him with you in due time." They believe revisionist bishops will be "reticent to play 'hardball' [on property disputes and clergy placement] for a while." These recalcitrant and unorthodox bishops have managed to "radicalize all the orthodox in our communion and taken away the 'middle ground' where so many of our members have hidden!" They will be pressured to cooperate with the ABC and the Primates. Chapman also calls for "redirected funds" from parish budgets going to Anglican missions. In doing this, he suggests that the participants argue for "freedom of conscience" and the honoring of donor intent. But, he warns, do not overtly declare yourself "out of communion." (You can bring charges of abandonment of communion, however, against the bishop.) Use words like "impaired" or "damaged" communion. The key is to wait for the supportive Primates who are building a solution to the crisis. As we shall see, this Chapman scenario almost exactly predicts the actions that six conservative parishes and their rectors would follow in the Diocese of Connecticut.

On January 20, 2004, at the epicenter of the conservative movement, Christ Church, Plano, TX, an official announcement is made of the creation of the Network of Anglican Communion Dioceses and Parishes identified in the Chapman memo. Spokesmen for the Network say it will "operate in good faith within the constitution of the Episcopal Church" and will "constitute a true and legitimate expression of the worldwide Anglican Communion."[2] Bishop Robert Duncan of Pittsburgh is elected moderator and a 12 member steering committee is created. The Network calls itself a "united missionary movement of Anglicans" in North America. As if expecting something like a violent apocalyptic battle with the forces of evil, the founders claim that they will "lay down our lives for one another in the face of risk and opposition."[3] The hyperbolic rhetoric of apocalyptic martyrdom will be a thread tying together a number of statements by conservatives, especially Duncan, over the next few years.

Money was, of course, an important issue for many parishes and dioceses. On February 20 the Diocese of West Texas gave its congregations the option of giving no money to the national church. Southwest Florida had previously permitted this financial option. The Episcopal Church's national headquarters in New York admitted that contributions from local dioceses had dropped 7 percent ($1.9 million) since August 2003. Forty dioceses said they would meet their pledges, while 42 would send a lower amount.[4] Virginia's giving was down about 18 percent in pledges from the previous year.[5]

Later, following its March 19–25 meeting in Camp Allen, TX, the House of Bishops issued a document entitled "Caring for all the Churches" in which they addressed directly the question of "oversight" of dissenting congregations. They say that they will commit themselves "to providing and to making provision for pastoral care for dissenting congregations, and we recognize that there may be a need for a bishop to delegate some pastoral oversight." But they lay down a clear marker: oversight does not mean "jurisdiction." We will continue to

> recognize the constitutional and canonical authority of bishops and the integrity of diocesan boundaries. ... the provision of supplemental episcopal pastoral care shall be under the direction of the bishop of the diocese, who shall invite the visitor and remain in pastoral contact with the congregation. This is to be understood as a temporary arrangement, the ultimate goal of which is the full restoration of the relationship between the congregation and their bishop.[6]

This approval of delegated episcopal pastoral oversight (DEPO) was already being contested by many conservatives, in line with the Chapman memo.

In mid-April 2004 the Primates of the Council of the Anglican Provinces of Africa (CAPA) met in Nairobi and reaffirmed Resolution 1.10 from Lambeth 1998.[7] The Primates urged the Lambeth Commission appointed by ABC Williams to "consider the serious implications of not taking strong disciplinary action against ECUSA, which will definitely tear the Communion apart. . . ." The African Primates call ECUSA to "repentance," and say that they will give it three months to do so, and after that "discipline should be applied." The language of discipline will become increasingly common in the months ahead. The CAPA bishops also pledged not to accept donations from any "pro-gay American diocese."

In late April Archbishop Eames issued an update for the Primates on the work of the Lambeth Commission on Communion, which he was chairing. He stressed the importance of maintaining "the highest possible degrees of communion among those who adopt differing views at this time . . . as long as these dissenting groups do not initiate schism in their own Churches." He reminded the Primates of the "very clear guidelines concerning jurisdictional boundaries that we have agreed to adopt" at successive Lambeth Conferences.[8] Drexel Gomez, Archbishop of the West Indies, responded on May 7, noting that "liberal viewpoints are [being] allowed to claim too much territory." Eames replied by asking, in reference to issues of sexuality, "are these the sorts of issues we really want to divide us or to weaken our mission to suffering humanity?" [9]

On June 9 a group of 22 archbishops of the Global South demanded the ouster of the Anglican Church of Canada and the Episcopal Church from the Anglican Communion for approving the blessing of same sex unions. At the same time a group of 700 self-described orthodox Episcopal priests and bishops wrote a letter to Archbishop Eames that previous attempts to make the U.S. Church "account-able" have not worked. "Without the imposition of discipline, the situation will continue to deteriorate. We ask you to declare the need for immediate interven-tion to establish discipline, order and accountability for the Episcopal Church." [10]

The Windsor Report

Things remained relatively quiet in the Church until October 18, when the long-awaited (and much feared) report of the Lambeth Commission on Communion (known as the Windsor Report) was finally issued. It was to become so important in the life of ECUSA that bishops would soon be found declaring themselves "Windsor compliant" in order to fend off conservative attacks. Its importance in the life of the Church is so significant that it deserves detailed attention.

The charge to the Lambeth Commission on Communion had been to consider "ways in which communion and understanding could be enhanced where serious differences threatened the life of a diverse worldwide church." [11]

Ironically, given the tenor of much of the debate leading up to its work, the Report does not take a position on the morality of homosexuality, the ordination of gay persons, same sex blessings, or the legitimacy of any particular interpreta-tion of Scripture. Instead, it focuses exclusively on actions that might impair the unity of the Anglican Communion. As has been typical of much of the debate surrounding the election of Gene Robinson, the underlying issue is more often than not asserted to be that of maintaining communion between the various bodies that comprise the Anglican Communion. The substance of the dispute on Biblical interpretation and the moral legitimacy of homosexuality are rarely addressed directly. Everything seems to hinge on whether Anglicans can first find a way to discuss substantial differences over the Bible and morality without breaking apart and destroying whatever exists of an underlying fellowship.

Nevertheless, implicit appeal to specific interpretations of the Bible and moral teaching is made throughout the Report. Eighteen of the 38 Primates had declared that the actions of the United States and Canada are "contrary to biblical teaching" and as such, unacceptable; and several dioceses and bishops had declared that a "state of either impaired or broken communion now exists." [12]

At the heart of the Report is the attempt to clarify the exact relationships that ought to exist between the constituent parts of the Church: parishes, bishops, diocesan conventions, General Conventions or Synods, laity, Primates, the Arch-bishop of Canterbury, the Anglican Consultative Council, and the Lambeth Con-ferences. These relations should be guided by the "instruments of unity" (the Archbishop of Canterbury, the Lambeth Conference, the Anglican Consultative Council, and the Primates' Meeting) that are intended to foster unity among the various parts of the Communion.

The Report concludes that the central failure of the Diocese of New Westmin-ster and ECUSA was their refusal to employ *all* of these instruments of unity before taking unilateral actions on issues of sexuality that had not received the proper consultation and advice from the other churches in the Communion. "This, we conclude, lies at the heart of the problems we currently face." [13]

The Report also places the actions of ECUSA and New Westminster in the context of previous Lambeth resolutions on sexuality, especially those of 1978 and, most importantly, Lambeth 1998. Lambeth 1978 had reaffirmed "heterosex-uality as the scriptural norm" even while calling for "deep and dispassionate study of the question of homosexuality which would take seriously both the teaching of Scripture and the results of scientific and medical research." Lambeth 1988 had reaffirmed the 1978 resolution in its entirety.[14] But, the Report reminds the Communion that Lambeth '88 had also called for adherence to the "historical position of respect for diocesan boundaries and the authority of bishops within these boundaries," and declared that it was "inappropriate behaviour for any bishop or priest of this Communion to exercise episcopal or pastoral ministry within another diocese without first obtaining the permission and invitation of the ecclesial authority thereof." [15]

The Report also reaffirms the infamous Lambeth 1998 Resolution 1.10, which asserted that abstinence is the right option for those not called to marriage between a man and a woman, which rejected homosexual practice "as incompat-ible with Scripture," and which rejected legitimizing same sex unions and ordaining those involved in such unions, even while calling on the Communion to listen to the experience of homosexual persons and to avoid irrational fear of homosexuals.[16]

The Report reminds the Communion that the Lambeth resolutions on sexuality should be considered, in the words of the Primates at their October 2003 meeting at Lambeth Palace, "as having moral force and commanding the respect of the Communion as its present position on these issues." [17] Significantly, this phras-ing does not foreclose the possibility that the "present position" might someday change. It implies the possibility of an evolution in belief on these topics in ways that would not, presumably, be true of "core" doctrines like the Trinity or the Incarnation.

There are six key features underlying the common life of the Communion that the Report considers to be at stake in the current crisis. The first is the recognition that there is theological development in the Church over time. One way for development to occur, according to the Report, is through the process of "recep-tion," by which a church pronouncement is received by the faithful over time.

The *consensus fidelium* ('common mind of the believers') constituted the ultimate check that a new declaration was in harmony with the faith as it had been received. . . . It is a key way of maintaining the unity of the Church through a time of experiment and uncertainty.[18]

One thing the Report faults ECUSA and New Westminster for, in keeping with the principle of theological development, is their failure to make "a serious attempt to offer an explanation to, or consult meaningfully with, the Communion as a whole about the significant development of theology which alone could justify the recent moves. . . ." [19] This also opens up the possibility that such an explanation can in principle be developed and the House of Bishops will soon offer one.

The second feature of unity is adherence to appropriate ecclesiastical procedures. Failure to observe these procedures, especially those involving consultation among the members of the Communion and reference to the Instruments of Unity can be laid at the doorstep of ECUSA and New Westminster.

A third feature is what the Church likes to call by the Greek name "adiaphora," meaning variable practices and beliefs that do not make an important difference to the faith. Unfortunately, the Report claims, what ECUSA and New Westminster regard as adiaphora the rest of the Communion regards as essential to the faith. A fourth feature of common life is subsidiarity. This means that, in principle, matters should be decided as close to the local level as possible. Nevertheless, the guilty parties are accused of acceding *too much* to the local level and not enough to the Communion as a whole.

A fifth feature is trust: the Communion trusts each province to "exercise its autonomy appropriately within our mutual fellowship." [20] There must be more attention paid by the offending provinces to listening respectfully to what other members of the Communion have to say on these controversial issues. At the same time, the Report does not foreclose but actually invites an opening into new ways of interpreting the Bible. "We clearly need more mutual exploration and explanation of our theological beliefs, our understanding of the Bible. . . ." [21]

The sixth principle is that of authority. The Report reaffirms that the Church's supreme authority is Scripture. Nevertheless, Scriptural authority "demands . . . appropriately sensitive and fine-tuned systems of decision-making" as well as "urgent fresh thought and action." [22] As in its earlier statement, this suggests that the Report rejects a simplistic reading of Scripture while continuing to acknowledge its authority. It notes, for example, that Scripture itself does not claim to be itself the supreme authority but instead points to God as the supreme authority for belief and practice. God's authority may be exercised *through* Scripture and the implications of the difference between Scriptural authority and God's authority "need to be thought out more fully." [23]

The Report's reading of Scripture is much more nuanced than many of the conservative arguments tend to be. It rejects the notion that Scripture's primary purpose is to provide true information, or to prescribe in matters of belief and conduct (which is certainly how it is used in the conservative attack on homosexuality), or merely to serve as a court of appeal. Instead, the Report claims, Scripture is to be "part of the dynamic life of the Spirit through which God the Father is to be "operative within the world and in and through human beings." [24] This last phrase suggests that fallible human authors are responsible for the writing of Scripture and their historical, cultural, and psychological contexts cannot be dismissed when interpreting what they have written.

The Report reminds its readers that the Church needs academic researchers even though the authoritative *teaching* of Scripture cannot be left to them. We need historical hermeneutics, they assert, so that we hear what Scripture is saying and not just what we want it to say. Biblical scholarship at its best "can be deeply challenging to entrenched views of what scripture is thought to be saying [presumably to both liberals and conservatives], not least where it has been read within an unchallenged philosophical or cultural matrix." [25] As to any particular interpretation, once it is subjected to critical analysis, it is up to the Church "to be prepared to change its mind if and when a convincing case is made." [26] At the same time, each community within the Communion is "called to read scripture within, and apply it to, [its] own particular setting—and to respect the fact that other churches face the same demands within their own contexts." [27] This does not mean an "unquestioning acceptance of another's readings, but rather a rich mutual accountability." Nevertheless, as latitudinous as the notion of reception may be in principle, Windsor, somewhat contradictorily, stops short of endorsing it in those cases "which are explicitly against the current teaching of the Anglican Communion as a whole." [28]

The Report goes out of its way to highlight what it calls "diversity within communion" and the hallowed notion of the autonomy of individual provinces. The tension between Communion and autonomy lies at the heart of the ecclesial debate. The Report addresses this tension by rejecting any identity between autonomy and "isolated individualism." Autonomy is freedom *within* interdependence, freedom to "determine one's life within a wider obligation to others." [29] Communion is "the fundamental limit to autonomy." [30] Just how autonomy and interdependence are to be reconciled was of concern to the authors of the Report but it is not entirely clear whether they were able to articulate that reconciliation persuasively. They do envision the possibility of a church departing

> on the basis of its own corporate conscience and with the blessing of the communion, from the standards of the community of which it is an autonomous part, *provided such departure is neither critical to the maintenance of communion nor likely to harm the common good of the Anglican Communion and of the Church universal* (again, as determined by the Instruments of Unity).[31]

What remains unclear are the following: what constitutes "criticality"; who determines "corporate conscience"; and what if the Instruments of Unity are divided as to what harms the common good? The rhetoric of Communion is stronger than the practical means laid out for determining when autonomy has violated the principles of unity and when diversity of practice is to be permitted.

Immediately after asserting the need to honor the common good, the Report goes on to acknowledge the reality of what it calls "inculturation." This is the recognition that "the eternal truth of the gospel relates in different ways to the particulars of any one society," leading to an appreciation of diversity within the life of the church, a diversity that is "to be welcomed and celebrated as normal and healthy." [32] But when diversity ought to trump uniformity and when the maintenance of the Communion trumps diversity is never made entirely clear.

Although some within the Communion were calling for the Instruments of Unity to be given stronger authority and judicial power, the Windsor Report supports the view that the Lambeth Conference should remain an advisory body without legislative powers.[33] The same should be true for the Anglican Consultative Council. And the Primates themselves, up to the present, have regarded their meetings as having no more than "consultative and advisory authority." [34] Having delimited the judicial or legislative authority of the Instruments of Unity, however, the Report calls for a clearer articulation of their "moral authority." The Archbishop of Canterbury, for example, should be regarded as "the focus of unity" and, given the overriding concern to hold the Communion together, that the other Instruments of Unity be regarded more appropriately as Instruments of Communion.[35] As the official convener of the Lambeth Conference, the Archbishop of Canterbury should feel free not to invite certain participants to those meetings "where full membership of the Conference is perceived to be an undesirable status, or would militate against the greater unity of the Communion." [36] Not surprisingly, perhaps, when the first list of invitees to Lambeth 2008 was released by the ABC, Bishop Gene Robinson's name was not included, nor was that of a dissident U.S. priest (Martyn Minns) who had defected from ECUSA and been ordained, against the ABC's advice, a bishop in the Church of Nigeria to serve in the United States. (The number of such bishops ordained by bishops outside ECUSA has continued to grow since then.)

As if four instruments of unity (now being recommended to be instruments of communion) were not enough, the Windsor Report also calls for a fifth body, a Council of Advice, to help the ABC exercise his ministry of unity for the Communion.[37]

One of its most controversial recommendations urges the adoption of a "common Anglican Covenant which would make explicit and forceful the loyalty and bonds of affection which govern the relationships between the churches of the Communion." [38] Covenants are not normally associated with Anglicanism, being more commonly found in presbyterian and congregational polities. But the urgency of holding the Communion together drove the authors of the Windsor Report to suggest this remedy for its present crises. While acknowledging that any covenant would have no binding authority, its mere development (through a "long-term process") would, according to the Report, be highly educational and would serve, in its own way, as an instrument creating a greater sense of interdependence and communion among the different churches. (But it should be noted that the first draft would be initiated by the Primates and would end with final approval by them, with the only body that includes priests and laity in addition to bishops the ACC, being used only for consultation and reception.) A covenant carrying the "weight of an international obligation," in the minds of the authors of the Report, would put a halt to covenanted churches proceeding unilaterally. In its own sketch of such a covenant, the Report significantly does not require acceptance by every church in the covenant relationship "of all theological opinion . . . characteristic of the other[s]" and asks that every church have the same concern "for a conscientious interpretation of scripture in the light of tradition and reason, to be in dialogue with those who dissent from that interpretation, and to heal divisions." [39] This certainly suggests that the Report recognizes that within the fellowship there can be legitimately different interpretations of Scripture and that the claim of some conservatives that Scripture's meaning is clear on its face is not *prima facie* acceptable. It explicitly asks of each church that while ensuring that the Biblical texts are handled "respectfully and coherently," its understanding of those texts must build on "our best traditions and scholarship believing that scriptural revelation must continue to illuminate, challenge and transform cultures, structures and ways of thinking" [40] (presumably including those that presently deny the legitimacy of same sex relationships).

The final section of the Report ("The Maintenance of Communion") gets down to specific recommendations growing out of the actions that in its opinion have unjustifiably disturbed the waters of the Communion. It notes that it has given serious consideration not only to submissions from ECUSA, New Westminster, and the General Synod of the Anglican Church of Canada, but also to "various primates who (without consultation with their fellow primates) have accommodated clergy who are at odds with their own bishops." All of these, in the opinion of the Report, "have acted in ways incompatible with the Communion principle of interdependence." As a result, the fellowship has "suffered immensely." [41] The Report then expresses a series of "regrets": interestingly, the first regret is that some Primates and Provinces have declared themselves in impaired or broken relationships with ECUSA and New Westminster. It then goes on to regret that, "without attaching sufficient importance to the interests of the wider Communion," ECUSA proceeded with the consecration of Gene Robinson, declared that the exploration by local faith communities of liturgies for blessing same sex unions is within the bounds of the common life of ECUSA, that New Westminster approved public Rites of Blessing for such unions, and (echoing its first regret) that a number of Primates and other bishops "have taken it upon themselves to intervene in the affairs of other provinces in the Communion." [42] A careful reading of the Report suggests that it is as concerned with "interventions" as it is with the precipitous actions on sexuality from Canada and the United States. Yet in the publicity that followed the issuance of the Report the greatest attention was given to its chastisement of those two churches and not to its criticism of the intervening bishops.

Yet its reprimand of ECUSA was quite clear. The very fact that the U.S. House of Bishops meeting in October 2003 would have had full knowledge that many people in the Communion "could neither recognize nor receive the ministry" of an openly gay man in a same gender union, "raises the question of their commitment" to ECUSA's interdependence as a member of the AC. In effect, the consecration of Gene Robinson indicates that those involved "did not pay due regard . . . to the wider implications of the decisions they were making." [43] In the future, the Report recommends, the acceptability of any candidate for the episcopate by all the Provinces in the Communion should be taken into account by those at the local level.

It also recommends that ECUSA "be invited to express its regret that the proper constraints of the bonds of affection were breached" in the election and consecration of Gene Robinson. Assuming the expression of such regret, Windsor also recommends that "those who took part as consecrators of Gene Robinson should be invited to consider in all conscience whether they should withdraw themselves from representative functions in the Anglican Communion" and ECUSA should "be invited to effect a moratorium on the election and consent to the consecration of any candidate to the episcopate who is living in a same gender union until some new consensus in the Anglican Communion emerges." [44] (Note that once again the Report implicitly refuses to characterize rejection of same sex relationships or homosexuality as constitutive of the faith itself. If a new consensus could accept them, the possibility of which the Report does not rule out, then they cannot be of the essence of the faith nor matters of orthodox belief or practice, which presumably are not subject to change by consensus. This implication, however, is not spelled out by the Report.)

Nevertheless, the Report does ask for ECUSA to make a contribution "which explains, from within the sources of authority that we as Anglicans have received in Scripture, the apostolic tradition and reasoned reflection, how a person living in a same gender union may be considered eligible to lead the flock of Christ." [45] Of course, one must assume that conservatives do not think such an explanation is even possible. But the fact that Windsor asks for it suggests that it does not rule out the possibility that it can be done. This reinforces the idea that no final position on the acceptability of same sex relationships has been taken by the Report. And the House of Bishops would soon commission a response, known as *To Set Our Hope On Christ,* which would be released in June 2005 and which would do exactly what Windsor asks for, though not necessarily to the satisfaction of conservatives.

The Report notes that the Canadian Church is in the process of ascertaining to what extent the blessing of same sex unions is a doctrinal matter. They are asked to demonstrate "how public Rites of Blessing for same sex unions would constitute growth in harmony with the apostolic tradition as it has been received." [46] In the meantime, the Report calls for a moratorium on all such blessings and invites bishops who have done them to express regret that the bonds of affection were breached. Nevertheless, continuing the theme of openness to the possibility of future justification for such actions, the Report calls for continuing study of Biblical and theological rationales for and against such unions.[47] In the meantime, it requests Provinces to reassess their care for and attitude toward persons "of homosexual orientation." It also calls for "conditional and temporary provision of delegated pastoral oversight for those who are dissenting" and commends the Canadian House of Bishops for doing precisely this.[48]

Finally, as if to echo the first regret it had articulated, it criticizes any attempt to establish two ecclesiastical jurisdictions in one place (as intervening bishops seem intent on doing) and it once again calls on those bishops who have (believing it is their conscientious duty to do so) intervened in Provinces, dioceses, and parishes other than their own "to express regret for the consequences of their actions, to affirm their desire to remain in the Communion, and to effect a moratorium on any further interventions." [49]

Immediate Response to the Windsor Report

One of the first to respond to the Report in the United States was Presiding Bishop Frank Griswold who, because of his position, was in London at the Primates' meeting that first received the Report. He reaffirmed the importance of recognizing the "multiple contexts" in which the Gospel is interpreted and lived. He also underscored the "positive contribution" gay and lesbian persons have made to every aspect of the life of the Church and its ministry even though he expresses "regret" at how difficult and painful the actions of the Church in the United States have been to other provinces.[50]

Not surprisingly one of the harshest and most negative reactions to the Report was that of Archbishop Akinola of Nigeria. He claimed that it "falls far short" of what is needed and fails to "confront the reality that a small, economically privileged group of people has sought to subvert the Christian faith and impose their new and false doctrine on the wider community of faithful believers." Those who have maintained their allegiance to "the faith once delivered to the saints" (a phrase that has now become a virtual mantra among conservatives) have been "marginalized and persecuted for their faith." He does not specify which acts of persecution he is referring to. The problem with the North American Church, according to Akinola, is its "deadly embrace" of the spirit of the age. Akinola was also upset by the rebuke of those bishops like himself who, in "trying to bring the church back to the Bible," have crossed provincial and diocesan boundaries and whose lives are now at risk because of the actions of ECUSA. "Where is the language of rebuke for those who are promoting sexual sins as holy and acceptable behavior?" [51]

A more thoughtful but no less forceful commentary on the Report was given the following year by the Reverend Paul Zahl, then dean and president of the conservative Trinity Episcopal School for Ministry in Ambridge, Pennsylvania. His remarks are found in a published conversation with Ian T. Douglas, a professor of World Mission and Global Christianity, the director of Anglican, Global and Ecumenical Studies at the Episcopal Divinity School in Massachusetts, and a member of the Anglican Consultative Council.

Both, ironically, are critical of the "institutional/hierarchical" slant of the Report, which uncritically reifies the primacy of the traditional Instruments of Unity, thus giving greater weight to a "structuralist/instrumentalist" approach to the issues of the Communion. One of Zahl's reasons for opposing the overly episcopal slant of the Report is that it can be used to justify a prohibition on the crossing of geographical boundaries. "There is an impermeable ecclesiology to many of our diocesan leaders" that makes it difficult for bishops who want to aid the besieged faithful minority to do so.[52] The issues are so serious, according to Zahl, that even the principle of subsidiarity (which permits much more latitude in practice at the local level) needs to be overridden by "outside agitators" like the African Primates, "to help us come to our senses!"[53] Zahl also points out that the Report excised language such as "alternative Episcopal oversight" and kept "delegated pastoral oversight," indicating that in its opinion the current bishops of ECUSA are responding appropriately to the concerns of their aggrieved parishes, an opinion Zahl clearly does not share. Zahl is also concerned that the issue of process has trumped that of the substance of the Church's and Bible's teaching on homosexuality. If the choice comes down to unity versus truth, truth should win. (Ironically, the liberals are inclined to say the same thing, except for them the truth is full justice for gays and lesbians in all aspects of the Church, not a literalist view of the Bible that condemns homosexuality without exception.) Zahl sees the crisis in the Church as one of faith and selfishness. He believes that ECUSA has become too slavish to the fads of the secular world. It has abandoned the reality of original sin for a much more generous view of human nature. Liberals, in effect, avoid dealing with "the darkest, deepest questions of the problem of being human"[54] and thus make themselves vulnerable to the latest and most optimistic social panaceas. The real problem, he insists, is homosexuality, and he even accepts, to a point, the Islamic critique of "western lifestyles" in which homosexuality is playing a major role.[55]

Zahl is also heavily critical of the Report's openness to a variety of interpretations of Biblical texts, believing that what it says on homosexuality is "unmistakable and clear." The Report, he laments, "seems not to allow for the Bible's speaking with verbal and unchanging force and authority on a given question."[56] Instead, he calls for "at least a few absolute statements, both to affirm and reassure."[57] Zahl admits that on some issues, such as the ordination of women, the Bible speaks in different ways, but on sexuality its teaching is crystal clear, as is the "inherited teaching" of the Church. Zahl rejects any notion that the Bible may not be completely transparent in its meaning regarding sexuality. He calls the failure of the Report to accept this view an evasion and wonders why it has not been "more vividly lanced in the media." [58] At the heart of Zahl's reading of the Report is his insistence that the position on homosexuality found in the Biblical texts is a subject "on which Bible-Christians are not able to change their minds. Not because we are dinosaurs—but because we believe God has already spoken." [59]

Zahl, in light of his concern over the failure to treat homosexuality with the seriousness it deserves, calls for a "formal act of felt regret—let's even say penitence or heartfelt apology for hurt causes" if the fragile bonds of unity are not to be stretched to the breaking point.[60] How far those bonds would be stretched in the coming months would be seen in the subsequent actions of the provinces of the United States and Africa. That story will be told after a brief examination of how the issues have played themselves out in one dioces in ECUSA.

The Connecticut Story

Although not unique in the way in which it handled events following the election of Gene Robinson, the Diocese of Connecticut became a paradigm of how conservative clergy and laity attempted, in many ways conforming to the Chapman Memo's recommendations, to respond to Robinson's election and how its bishop attempted to deal with their actions.

On March 29, 2004, the bishop of Connecticut, Andrew D. Smith, announced that he would implement a DEPO plan in his diocese. Smith, however, laid down very clear conditions for such delegation.[61] Any bishop delegated by him would remain under his jurisdiction. A parish receiving a delegated bishop would agree to continue making a financial contribution to the diocese. Once a delegated bishop had been selected by the diocesan bishop, he would consult with him before and after each parish visitation.

Less than a month later, on May 27, 2004, six parishes and their rectors (who will come to call themselves the Connecticut Six or the CT6) wrote a letter to Bishop Smith criticizing his DEPO plan for being "more restrictive" than the House of Bishops plan outlined in its "Caring for All the Churches." One of the first demands they made to Smith is that he deal with them as a group, not as individual parishes.

They say that they are seeking reconciliation with him but it would involve "a heartfelt repentance" for his personal support for Robinson, for his ordination of other "unchaste homosexuals," as an acknowledgement by him that his actions "have done serious damage to the worldwide Anglican Communion." They say that they can only accept a delegated bishop who "affirms Holy Scripture, the ancient creeds, and the 39 Articles," who "upholds the 1998 Lambeth resolution on human sexuality," and who did not support the election of Robinson or of any other "unchaste homosexuals." They also ask for a suspension of the canons regarding the assessment of parish funds given to support the diocese. And they insist that the succession of clergy in their parishes must be determined by their vestries, search committees, and the delegated bishop, not by Smith. Smith refused to accept their demands because, in his opinion, to do so would subvert his authority and duty as the diocesan bishop.

On February 17, 2005, Smith reported to the Standing Committee (the body that serves as a Council of Advice to the Bishop and certifies abandonment of communion by any priest in the diocese) that none of the six parishes or their rectors had chosen to exercise either of the options he had given them: either to return to pastoral oversight by the bishops of the diocese or to accept delegated episcopal pastoral oversight under the conditions he had laid out. Less than a month later, on March 9, 2005, Smith submitted documentation to the Standing Committee that, in his words, "led me to believe the six parishes and their rectors have abandoned the communion of this Church."

On April 14, 17 ECUSA bishops, including Bishops Duncan, Iker, Salmon, and Stanton, wrote an open letter to Smith and the Standing Committee expressing their "deepest grief and concern" that his action against the CT6 regarding abandonment of communion was a violation of the canons. A few days later Smith did meet with the CT6 as a group, but they left the meeting without having acknowledged his authority as their bishop and had therefore, in Smith's opinion, placed themselves under the threat of inhibition by refusing to live within their priestly vows. Smith stated in an interview the following day that he believes the CT6 were following the guidelines in the now-infamous Chapman Memo, though at least one member of the group denied that it was serving as their "playbook."[62]

On April 29, the Standing Committee announced that the actions of the six clergymen had convinced the Committee that they were seeking to move their parishes "out of communion with the discipline of the Diocese of Connecticut. The six priests have intentionally prevented the diocesan bishop from exercising all the prerogatives and responsibilities set forth in the Constitution and Canons directly."[63]

The six rectors responded by denying they had rejected Smith's episcopal authority but acknowledged that they had not reached agreement with him on DEPO. They then asked for AEO and the use of the Panel of Reference.[64] On May 6, 2005, the ABC referred their complaint to the Panel.

On July 12, 2005, Smith put one of the CT6, the Reverend Mark Hansen of St. John's, Bristol, under inhibition for six months for having made "an open renunciation of the Doctrine, Discipline, or Worship of this Church or [sought] . . . formal admission into any religious body not in Communion with this Church" and for having abandoned the Communion of the Church. The following day Smith and other members of the diocesan team went to St. John's, Bristol, to recover church property and deliver copies of the inhibition of Hansen. Smith also installed a priest-in-charge.

Smith's actions were immediately condemned by the American Anglican Council for what it called the illegal seizure of St. John's. On July 15 the moderator of the AAC, Bishop Robert Duncan, accused Smith of having broken the status quo as regards actions against the conservative minority in the Church and in the process "jeopardized the future of a faithful Episcopal parish." Duncan claimed that he must now challenge Smith's action.[65]

On July 27, 17 bishops attacked Smith for his actions regarding St. John's, Bristol, saying that they will prepare charges against him for conduct unbecoming a bishop of the Church. They also promised to raise money for the six parishes, provide "episcopal care" to them, and license Hansen to work in their dioceses.

The next day Smith replied to the accusing bishops, saying that their public letter "is filled with assumptions, conclusions, and emotional, highly charged language. In it you have passed judgment on a brother bishop and a diocese without even attempting to ascertain the facts." [66]

On August 19, 2005, the CT6 filed a complaint against Smith with the Presiding Bishop. It attacks his ordination of gay persons, his participation in the consecration of Robinson, his support at the General Convention for "denying historic doctrines of the Episcopal Church," his adopting a liturgical form for celebration of same sex unions, his countenancing of the same, his refusal to discuss any other form of DEPO than the one he proposed, and his requirement that each parish in the diocese pay its assessed financial contributions.

On September 27, 13 bishops asked PB Griswold to forward their complaint against Smith to the Title IV Review Committee and added five additional charges of "conduct unbecoming a member of the clergy." That same day the CT6 clergy and parishes filed a civil lawsuit against Smith and the diocese in the U.S. District Court, accusing him of depriving their parishes of their rights under the First, Fifth, and Fourteenth Amendments. They ask to have a state law that provided for the corporate organization of the Episcopal Church declared unconstitutional. On January 13, 2006, Smith officially deposed Hansen for "abandonment of communion."

The following year, on May 15, 2006, the Panel of Reference appointed by the ABC announced that the ABC had withdrawn the CT6's request to hear their case because a civil case is pending (which the six themselves had initiated). The six had also initiated ecclesiastical charges against Smith, which would render their appeal to the Panel moot.

Some good news for the Bishop came on August 21, 2006, when it was announced that the civil lawsuit against Smith and the diocese had been dismissed by U.S. District Judge Janet B. Arterton, who concluded that Smith had acted appropriately under canon law. Smith responded by saying that

non-interference by civil authorities in religious matters is a constitutional foundation of our nation and I trust that those members of the Episcopal Diocese of Connecticut who appealed to the courts will recognize the significance of this ruling and will seek to live in communion with their Bishop and this Church.[67]

The civil ruling did not, however, deter the CT6 entirely. On August 31, the Reverend Christopher Leighton of St. Paul's, Darien, said that Smith had been taking over the churches and must be confronted.[68] Nevertheless, by October, the CT6 were prepared, they said, to negotiate a settlement with the bishop. Such a proposal, however, ran headlong into the Diocesan Convention held on October 21–22 at which Bishop Smith gave a major address attempting to put the issue to rest.

In his "Bishop's Address" [69] Smith told the convention delegates that the issues in relation to the CT5 (down from the original six following the inhibition of Father Hansen) are "diocesan episcopal oversight" and the "obedience of the rectors to their ordination vows." Their demands for "alternative" or "adequate" episcopal oversight "lie outside any possibility for the Episcopal Church." He lamented the fact that in having to respond to the legal and ecclesiastical actions taken against him and the diocese, the "nurture of our diocesan life and witness" had been diverted. He also noted that the dissident parishes and their clergy, even while bringing him and the diocese into court, are continuing to enjoy the benefits of the Church while refusing to contribute to it. The dissidents, he claimed, continue to make contributions to their own pension funds, purchase insurance through a diocesan plan, and profit from a tax privileged status while challenging the basis of that privilege (a diocesan exemption) in court. They retain the use of property held in trust for the very diocese and bishop whom they repudiate. Smith interpreted their actions as a way of forcing the diocese into expensive legal responses, backing it into a corner, and bullying it into submission. He estimated that responding to their charges has cost the diocese more than $350,000 in legal fees. But he asked, "is this really a matter of winning and losing or 'calling it a draw'? And this is of Jesus?"

Finally, Smith concluded, it is time to say "enough."

> The passive nonsupport and the active sabotage of the diocese by the leaders of these five congregations and those who support them from the outside are a scandal in the community and before the Lord, and they cannot continue.

He laid down the options very forcefully: either return to the life, mission, and communion of the Church or, "if you cannot tolerate the life and openness of the Episcopal Church, then honorably move on. Above all, stop the whining and the destructive behavior which diminish all of us and the Lord Jesus."

Smith then addressed head-on the question of gay and lesbian persons. He asserted that it is now time for this church and diocese "formally to acknowledge and support and bless our sisters and brothers" who are gay and lesbian, "including those who are living in faithful and faith-filled committed partnerships, as followers of Jesus and faithful members of the Church." It is the "witness of the focused faith and pure charity of so many gay and lesbian companions," their "patience and endurance," and their "struggles and their sacrifices" that have brought him to say "yes" to their requests.

While not ready to endorse clergy officiating at civil unions, he did indicate his willingness to give the green light for blessings on relationships under limited conditions.

On April 11, 2007, the Review Committee, considering charges of presentment against Bishop Smith, announced that it was rejecting the charges.[70] According to the authors of the Review Committee's findings, the charges were based on a "concerted" challenge by six priests to the "coherence of the Diocese and the authority of Bishop Smith." Over time, the Committee found, the six priests had "separated themselves by degrees from the Diocesan community."

The Committee was cognizant of the AAC's strategy for replacing the Episcopal Church and finding a foreign Primate to exercise episcopal authority over the dissenting parishes in ECUSA. While the six priests denied that they were being guided by the AAC, the Committee was not convinced. According to the Committee's report, the minutes of vestry meetings in the six parishes in February 2005 indicated that all six parishes were making plans to leave the diocese and the Episcopal Church. They were exploring with a lawyer incorporation as 501(c)3 organizations, joining an existing church or network, or aligning themselves with an offshore bishop and securing liability insurance.

The Review Committee also pointed out that it was the Standing Committee, not the bishop, who decided to proceed under Canon IV.10 against the rectors of the six parishes. Once the Standing Committee had found that they had abandoned the communion of the Church, the canons permitted Smith to affirm the Standing Committee's findings and to inhibit any priest found guilty under them. Smith himself did not even know all the evidence the Standing Committee had considered in reaching its decision. Smith did not affirm the Standing Committee's findings for any priests other than Hansen. Thus the Review Committee found that Smith had committed no offense.

With the release of the Review Committee's report Smith was now free from both the civil suit and the possibility of a presentment. But his troubles were not over. On May 27, 2007, Trinity Church, Bristol, announced that it had joined the Anglican Church of Nigeria. In doing so it became the first parish in the diocese to officially split with the diocese and the national Church. As part of its action, Trinity claimed that its property belonged to it because it had existed as a parish before there was a diocese or a national Church. The following month, its rector, Donald Helmandollar, announced that he had affiliated with the Convocation of Anglicans in North America (CANA) and was subsequently deposed by Bishop Smith on the advice and consent of a majority of the Standing Committee for having abandoned the Communion of the Church. As a result of the parish's and Helmandollar's actions, Smith announced that the diocese intended to recover its property by taking Trinity to court. At his bishop's address to the Diocesan Convention in October 2007, Smith reported that the issues between him and the CT6 (now down to four with the deposition of Hansen and Helmendollar) had now reached a new stage in his relationship with them.

—— 6 ——

From Dromantine to San Joaquin

"The worst are full of passionate intensity"

Shortly after the start of 2005 the first official response to the Windsor Report from the House of Bishops of ECUSA was issued from Salt Lake City in a document called "A Word to the Church." The bishops accepted the Report "with humility" and expressed their "sincere regret for the pain, the hurt, and the damage caused to our Anglican bonds of affection by certain actions of our church . . . [W]e express this regret as a sign of our deep desire for and commitment to continuation of our partnership in the Anglican Communion." [1]

But the Primates, meeting at Dromantine Retreat and Conference Centre in Northern Ireland, released a communiqué on February 24 asking the Episcopal Church and Canada to voluntarily withdraw from the Anglican Consultative Council until Lambeth 2008.[2] The conservative Primates also expressed alarm that Lambeth 1.10 "has been seriously undermined" by the actions in North America. Nevertheless, they expressed cautiousness about any development that would imply the "creation of an international jurisdiction which could override our proper provincial autonomy." They also recommended that the ABC appoint a Panel of Reference "to supervise the adequacy of pastoral provisions made by any churches" who are in serious theological dispute with their diocesan bishop or dioceses in dispute with their provinces. And they commit themselves "neither to encourage nor to initiate cross-boundary interventions." But, consistent with the recommendations of the Windsor Report, they asked for a moratorium on the authorization of public rites of blessing same sex unions and any election or consecration of a bishop in a sexual relationship outside Christian marriage.[3]

Less than a month after the Dromantine meeting the U.S. House of Bishops met at Camp Allen, Texas. They once again expressed "deep regret for the pain that others have experienced for [ECUSA's] having breached the bonds of affection . . . ," etc. But they also stated that their "polity does not give us the authority to impose on the dioceses of our church moratoria based on matters of suitability beyond the well-articulated criteria of our canons and ordinal." They did encourage dioceses to delay episcopal elections and to withhold consent to consecration of "any person elected" to the episcopate after this date and before the General Convention 2006.[4]

To Set Our Hope on Christ

Three months later, on June 21, 2005, ECUSA's response to Windsor's request for an explanation of how a person "living in a same gender union may be considered eligible to lead the flock of Christ" was released. It is called *To Set Our Hope on Christ*. It is probably the most important official document from within ECUSA responding to the Windsor Report and directly addressing the issue of homosexuality.[5] It reflects the capacious or comprehensive vision of the inclusion of different views and persons within a single Church, and an openness to the complexity of Biblical interpretation.

The authors assert that many members of ECUSA over time "have discerned holiness in same-sex relationships" and they have "evidenced the fruit of the Holy Spirit: 'joy, peace, patience, kindness, generosity, faithfulness, gentleness, and self-control' (Galatians 5:22–23)."[6] This holiness, they contend, stands in stark contrast to many sinful patterns of sexuality, including heterosexuality, throughout the world.

They exploit the early church's experience of including gentiles in what was originally an all Jewish community. This inclusion, they argue, "has allowed us to interpret our experience in the light of the early Church's experience."[7] They also place Scripture within an historical process. The Church received the Bible as the product of a long tradition, suggesting that it did not come down in some pristine noninterpreted way directly from heaven.

> From the beginning, Scripture was seen as complex and contested: . . . Scripture itself corrected and amended earlier versions of Scripture in some cases; in other cases, rival arguments were allowed to stand side by side unresolved. The idea that there is only one correct way to read or interpret Scripture is a rather modern idea.[8]

Acknowledging the diversity of the early Church, they claim that some conflicts "were more difficult to resolve because they were good faith attempts to live out different visions and different values, all of which could be rooted in scripture and defended by biblical arguments." Even St. Paul argued that churches need to respect one another's honest differences of opinion about important matters.[9] Paul himself, according to the authors, criticized the certainty Peter seemed to feel regarding the absoluteness of some of the prohibitions set out in Leviticus, the same text on which the conservatives today draw for their attack on homosexual acts.[10]

As to the conservative claim that "the scriptures are perfectly clear and do not need interpretation" on issues of sexuality, the authors simply deny the claim outright. Whether the issue is the morality of usury, slavery, the use of violence, abortion, the death penalty, war, contraception, the nature of marriage, the rights of women, etc., the fact is that "the Church's appropriation of Scripture has been complex and in many cases even at odds with the most obvious sense of the biblical text." [11] We live in different cultural situations, and "not all biblical commandments or proscriptions apply simply or in the same way to any one person or situation." Nevertheless, the authors are bold enough to say that their reading of Scripture clearly reveals "overwhelming concern" for justice for the poor. According to Biblical scholar Richard B. Hays, the Bible hardly ever discusses homosexual behavior in comparison with the vast number of Biblical texts on wealth and poverty, greed, and the right use of possessions. [12]

On the issue of sexuality, the authors note that "it seems very likely that there was no phenomenon in the time of the Biblical writers directly akin to the phenomenon of Christians of the same gender living together in faithful and committed lifelong unions" and that the cultural context of Leviticus is "so different from our own" that we cannot assume that a selective number of "its texts are more binding on us today than all the other of its proscriptions that we, in fact, do *not* any longer follow." [13] (We will return to the Biblical treatment of sexuality in Chapter 10.)

Beyond the Bible, the document observes that modern science is tending toward the view that same sex affection is "simply another way in which human nature exists." It has a genetic-biological basis, and sexual orientation "remains relatively fixed and generally not subject to change." What was once seen as a crucial and defining division among human beings might now be "in fact a biological or cultural difference . . . that has been overtaken by our common Baptism. . . ." [14] (The appeal to a common Baptism will be developed in the Conclusion.)

From these observations and analyses, the authors boldly declare that "this has led us to the conviction that covenanted same sex unions can be open to God's blessing and holy purposes in an analogous way to that of marriage between a man and a woman." Procreation is not the exclusive end of human sexuality. Another purpose (lifelong fidelity and self-giving love), according to Jesus, "would call for the continuance of the marriage even in the absence of children" and implicitly opens the door for persons of the same gender meeting this particular intent of marriage. They cite the 1997 report of the Standing Liturgical Commission and Theology Committee of the House of Bishops, which affirmed that "the Church's theology of marriage according to its purpose and nature has been open and evolving historically." [15]

Consequently, they argue, a blessing of same sex unions signifies the taking of vows of fidelity and commitment, giving praise and thanks to God. A public blessing is an "evangelical message to persons of same-sex orientation and to the culture-at-large." [16] Drawing on their earlier claim that the Bible's social message is one of justice for the poor, they acknowledge that the Church is presently one in which the dominant groups have not been "eager to accept" the lowly or oppressed.[17]

Finally, the document turns to the role of bishops and their authority in the Church. A bishop duly elected in one locale need not be acceptable everywhere, and his/her election is not subject to confirmation by the whole Communion. Anglicanism is, in fact, characterized by (quoting from the Virginia Report) "differences which arise from a variety of reactions to critical studies of the Bible, particular cultural contexts, different schools of philosophical thought and scientific theory." [18]

Speaking directly to the issue of closure in the development of Christian belief, the authors claim that God "ever calls us beyond our narrowness of vision for human life" and a premature stopping point of unity in the form of an already established consensus "might inhibit us from following in faithfulness the lead of the Spirit who moves ahead of us in surprising ways." Our part of the Church (i.e., ECUSA) "is calling the rest to 'come and see' if this isn't in fact the work of the Holy Spirit." Again in the context of justice this calling benefits the whole community by the "raising up of previously marginalized persons into leadership positions." In that light, they conclude by praying that the " 'lived experience' of this 'particular community enables Christian truth to be perceived afresh for the whole community.' " [19]

In these final words, *To Set Our Hope On Christ* is evoking a cherished Anglican principle that permits one part of the Communion, if that part is generally of a common mind, to practice a new way of doing Christianity before the rest of the Communion is prepared to join it in doing so. To claim that the Levitical teaching on homosexual acts, and some scattered comments by Paul suggesting that homosexual acts are shameful, are at the heart of Christian belief and practice goes against the consensus of Biblical scholarship and the historical traditions of the Church. One might also invoke the fact that the Lambeth Conference in 1988 permitted the continuance of polygamy as a concession to certain historical practices in some African communities, and continues to permit remarriage after divorce throughout the Communion despite Jesus's prohibition of remarriage except for adultery. No one seems ready to split the Communion over polygamy, divorce, or remarriage, and yet some seem more than eager to do so over homosexual acts.

The Year 2006: The General Convention

The year 2006 was relatively quiet until the precedent-shattering General Convention held between June 12 and 21 in Columbus, Ohio. At this convention not only was the first woman Presiding Bishop for ECUSA elected but she also became by virtue of her election the first woman Primate in the Anglican Communion. At the same time the Convention also passed, in the aftermath of the Windsor Report, a series of resolutions on sexuality that ended up pleasing no side fully.[20]

With little opposition, the Convention voted to reaffirm ECUSA's commitment to the Anglican Communion and expressed its desire "to live into the highest degree of communion possible." It even voted to ask the Presiding Bishop to explore ways by which there might be inter-Anglican consultation and participation on the Standing Commissions of the General Convention.

With respect to its response to the Windsor Report, perhaps the most significant resolution was A160, which said that the Convention "expresses regret for straining the bonds of affection in the events surrounding the General Convention of 2003 and the consequences which followed," and it offered "its sincerest apology to those within the Anglican Communion who are offended by our failure to accord sufficient importance to the impact of our actions on our church and other parts of the Communion." It then went on to ask forgiveness, though it was somewhat unclear if it wanted forgiveness for the actual content of its 2003 actions or only for causing offense by those actions.

A noncontroversial resolution commending the listening process, as recommended by the Windsor Report, was easily passed, though many were skeptical whether this would result in significant changes of mind toward gay and lesbian persons. The Convention also voted to support the process of the development of an Anglican covenant.

The most controversial resolution proved to be A161, which in its original form directed the Church not to develop official rites for blessing same sex relationships. It also urged those in authority to "*refrain* [emphasis mine] from the nomination, election, consent to, and consecration of bishops whose manner of life presents a challenge to the wider church." In this form the resolution was defeated, in large part because liberals generally felt the word "refrain" was too restrictive. After some behind the scenes maneuvering by the newly elected Presiding Bishop and the outgoing PB, a substitute motion (B033) was introduced to help smooth the ruffled feathers that a complete rejection of any restraint on electing openly gay bishops would have on the wider Communion, possibly even leading to an attempt to oust ECUSA from the Communion and cause the ABC not to invite its bishops to Lambeth '08, only two years away. The substitute resolution called on standing committees and bishops with jurisdiction "to exercise *restraint* [emphasis mine] by not consenting to the consecration of any candidate to the episcopate whose manner of life presents a challenge to the wider church and will lead to further strains on communion." Some progressives saw "restraint" as somewhat less restrictive than "refrain." Neither extreme conservatives nor liberals were ultimately happy with the resolution using the word "restraint." Conservatives said it had enough wiggle room to permit openly gay bishops to be elected; liberals thought it was a shameful denial of the rights of gay and lesbian persons to be the choice of their dioceses as bishops. Supporters of gay and lesbian persons in the Church argued that they were the ones still paying the price for the Church's attempt to hold together people of widely varying views on the issue. Bishop Jon Bruno, liberal bishop of Los Angeles, while see-ing the resolution on restraint as a "detour" to full inclusion of gays and lesbians, was told by the Archbishop of York, who was attending the Convention, that it would be enough to keep ECUSA from being excluded from Lambeth '08. (And it turned out he was right.[21])

In the spirit of the Anglican principle of the dispersion of authority, the Con-vention also passed a resolution stating that no action of the Convention was intended to affect the historic separate and independent status of the churches of the Anglican Communion or the legal identity of the Episcopal Church.

The First Woman Primate

Clearly the most momentous moment of the Convention was the election of Katharine Jefferts Schori as the new Presiding Bishop (or Primate) of ECUSA. At age 51, she was one of the youngest candidates standing for election as PB. She had been a priest for only 12 years, with 6 years as bishop of one of the smallest dioceses (Nevada) in ECUSA. Jefferts Schori had consented to Robin-son's election and participated in his consecration. She was publicly known as supportive of the blessing of same sex relationships, had authorized them in her diocese, and was on record as saying that she was "fully committed to the full inclusion of gay and lesbian Christians in this church." Her critics seemed very uncomfortable with the fact that she had referred to "our mother Jesus [who] gives birth to a new creation" in her first sermon as PB-elect. Primarily for these reasons her election was not received well by conservatives, not so much (at least officially) because of her gender but because of her views on gay and lesbian per-sons' roles in the Church.[22]

After welcoming her to her new position, ABC Williams issued an official let-ter to the Primates on June 27. Entitled "Challenge and Hope of Being an Angli-can Today," [23] the letter insisted that the current debate in the Church has to be resolved on the basis of arguments drawn from the Bible and the historic teach-ing of the Church. The question, according to Williams, is

> what kinds of behaviour a Church that seeks to be loyal to the Bible can bless, and what kinds of behaviour it must warn against—and so it is a question about how we make decisions corporately with other Christians, looking together for the mind of Christ as we share the study of the Scriptures.

He observes sadly that listening to the experience of homosexual people had not advanced very far. He then addresses the difference between the debate over women's ordination and that of gay and lesbian persons. Committed to the notion that the individual members of the Communion should not move too far out in front of the vast majority of the fellowship, Williams argues that the con-tinuing division over women bishops "can still be understood within the spec-trum of manageable diversity about what the Bible and the tradition make possible. On the issue of practicing gay bishops, there has been no such agreement" and it is not unreasonable to seek for a wider consensus before adopting any change even within one or two Provinces. He also claims that the resolutions of the 2006 General Convention "have not produced a complete response to the challenges of the Windsor Report." He says no member church can make significant decisions unilaterally and still expect this to make no difference to the fellowship. Even those actions "believed in good faith to be 'prophetic' in their radicalism are likely to have costly consequences."

Still focusing on issues of process and institutional identity that had also occupied the authors of the Windsor Report, Williams goes on to assert that "what our Communion lacks is a set of adequately developed structures which is able to cope with the diversity of views that will inevitably arise in a world of rapid global communication and huge cultural variety." Williams seems determined not to address the substance of the question of whether ordaining homosexual persons or blessing their relationships is consistent with Biblical and church teaching.

As part of his focus on institutional unity, he pushes the Windsor Report's recommendation for a covenant between Provinces that would require limiting their "local freedoms for the sake of a wider witness." Those willing to do this, he suggests, would be known as "constituent" or covenanted churches and noncovenanted churches would be "churches in association," not bound in a single unrestricted sacramental communion, and not sharing the same constitutional structures. Associated churches would have no direct part in the decision making of the constituent churches. Any one component of the Anglican heritage, he warns, if "pursued on its own would lead in a direction ultimately outside historic Anglicanism." He concludes by reminding the Primates that their suggestion that the ABC resolve all these issues is not appropriate.

The Archbishop of Canterbury: The Office and the Man

This is an appropriate time to briefly summarize the role of the Archbishop of Canterbury and the man who presently occupies it, Rowan Williams. The ABC, as the occupant of the office is known, is the ecclesiastical head or Primate of the Church of England and, as such, an officer of the government of England. He (and it always has been a man) convenes the Lambeth Conferences of bishops, the Anglican Consultative Council, and the Primates' meetings. As the *primus inter pares,* the first among equals, his voice carries great weight in the Anglican Communion but it is not absolutely authoritative. He can refuse to invite certain persons to the Lambeth Conferences, but he cannot determine doctrine or policy for the churches in the Communion, nor even for the Church of England itself. As one writer has said, the position of the ABC has never been fully defined and remains under the shadow of past empires, carrying with it an "imperial flavor." [24] As Church historians John Booty and Stephen Sykes have put it, the international role of the ABC "fits uneasily with his position as Primate of a national and established Church." [25]

The job of the ABC has built into it ineluctable tensions: the expectation of powerful, persuasive teachings, actions that foster unity among diverse parts of the Communion, and no ability to impose those teachings or ensure that his actions will be accepted. These tensions have now been stretched almost to the breaking point because the divisions within the Communion are as extreme as they ever have been. And Williams has, in effect, himself been stretched between the extremes. As one bishop, Idris Jones, Primate of the Scottish Episcopal Church has put it, Williams is currently occupying a Christlike position: "He is crucified between extremes and they're pulling him apart." [26] That crucifixion is exacerbated, I believe, by the fact that Williams has a great deal of the college professor in him (a position he once occupied). As such he was given to seeing all sides of an issue and engaging in provocative exchanges with his students in the hope that the free and open expression of alternative views will lead to greater understanding. But as Primate and one "instrument of unity" for an entire Communion of churches, such openness and tolerance for diversity are not always helpful and may even be impediments to carrying out his function as ABC.

Williams was born in Wales, read theology at Christ's College, Cambridge, and from 1986 to 1992 held one of the most distinguished academic chairs in the world as Lady Margaret Professor of Divinity at Oxford. He became Bishop of Monmouth in 1992 and Archbishop of Wales in 2000. He was elected Archbishop of Canterbury in 2002 at the age of 52, one of youngest so elected and the first from outside the Church of England for the past 450 years. He was present at Lambeth 1998 but, ironically, abstained from the controversial vote on 1.10.

Shortly before his election as Archbishop of Wales, he had spoken out and written on the question of homosexuality. In 1989 he had referred to a "fantasy version of heterosexual marriage as the solitary ideal, when the facts of the situation are that an enormous number of 'sanctioned' unions are a framework for violence and human destructiveness." He also claimed, in words that would come back to haunt him in the eyes of a number of conservatives, that

> the absolute condemnation of same-sex relations of intimacy must rely either on an abstract fundamentalist deployment of a number of very ambiguous texts or on a problematic and non-scriptural theory about natural complementarity, applied narrowly and crudely to physical differentiation without regard to psychological structures.[27]

Later, as the issue of homosexuality heated up after he became the ABC, he began to back away publicly from these views which, he stressed, he had offered when he was a professor seeking to stimulate debate. Now, he confessed, "my personal ideas and questions have to take second place." [28] In the interview from which these remarks were taken he also said that "inclusion" is not a value in itself. Conversion means a change in behaviors, and this applies to sexual ethics. He accepts the authority of Scripture but while acknowledging that there is "a bit of room for manoeuvre [*sic*]" in the Bible on divorce, "it is harder to say that about homosexuality." He says he accepts Lambeth 1.10 as the standard of teaching on matters of sexuality for the Communion. At the same time he is willing to ask publicly whether there is "more than one form of covenanted sexual union that is sacramental of God's grace?" This suggests that for him the issue is not closed even though he is not willing to press the Communion to consider the question since its teaching has already been expressed in Lambeth '98 1.10.

He is also reluctant to commit himself on how the Anglican Communion should deal with the issue. But he does not want any final decisions to be "foreclosed by a radical agenda." He has bought into the notion of an Anglican covenant in which (should it ever be adopted), he argues, one would draw a distinction between "constituent" churches and associated churches, a distinction that has no precedent in the history of the Communion.

Hammered on the right by conservative evangelicals who think he is too liberal on issues of sexuality (and who remind themselves that he had originally approved of openly gay Jeffrey John's election to the episcopate before asking him to withdraw) and by liberals who think he has caved into evangelical pressure, Williams essentially sees himself almost entirely in the role of the unifier of the Communion who has to put aside any personal views he has on the morality of homosexual relations. He no longer feels he has the luxury of espousing prophetic change in the Church. If people want to act radically and prophetically they must be prepared to "risk the breakage of a unity they can only see as false and corrupt. But the risk is a real one" and "the nature of prophetic action is that you do not have a cast-iron guarantee that you're right." [29] In short, Williams is focusing almost entirely at this point on maintaining the unity of the Communion, even if it means putting on the back burner moral issues that many consider to be ones of justice.

What he does not address (nor do any conservative members of the Communion) is the question of how one can reconcile appeals to the authority of Scripture with the consensus of the community. Surely if something is taken as morally absolute from Scriptural texts, how could a contrary "consensus" opinion alter its moral standing? If something is absolutely wrong (e.g., rape), no consensus could make it right. So it is rather disingenuous to suggest, as Williams seems to do, that he cannot accept homosexuality now because there is no consensus for its acceptance within the Communion. Is he suggesting that at some point in the future a consensus might emerge that accepts loving homosexual relations as morally permissible? If so, what happens to the authority of Scripture, which many believe absolutely condemns homosexuality no matter what the context or the number of people who might (erroneously) believe it to be morally acceptable? This contradiction also extends to the notion, which Williams continually stresses, of listening to the experiences of homosexuals and to arguments on behalf of the morality of same sex relationships. He wants the Church to be a safe place for gays and lesbians. But if you believe in the absolute prohibition on homosexual acts, what might you expect to hear during the listening process that would undermine your confidence in your interpretation of Scripture as absolutely condemning homosexual acts? Williams never clarifies the answer to these questions even though he has one of the most finely honed theological minds in the entire Anglican Communion.

It seems that Williams wants to do two difficult, perhaps mutually contradictory, things: keep raising the question of the proper Biblical interpretation of what same sex relations might be in the eyes of God, and keep maintaining the unity of the Communion by not encouraging the first question to become a make or break one. The truth of the matter, he believes, must be decided only after unity has been preserved. Unity is the way of coming closer to the truth and must precede the perception of truth.[30]

In an interview with John Wilkins of the *National Catholic Reporter* in September 2007, Williams reveals that what has held him together and even hopeful during these extremely trying times is a deep faith and his ability to draw on its spiritual resources. Williams sometimes sounds like the whole issue of the unity of the Anglican Communion is secondary to the larger mission of the Church.

> What matters is not the Church of England or the Anglican Communion but the act of God in Jesus Christ for the salvation of the world. . . . the transforming thing has got to be . . . a renewing sense of gratitude. Whether the Church of England survives or not, whether the archbishop of Canterbury survives or not, Christ still died on the cross and rose again, and that's enough to keep you going for quite a few lifetimes.[31]

Conservatives generally applauded Williams's June 2006 letter. Robert Duncan said, "for the first time, the archbishop himself is acknowledging that some parts of the communion will not be able to continue in full membership if they insist on maintaining teaching and action outside of the received faith and order." Liberals pointed out that it said nothing about homosexuality.[32]

After the Convention

Following the 2006 Convention the issue of "oversight" for dioceses dissenting from the actions of the Convention gained renewed importance. Seven dioceses (Fort Worth, South Carolina, Pittsburgh, San Joaquin, Springfield [Illinois], Central Florida, and later Dallas)[33] were reported to have petitioned ABC Williams for "alternative primatial oversight" by a Primate outside ECUSA.

In August, the Reverend Martyn Minns, conservative rector of Truro Church in Fairfax, Virginia, was consecrated in Nigeria as a bishop for Convocation of Anglicans in North America (CANA) under the authority of Archbishop Akinola. CANA, originally created for ministry to Nigerians living in the United States, will now welcome any creedal "orthodox" Episcopalians dissatisfied with the Episcopal Church in America. Akinola claims that he intends "not to challenge or intervene in the churches of (North America) but rather to provide safe

harbor for those who can no longer find their spiritual home in those churches."
Peter Lee, bishop of Virginia, said Minns's consecration is "an affront to traditional Anglican provincial autonomy." [34]

In mid-September, at the invitation of the ABC a group of bishops meet in
New York to discuss current conflicts in the Church.[35] They could not reach consensus on a plan to meet the needs of dioceses asking for Alternative Primatial
Oversight (APO).[36] It was pointed out in one of the many excellent and infor-
mative reports filed for the Episcopal News Service by Mary Frances Schjonberg
that none of the bishops asking for APO have had diocesan conventions ratify the
requests as would be required by canon law.[37] Bishop Jack Iker of Fort Worth
said in response to the meeting that "the time for endless conversations is coming
to a close and that the time for action is upon us."

One issue emerged during this period that would continue to haunt the Church
down to the present—the disposition of church property in those parishes seeking to disaffiliate from ECUSA. An opening salvo came on September 15 from
Christ Church, Plano, Texas, which announced that it would pay the Diocese of
Dallas $1.2 million for title to parish property and sever itself from the Episcopal
Church. Bishop Stanton of Dallas accepted the deal. By this time (September
2006) about 30 of 7,600 congregations in ECUSA had had majority votes by
their members supporting affiliation with an overseas diocese.[38]

Outside ECUSA the African bishops were still showing a deep interest in its
internal affairs. On September 19, the Council of Anglican Provinces in Africa
(CAPA) received a report it had commissioned earlier in February called "The
Road to Lambeth." [39] Claiming that the "evangelical and spiritual dynamism"
of the AC is now in the Global South where a majority of Anglicans live, it criticizes the retention of power in the AC in the hands of those with the money, i.e.,
the Global North. It refers to the Lambeth '98 1.10 resolution and says, "here is
an issue on which we cannot compromise without losing our identity as a Christian body." In commenting on the Windsor Report, it claims that it presented "a
thorough expose of the ways in which the Episcopal Church arrogated to itself
unilaterally a practice condemned in Scripture, tradition, and the Resolutions of
this Communion." Now, it says, "the time has come for the North American
churches to repent or depart. . . . They must reverse their policies and prune their
personnel." The problem, as the document sees it, is that there has been a break-
down of discipline and a willingness to accept the proclamation of two Gospels:
one the Gospel of Christ, the other the "Gospel of Sexuality." Claiming to
believe that clergy in the Church of England are "obliged" to recognize immoral
unions of homosexuals, the writers of the document attack the authority of the
present ABC, saying that he "has failed to oppose this compromising position
and hence cannot speak clearly to and for the whole Communion."

They then insist that they

must receive assurances from the Primates and the ABC that this crisis will be
resolved *before* a Lambeth Conference is convened. . . . We will definitely not attend

any Lambeth Conference to which the violators of the Lambeth Resolution are also invited as participants or observers.

They also argue that the next Lambeth Conference should be in the Global South rather than, as it has been traditionally, in England.

The document concludes by saying,

> We Anglicans stand at a crossroads. One road, the road of compromise of biblical truth, leads to destruction and disunity . . . but surely the second road is God's way forward. It is our sincere hope that this road may pass through Lambeth, our historical mother.

Following its receipt of the "Road to Lambeth," the Primates of the Global South, meeting in Kigali, Rwanda, under the leadership of Archbishop Akinola, issued the now infamous "Kigali Communiqué" on September 22, 2006. The Communiqué expresses their regret that ECUSA "gave no clear embrace of the minimal recommendations of the Windsor Report" at its General Convention earlier in the summer. They note with dismay that the new Presiding Bishop Katharine Jefferts Schori holds a position on sexuality "in direct contradiction" to Lambeth '98 1.10. Nevertheless, they say that they are encouraged "by the continued faithfulness of the Network Dioceses." They also acknowledge that they have received requests for Alternative Primatial Oversight from some ECUSA bishops and dioceses. The time has now come, they declare, for a "separate ecclesiastical structure of the" Anglican Communion in the United States. This may indicate a decision to no longer seek the reformation of the Episcopal Church but instead to create a new Province of the Communion, separate from the Episcopal Church, that would be strictly orthodox on the issue of sexuality. This indication would be borne out later in 2007.

The self-styled Global South Primates also say that they will not recognize Jefferts Schori "as a primate at the table with us" at the next Primates' meeting scheduled for February 2007. This was a threat that many of them carried out. There was uncertainty as to who signed the Communiqué: some believe that all those in attendance, whether or not they agreed with the Communiqué, were listed as signers simply because they were present at the meeting, but some on that list claimed that they did not see it, sign it, or agree with it.[40]

At the same time as the meeting in Kigali, conservative ECUSA bishops met at Camp Allen, Texas. They issued a letter to other bishops in ECUSA claiming that the General Convention "did not adequately respond" to the Windsor Report or the Primates' Communiqué from Dromantine. To attend this meeting in Texas, bishops had to agree ahead of time that Lambeth '98 1.10 now constitutes the teaching of the Anglican Communion, that commitment to the Windsor Report marks the way ahead, and that one must accept its recommendations with respect to blessing same sex unions and ordination; accept the Communiqué from Dromantine; and agree that ECUSA's General Convention did not go far enough in response to the Windsor Report.[41]

Bishop Duncan, apparently still reluctant to break with ECUSA, said he was still waiting on the ABC and the Primates to answer the request for APO from those dioceses that want it. Bonnie Anderson, a layperson who is president of the House of Deputies, reminded everyone that the Executive Council and the Deputies need to be in the conversation. Bishops alone, she warned, ought not to be deciding the future of the Church and the Communion.[42]

Shortly after the Kigali and Camp Allen meetings, outgoing PB Frank Griswold sent one of his most forcefully written letters to ECUSA bishops on September 28.[43] Griswold reminded the bishops that it is not the responsibility of "self-chosen groups" within the Communion to determine the adequacy of the responses of the Episcopal Church to the Windsor Report. He rejects as inconsistent with Windsor any portions of the Kigali Statement that take issue with the actions of ECUSA before hearing from an advisory group that had been established by the primates and the ACC, and criticizes "continuing incursions of bishops from other provinces into our dioceses." He believes "profound questions" are raised by the Kigali recommendation that a separate ecclesial body within the province of ECUSA be created. He also rejects a proposal by the conservative Anglican Communion Institute for creating a "constituent body" in the United States, other than the Episcopal Church, and believes that not all the signers of the letter from Camp Allen agree with that proposal. He concludes by saying, in words that mark the sharp divide between those who want to avoid change and those who are not afraid of it, that

> those who cling to tradition and fear all novelty in God's relation to the world deny the creative activity of the Holy Spirit, and forget that what is now tradition was once innovation; that the real Christian is always a revolutionary, belongs to a new race, and has been given a new name and a new song. [emphasis mine]

Meanwhile defections of some parishes continued apace. On October 15 a church in Virginia decided to dissolve itself and reform under the authority of the Church of Uganda. On November 17–18 the Diocese of Fort Worth resolved in convention to withdraw the diocese's consent to membership in Province VII of TEC and another that provided a mechanism for parishes to remove themselves from membership in the Network with two-thirds majority of its vestry and two-thirds majority of its voting members.

On November 4, 2006, Jefferts Schori was consecrated as Presiding Bishop in Washington, D.C. On November 20 she sent conservative Bishop of San Joaquin John-David Schofield a letter reminding him of his vows to uphold the doctrine, discipline, and worship of TEC. If he cannot do so, she suggested, "the more honorable course would be to renounce your orders in this Church and seek a home elsewhere." She also reminded him that the property held by the Church was received by it as stewards. "Our forebears did not build churches or give memorials with the intent that they be removed from the Episcopal Church" nor fund endowments "with the intent that they be consumed by litigation."[44] On December 2, despite Jefferts Schori's warning, the Diocese of San Joaquin voted to remove all references to the Episcopal Church in its Constitution and to make its Standing Committee the ecclesiastical authority in the absence of sitting bishops, to put all diocesan trust funds under the bishop, and to permit the diocese unilaterally to extend itself beyond its current geographic boundaries. Jefferts Schori and Bonnie Anderson expressed their "lament" over these "extracanonical actions" of the diocese.[45]

On November 30 Jefferts Schori announced that she would as of January 1, 2007, dispatch a deputy or "primatial vicar" into dioceses where she is unwelcome. Some conservatives immediately rejected the idea because they would have no say in whom she would appoint. That same day Jefferts Schori and a group of bishops developed a response to the request by some dioceses for APO called "An Appeal to the Archbishop of Canterbury." She noted that she would appoint a Primatial Vicar, accountable to her and an advisory panel, which would consist of a designee of the ABC, her designee, a bishop of ECUSA selected by the petitioning dioceses, and the president of the House of Deputies (or her designee). She insisted that DEPO was also still available. The president of Integrity, Susan Russell, commended the APO proposal of Jefferts Schori.[46]

Two weeks later, on December 17, 8 of Virginia's 195 congregations (about 8,000 of 90,000 Episcopalians in Virginia) announced that their members had voted by margins over 90 percent, to sever ties to TEC and affiliate with Uganda or Nigeria by way of the Anglican District of Virginia created by CANA. According to the Constitution and Canons of TEC, dioceses are created or dissolved only by acts of the General Convention and diocesan conventions create or dissolve congregations in their midst. Previously four other Virginia congregations had announced their disaffiliation with the diocese and two others indicated they intended to put their continuing membership in TEC to a vote.[47] Virginia Bishop Peter Lee tried to accommodate these parishes by allowing them to keep their seats on diocesan councils (even though they had stopped contributing to the diocesan budget) and had brought in former ABC George Carey to administer confirmations in their parishes.[48]

The year ended with the release of the "Report of the Panel of Reference" appointed by the ABC in May 2005 in response to concerns expressed by the Primates at Lambeth Palace in the fall of 2004 and Dromantine in the winter of 2005, seeking guidance with respect to the acceptance of women in the priesthood, and regarding delegated or extended episcopal oversight for those parishes that "find it impossible in all conscience to accept the direct ministry of their own diocesan bishop or for dioceses in dispute with their provincial authorities."[49] The Panel, responding specifically to a submission from the Diocese of Fort Worth, recommended that while the Communion was still in a process of reception "no diocese or parish should be compelled to accept the ministry of word or sacrament from an ordained woman; and that provision has to be made to meet the conscientious objection to ministry by women." It also recommended that one's views on the legitimacy of women's ordination should not be a basis for denying consent to an individual elected a diocesan bishop. These recommendations were based on what was known as the "Dallas Plan," which permits a parish seeking a woman priest to have her placed under the oversight of a neighboring diocese (in this case Dallas), which does allow female clergy.

2007 Events from the Covenant Design Group to New Orleans

Very early in the new year Bonnie Anderson, president of the House of Deputies, wrote to the Panel of Reference and the Archbishop of Canterbury "to clarify apparent misconceptions regarding the polity of the Episcopal Church" in the Panel's recent report about the Diocese of Fort Worth's handling of the issue of recognizing ordained women. The misconception, she said, is based on its belief that ultimate authority in TEC rests with the bishops, not with the General Convention composed of bishops, priests, and laypersons.

In the middle of January the Covenant Design Group appointed by Archbishop Williams to explore the Windsor Report's recommendation on an Anglican covenant received a progress report from the Joint Standing Committee of Primates and the Anglican Consultative Council called "Towards an Anglican Covenant." [50] The final text of whatever Covenant eventually emerges, the Group cautioned, was not to be the "invention of a new way of being Anglican, but a fresh restatement and assertion of the faith which we as Anglicans have received, and a commitment to inter-dependent life such as has always in theory at least been given recognition." The enforcement of such a Covenant is to be vested in episcopal authority. The Report also recommended that all matters in serious dispute should be submitted to the Primates who would offer guidance and direction.

A form of discipline is suggested in the Report's proposal that in those cases where churches

> choose not to fulfill the substance of the covenant as understood by the Councils of the Instruments of Communion, we will consider that such churches will have relinquished for themselves the force and meaning of the covenant's purpose, and a process of restoration and renewal will be required to re-establish their covenant relationship with other member churches.

The issue of granting to requesting conservative dioceses a Primate other than the Presiding Bishop of their Province (an APO) continued to gain momentum during these early months of 2007. On February 14, however, a group of moderate and liberal clergy and laity (more than 900, including many from dioceses seeking APO) sent an open letter to the ABC asking him to reject requests for APO because it would "pose a grave danger to the AC." [51] The letter says that those seeking APO are in effect "asking to walk away from the messiness and ambiguity of our current disputes" about gays and lesbians. The authors say that they do not view the Windsor Report "as an ultimatum dictating precise forms of response" by the Episcopal Church.

On February 15, 2007, the Report of the Communion Sub-group was released.[52] The group had been appointed by the Joint Standing Committee of Primates and the ACC to assist the ABC "in discerning the response of the Anglican Communion to the decisions" of the 2006 General Convention. The Report acknowledged that ECUSA had taken the Windsor Report and the Primates' recommendations "extremely seriously" and that its response to the Windsor Report "as a whole in its resolutions was positive." But it also noted that the language of Windsor asking ECUSA to "refrain" from electing openly gay persons was not used at the 2006 General Convention, being replaced at the last minute in Resolution B033 by the word "restraint." It cautioned that "we do not see how bishops who continue to act in a way which diverges from the common life of the Communion can be fully incorporated into its ongoing life." The group also noted with disapproval that ECUSA did nothing to "check" the development of same sex blessing rites. "It is therefore not clear whether, in fact, the Episcopal Church is living with the recommendations of the WR on this matter."

On the question of whether ECUSA has expressed sufficient regret for its actions, the report said that

> on the one hand, there does not seem to be any admission of the fact that the action of consenting to the particular election at the centre of this dispute was in itself blameworthy. On the other, there is the use of the strong language of "apology" and the request for "forgiveness." These words are not lightly offered, and should not be lightly received. Taken with the apparent promise not to repeat the offence [B033] we believe that the expression of regret is sufficient to meet the request of the primates.

In a possibly oblique reference to another issue that the moderate/liberal wing had been pushing, that of boundary crossing and intervention into diocesan affairs by bishops outside those dioceses, the sub-group's report stated that "we have to express our concern that other recommendations of the Windsor Report, addressed to other parts of the Communion, appear to have been ignored so far." And, as if to dampen somewhat the voices calling for greater episcopal power in the resolution of Communion debates, the report reminded the ABC that laity and nonepiscopal clergy need to fully participate in any discussions about these matters.

On the same day as the release of the interim report, the Primates began a four day meeting in Dar Es Salaam, Tanzania. From this meeting would emerge one of the most important manifestos challenging the Global North, and in particular ECUSA's House of Bishops, to conform more closely to the views developed in the Global South. The tone was set at the first eucharist of the meeting when seven Global South Primates, including Akinola, Nzimbi, Orombi, Venables, and Kolini, refuse to take communion with PB Jefferts Schori "because to do so [in their opinion] would be a violation of Scriptural teaching and the traditional Anglican understanding." [53] (No principle for determining with whom one shares communion was referred to.) On the last day of the meeting, the

Primates issued what would be called the Dar Es Salaam Communiqué.[54] The core of the Communiqué addresses the issue of sexuality and ECUSA. It reaffirms Lambeth 1.10 as the standard of teaching on sexuality but says it looks forward to receiving material that will aid in listening to the experience of homosexuals. Once again the question of how one might be open to changing one's mind about Scripture's teaching on the morality of same sex relationships based on listening is not even hinted at. They then addressed ECUSA's actions directly. "At the heart of our tensions," they claimed, is the belief the ECUSA has departed from 1.10. They express gratitude that ECUSA has taken seriously the WR's recommendations, but say that they believe "there remains a lack of clarity" about the stance of ECUSA on authorizations of same sex blessings, especially since "local pastoral provision" is made for these in some places.

The response of the Episcopal Church to the Primates' request made at Dromantine "has not persuaded this meeting that we are yet in a position to recognize that the Episcopal Church has mended its broken relationships." They go on to say that "we are deeply concerned that so great has been the estrangement between some of the faithful and the Episcopal Church that this has led to recrimination, hostility and even to disputes in the civil courts." The contrast between the "faithful" and the Episcopal Church, of course, seems to assume that "the faithful" are those in dissent. But the contrast is not explained or elaborated. Then addressing the issue of diocesan interventions, the Primates acknowledge that "the interventions by some of our number and by bishops of some Provinces, against the explicit recommendations of the Windsor Report, however well-intentioned, have exacerbated this situation." Nevertheless, these interventions, they argue, are tacitly justified until some alternative oversight mechanism is provided for the dissenters. "For interventions to cease, what is required [in the view of some who have done this] is a robust scheme of pastoral oversight" for those alienated from the Episcopal Church "with adequate space to flourish within the life of that church in the period leading up to the conclusion of the Covenant Process," the initial design of which they endorsed.

The Communiqué concludes with a series of recommendations. First, the Primates ask for the creation of a "pastoral council" consisting only of Primates to work in consultation with the Episcopal Church (two members of which would be nominated by the Primates, two by the Presiding Bishop, and a Primate nominated by the ABC to chair the council). The council would "negotiate" structures for pastoral care (and once it is in place, and only then, would the Primates "undertake to end all interventions"), advise the PB and the instruments of communion, and continue to monitor the response of ECUSA to the Windsor Report.

Then, in a direct challenge to ECUSA, the Primates request that its House of Bishops "make an unequivocal common covenant that the bishops will not authorize any Rite of Blessing for same-sex unions in their dioceses or through General Convention" and confirm that B033 "means that a candidate for episcopal orders living in a same-sex union shall not receive the necessary consent . . . unless some new consensus on these matters emerges across the Communion." (Again the question of how a new consensus could be reached on matters that most Primates think are non-negotiable, Biblically sanctioned prohibitions is not raised or dealt with.) And they request that the House of Bishops provide an answer to these demands by September 30, 2007. In the meantime, the Primates urge that all property disputes between ECUSA and dissenting or disaffecting parishes be suspended.

On her return from Dar Es Salaam, PB Jefferts Schori offered some reflections on the Primates' meeting.[55] She noted that an apparent conflict exists between a desire for justice and a desire for "fidelity to a strict understanding of the biblical tradition and to the mainstream of the ethical tradition." She said that what is being called for is a "season of fasting—from authorizing rites for blessing same-sex unions and consecrating bishops in such unions on the one hand, and from transgressing traditional diocesan boundaries on the other." She expressed her conviction, however, that justice for gays and lesbians will eventually prevail as did freedom from slavery, even though it did not happen overnight. She would later add that ECUSA is a "radical and anti-colonial expression of Christianity and we have trouble with assumptions that are purely hierarchical." [56]

Jefferts Schori's comments not withstanding, others within ECUSA were appalled at the tone and content of the Communiqué. New York Bishop Mark Sisk was quoted as saying that "if the price of that [being part of AC] is I have to turn my back on the gay and lesbian people who are part of this church and part of me, I won't do that." [57] House of Deputies President Bonnie Anderson[58] said the Communiqué "raises profound and serious issues regarding their [the Primates'] authority" to require any member Church to take the kinds of actions they recommend. She reminds them that the polity of ECUSA is one of "shared decision making" among laity, priests, deacons, and bishops and reaffirms the tradition of autonomous churches.

Early the following month, from March 2 to 4, the Executive Council of ECUSA met in Portland, Oregon, and made its own response to the Primates' Communiqué. They recognized that the requests from the Primates "raise important and unresolved questions about the polity" of the Episcopal Church, and they create a work group to study the issue and report back by the June 2007 meeting of the Council. They also wished to "reaffirm to our lesbian and gay members that they remain a welcome and integral part" of TEC.[59]

Other events in the Church continued to reflect the issues raised by the conservatives and responded to by the liberals and moderates. On March 3 the Diocese of New Jersey approved a resolution expressing regret for the passage of B033 because of the "pain and anguish suffered" by gays and lesbians. In late October the Diocese of Connecticut at its annual convention also dissented from the resolution. On March 14 a parish in Massachusetts decided not to perform any wedding ceremonies until the marriage rite is available to all people, including gay and lesbian persons.

On March 19 the House of Bishops met in Camp Allen, Texas, to consider its response to the Dar Es Salaam Communiqué. The meeting began with two very different analyses from Episcopal Church members of the Covenant Design Group. One was from Katherine Grieb of the Virginia Theological Seminary and the other from conservative Ephraim Radner (then Rector of the Church of the Ascension, Pueblo, Colorado).[60]

Grieb saw the report of the Design Group as a "conversation starter" for the covenant process. Her own view was that Anglicanism has a long tradition of "creating spaces where different points of view can be argued intelligently, coherently, and with attention to biblical interpretation in ways that we can move forward without everyone agreeing." She charged that the Primates are acting in an "unprecedented way" by attempting to set up a pastoral council and Primatial Vicars "as if the Proposed Anglican Covenant had been completed." This, to her, suggested the process for the covenant "has been ignored, bypassed, condensed, or otherwise made irrelevant by" the Primates' Communiqué because ECUSA is considered so "unreliable and so untrustworthy." She even suggested that ECUSA enter into a five-year fast from participation in the AC. We in ECUSA, she said, will be going into exile but "we might remember that our gay and lesbian brothers and sisters have long lived in exile and it will be a great privilege to go into exile in their company."

Ephraim Radner's take on the Communiqué was, not unexpectedly, quite different. He argued for holding on to the idea of a worldwide Church that could "balance unity and consent." And consistent with the conservative emphasis on episcopal hierarchical authority, he gives much greater weight to the Primates than does Greib. If we choose to distrust them and their communiqué, he charges, "that says a lot right there." The Primates *should* be given the authority of "appeal and final gateway of decision-making" because someone must do this; because Lambeth '98 requested that they take on this role (which he claimed came under the rubric of intervention in exceptional emergency); and because the Primates "represent, in themselves, the unity affirmed and upheld—the 'yes' of the Communion—to which the Covenant itself witnesses."

Following their reception of the reports from Grieb and Radner, and after further reflections, on March 20, 2007, the House of Bishops resolved as its collective "mind" that the proposed pastoral scheme of the Primates' Communiqué "would be injurious to the Episcopal Church and urges that the Executive Council decline to participate in it" and that the House of Bishops work to find ways to meet the pastoral concerns of the Primates that are "compatible" with ECUSA's polity and canons. The "scheme" proposed by the Primates would call for a delegation of primatial authority not permissible under the canons and would be a "compromise of our autonomy as a Church not permissible under our Constitution." It would violate the founding principles of TEC "following our own liberation from colonialism and the beginning of a life independent of the Church of England." It is also a serious "departure" from Anglicanism's Reformation heritage. "It abandons the generous orthodoxy" of our *Book of Common*

Prayer tradition, "sacrifices the emancipation of the laity for the exclusive leadership of high-ranking Bishops," and would replace the local governance of the Church "by its own people with the decisions of a distant and unaccountable group of prelates." Most importantly, it is "spiritually unsound" because it encourages one of the "worst tendencies of our Western culture, which is to break relationships when we find them difficult instead of doing the hard work necessary to repair them and be instruments of reconciliation." [61] Before their vote on the resolutions, PB Jefferts Schori had reported to the Bishops that the Communiqué from Dar Es Salaam was never printed for the Primates to see, and every time it was returned to the drafting committee it got stronger and harsher. [62]

At the same meeting the bishops agreed to write to the whole church acknowledging that TEC shares a common mother in the Church of England and expressing a desire to maintain full communion with the See of Canterbury and other constituent members of the AC. They also noted that TEC did not, as requested by the WR, send delegates to the ACC meeting in 2005. And in 2004 they adopted a policy of DEPO, which received a favorable response by the WR even though the Primates did not accept it. They also noted that some Primates and other Anglican bishops "have violated our provincial boundaries and caused great suffering and contributed immeasurably to our difficulties in solving our problems." At the same time they observe that the Communiqué is "distressingly silent" on the Gospel's opposition to violence against those being persecuted "because of their differences." Biting the bullet on the question of being rejected by the Communion, the bishops conclude by saying,

> we proclaim a Gospel that welcomes diversity of thought and encourages free and open theological debate as a way of seeking God's truth. If that means that others reject us and communion with us, as some have already done, we must with great regret and sorrow accept their decision.

At the end of April word is out that Archbishop Akinola intends to come to the United States to install newly consecrated Nigerian Bishop Martyn Minns for service to CANA on May 5 in Woodbridge, Virginia. PB Jefferts Schori released a statement stating her regret that Akinola has not given her notice nor has she given him permission to perform this action. (Both are required by Episcopal protocol precisely in order to prevent boundary crossing.) Such a failure on Akinola's part "is not the ancient practice followed in most of the church catholic. ... This action would only serve to heighten current tensions and would be regrettable if it does indeed occur." [63] Even ABC Williams had asked Akinola not to proceed with the installation of Minns.

Akinola, however, replied to Jefferts Schori, claiming "the usual protocol and permissions are no longer applicable." He proclaims that until ECUSA "abandons its current unbiblical agenda ... we have no other choice than to offer our assistance and oversight to our people and all those who will not compromise the 'faith once for all delivered to the saints.' " He directly addresses her appeal to the ancient customs of the Church by noting that it is her Province's "deliberate rejection of the biblical and historic teaching of the Church that has prompted our current crisis." He also takes the opportunity to criticize her for continuing her own "punitive legal actions against" CANA clergy and congregations (presumably referring to ECUSA's policy of retaining the property of formerly Episcopal congregations that have left to join overseas dioceses).[64] Akinola proceeded with the installation of Minns on May 5. The following day he responded to ABC Williams, claiming that "the decisions, actions, defiance and continuing intransigence of The Episcopal Church are at the heart of our crisis." CANA, he asserts, is a "bonafide branch of the Communion." He also takes the opportunity to label the House of Bishops' response to the Dar Es Salaam Communiqué "insulting and condescending." Casting himself in the role of the savior of the Church, he claims that if he fails to act "thousands of souls will be imperiled." [65]

Having announced on April 17 that Lambeth 2008 will proceed, ABC Williams sent out his invitations on May 22. As it turns out, he did not invite either Bishop Robinson or Bishop Minns (though he indicates that he will explore how Robinson might be present as a guest). Williams claims he has to "reserve the right to withhold or withdraw invitations from bishops whose appointment, actions or manner of life have caused exceptionally serious division or scandal within the communion." [66] Bonnie Anderson responded immediately, pointing out the obvious fact that Robinson is a duly elected and consecrated bishop of the Church. The Primates themselves had acknowledged his due election in 2005 despite their misgivings about the wisdom of that election. The problem with Minns, according to the Reverend Canon Kenneth Kearon, secretary general of the Anglican Communion, is that CANA, for which Minns was installed as bishop, is not officially recognized as a constituent member of the AC. Williams also reminded the bishops who did receive an invitation that attending Lambeth "does not commit you to accepting the position of others as necessarily a legitimate expression of Anglican doctrine and discipline, or to any action that would compromise your conscience or the integrity of your local church."

In his first response to not getting an invitation, Bishop Robinson pointed to the contradiction between the Church's insistence that it wants to listen to the experiences of gay and lesbian persons and its denial of a place for him at the table to which, as a bishop, he is entitled. If there is to be a true listening process, "it makes no sense to exclude gay and lesbian people from that conversation." [67]

Minns's response was somewhat more global and apocalyptic. He claimed that in considering ABC Williams's refusal to invite him it should be remembered that "this crisis in the Anglican Communion is not about a few individual bishops but about a worldwide Communion that is torn at its deepest level." Perhaps in a gesture to Williams, he says, truthfully I think, that he "faces an impossible task—he is confronted by two irreconcilable truth claims." [68] But having given with one hand, he takes back with the other: Minns says in no uncertain terms that "there is no moral equivalence between immoral living and a creative pastoral division." We are in "one more phase of a global conflict for the soul of the Anglican Communion." And he promises a great deal will happen before next July.[69] Akinola himself says that withholding an invitation to Minns will be viewed as withholding an invitation to the whole Church of Nigeria.[70]

Some bishops in ECUSA who have been supportive of Robinson responded with some anger to the refusal to issue him an invitation. For example, on May 24 Ohio Bishop Mark Hollingsworth posted on his diocesan Web site a statement saying he does not believe Robinson's "manner of life" has caused division but rather it is the "divisive actions of those who have used it in an intentional effort to divide" TEC and the AC that have brought about the division. Hollingsworth was also critical of those bishops who have come into his diocese without his permission "in contempt of the centuries old practice of jurisdictional respect."[71]

On June 1 Bishop Duncan of the Network invited bishops of seven self-identified Anglican organizations to gather in September, immediately following the House of Bishops' meeting in New Orleans, to "initiate discussion of the creation of an 'Anglican Union' " such as envisioned by the Primates of the Global South who had called for a new "ecclesiastical structure of the Anglican Communion" in the United States. The gathering called by Duncan the "first-ever Common Cause Council of Bishops." Common Cause was founded in 2004, connecting Anglican bodies working together for a "Biblical, missionary and united Anglicanism in North America." Duncan acknowledged that the Council lacks the voice of the laity, but this is not surprising given the heavy emphasis the conservatives are putting on episcopal authority to resolve what they see as the crisis of the Communion.[72]

In early June the Executive Council of TEC began a four day meeting. In a move not designed to assuage the feelings of AB Akinola, it agreed to hear from a gay activist from Nigeria, Davis Mac-Iyalla, who was the founder of Nigeria's only gay-rights organization "Changing Attitude Nigeria." At the conclusion of its meeting, the Executive Council warned dioceses that attempts to change their constitutions to bypass ECUSA's Constitution and Canons will be regarded as "null and void."[73] It also reminded the AC that no governing body other than TEC's General Convention can interpret Convention resolutions or overturn decisions by dioceses or previous General Conventions. It declined to give any support for or to participate in the pastoral scheme for alternative primatial oversight proposed by Primates in their Dar Es Salaam Communiqué, and it asked the Presiding Bishop to decline as well. The Council also questioned the authority of the Primates to impose any deadlines and demands on any of the individual churches in the Communion.[74]

Not surprisingly, conservatives were not happy with the Executive Council's statement. On June 19 the Fort Worth Standing Committee said that the Council's position was evidence of an "illegitimate magisterial attitude that has emerged in the legislative function" of ECUSA. This, in itself, is a bit surprising since the conservatives seem to want greater magisterial power to be exercised by the bishops. The issue, of course, is *who* shall exercise this power in the

Church: the laity and clergy in collaboration with the bishops, or the bishops alone. The Fort Worth Standing Committee went on to proclaim that no action of the General Convention contrary to Scripture or apostolic teaching shall have any force or effect in the Diocese of Fort Worth. At the other end of the spectrum, Progressive Episcopalians of Pittsburgh applauded the Council's statement because it "offers relief to faithful Episcopalians in this diocese who have been pressured to accept procedures or policies they knew were at odds with Episcopal Church canons." [75]

On July 18 the Steering Committee of Global South Primates issued a warning that they will continue to violate the boundaries of TEC and exercise authority over dissident congregations. They claimed that they have no choice because the House of Bishops had failed to embrace the pastoral scheme proposed by the Primates. Late in July, Trinity Church Wall Street convened a group of American and African bishops in Madrid, Spain, "for a consultation to strengthen relationships, develop mission partnerships, and to discover new opportunities to bear witness to the Gospel." [76] Initial reports from the gathering were positive, but the full implications were not immediately clear.

The bishops of two dioceses, Pittsburgh and Quincy, announced in September that they would seek to sever all ties with TEC if they get the approval of their diocesan conventions. Their actions were predicated, in part, on the anticipated actions of the House of Bishops scheduled to meet September 20–25. Bishop Duncan said he would ask his convention to remove all references to the diocese's connection with the Episcopal Church and to pass legislation that would allow the diocese to belong to another province of the Anglican Communion. It is not clear whether a diocese has the authority to remove itself from the national Church and a counterresolution to that effect would be offered at the Pittsburgh convention, and followed in 2008 by directives from Bishop Jefferts Schori raising questions about whether Bishops Duncan and Schofield may have abandoned the communion of the Church by leading their dioceses to reject the Constitution and Canons of TEC. Bishop of Quincy Keith Ackerman said in proposing the move to disassociate from TEC that two churches now exist in the United States. One is committed to the authority of Scripture and orthodoxy. The other "is a new culturally-driven religion that advocates revolutionary social change and has abandoned orthodox Christianity." [77]

Interventions also continued apace. On June 22 Ugandan Archbishop Henry Luke Orombi announced that he would consecrate Episcopal priest John A. M. Guernsey as bishop in the Church of Uganda to provide oversight to conservative congregations in the United States. A few days later retired bishop Andrew Fairfield of South Dakota was received by the House of Bishops in Uganda to assist Guernsey. [78] And on July 2 it was announced that the Reverend Bill Murdoch of the Diocese of Massachusetts would be consecrated as suffragan bishop in the Church of Kenya. He, along with the Reverend Bill Atwood, general secretary of Ekklesia, were consecrated as bishops for Kenya at the end of August. Guernsey was consecrated at the beginning of September. Nigeria announced in mid-September that four more bishops formerly serving as priests in episcopal parishes in TEC, including the head of the American Anglican Council, David Anderson, had been elected to serve as bishops for CANA. Later that month, Archbishop Akinola was sharply rebuked by the bishop of the Diocese of Ohio for visiting his diocese without prior notice, a protocol that is widely recognized throughout the Anglican Communion for outside visiting bishops.

At the end of August a story by Ken Howard for Episcopal Life Online was released regarding the actual number of defections from the Episcopal Church. Howard reported that contrary to some projections that between 200 and 250 churches had departed out of the 7,000 congregations that constitute TEC, the actual number in which a majority of their members have voted to leave the denomination came to around 45, or less than 1 percent of the total number.[79]

Also in August it was announced that, despite the B033 resolution from the 2006 General Convention and the Dar Es Salaam Communiqué counseling no further such actions, one of the candidates for the episcopate in the Diocese of Chicago was an openly lesbian priest.[80]

In mid-September the House of Bishops of the Anglican Church of Nigeria voted to ask the ABC to postpone the next Lambeth Meeting. Such a delay would "allow the current tensions to subside and leave room for the hard work of reconciliation that is a prerequisite for the fellowship we all desire." Following this somewhat irenic note, however, the Nigerian bishops expressed their concern at what they called "the abuse directed towards those who hold to traditional views on matters of human sexuality." An example of such abuse, apparently, was the fact that at the last Lambeth Meeting bishops were greeted by persons carrying placards. The bishops also asked for a special session of the Primates' Meeting to consider the "adequacy" of the responses of the U.S. House of Bishops to the Communiqués from Dar Es Salaam and Dromantine.[81]

The Response From New Orleans

On September 20, the long-awaited meeting of the House of Bishops that would take up the Dar Es Salaam Communiqué from the Primates began in New Orleans. The bishops first met briefly with the Archbishop of Canterbury but it was, according to most reports, not a ground breaking encounter with him. The more substantive part of the meeting revolved around how the bishops would address the demands expressed by the Primates in their Dar Es Salaam Communiqué. In the end the Bishops produced a "Response to Questions and Concerns Raised by our Anglican Communion Partners." [82] They reiterated their "passionate desire to remain in communion" with the rest of the Anglican world. Nevertheless, they pretty much stuck to their guns and did not alter positions they had taken earlier. They reconfirmed the B033 resolution of the 2006 General Convention to "exercise restraint" in electing anyone to the episcopate whose manner of life "presents a challenge" to the wider church and acknowledged that they included noncelibate gay and lesbian persons in that category.

They also pledged not to "authorize public rites" for the blessing of same sex unions. But here the wording of the document is a bit slippery. The bishops simply noted that no authorization for the creation of such rites had been approved by the General Convention, and that as a matter of record a majority of bishops do not make allowance for such blessings. Ironically, they quote from the May 2003 Communiqué of the Primates themselves which, while refusing to support the development of rites for blessing same sex relationships, nevertheless acknowledged the necessity of maintaining "a breadth of private response to situations of individual pastoral care." [83] The bishops in New Orleans (at least most of them) understood this to allow the blessing of same sex relationships in circumstances where it was seen as a pastoral response to same sex couples requesting such a blessing "with love and understanding."

The bishops also addressed the question of "episcopal visitors" by affirming PB Jefferts Schori's plan to appoint them at the request of dioceses that want them. The bishops saw this plan as consistent with the DEPO plan they had approved earlier. But they were forcefully opposed to "incursions" by uninvited bishops. Such incursions imperil the long-established ecclesial principles of the Communion and undercut "respect for local jurisdiction and recognition of the geographical boundaries of dioceses and provinces."

The proposed "pastoral scheme" of the Primates set forth in the Dar Es Salaam Communiqué was decisively rejected. They noted that in March they had expressed their concern that the scheme "would compromise the authority of our own primate and place the autonomy of the Episcopal Church at risk." Nevertheless, they expressed a willingness to engage in Communion-wide consultation with respect to the pastoral needs of those who have asked for alternative oversight.

Not surprisingly, of course, they endorsed the continuation of the "listening process" and an enhanced role for the Anglican Consultative Council, because it includes laity as well as ordained clergy, in facilitating this process. The bishops also expressed a hope that the ABC might find a way to include Bishop Robinson in the 2008 Lambeth Conference.

They concluded their response by a reaffirmation of the need for justice for gay and lesbian persons and a commitment to oppose any action that "violates their dignity as children of God" because they are "full and equal participants in the life of Christ's church."

Reaction to the bishops' response was quick and in some instances quite puzzling. Archbishop Akinola declared that it was unacceptable because it had failed to provide "unequivocal assurances" that the bishops are fully committed to the mind and teaching of the Communion.[84] He picked up on the wiggle room in the response with respect to same sex blessings, claiming that there was no outright moratorium on them as demanded by the Primates. The American Anglican Council, the Anglican Communion Network, and Forward in Faith North America issued a joint statement condemning the response's ambiguity and its "rejection of obvious Scriptural teaching." [85] Integrity USA, the advocacy group for lesbian, gay, bisexual, and transgendered (LGBT) Episcopalians, commended the report for not succumbing "to the pressure to go backwards." [86] And Gene Robinson, in an open letter to the LGBT Community, said that the goal of many of the bishops in New Orleans was "to do NOTHING." The bishops simply restated what had been said at the last General Convention. [87]

Perhaps the two most important follow-on responses came from a gathering of 13 bishops in Pittsburgh under the auspices of "The Common Cause Council of Bishops" [88] immediately after the House of Bishops' meeting in New Orleans. In fact, a number of the bishops meeting in Pittsburgh had walked out of the New Orleans meeting early. Their four day meeting in Pittsburgh was intended to begin the creation of an "Anglican union" that would, they hoped, eventually be recognized as a constituent member of the Anglican Communion by the Primates who are finding it difficult to accept the Episcopal Church under its present leadership. This union was compared to the more "perfect union" envisioned by the colonies that broke away from Great Britain in 1776, at least according to Martyn Minns. Duncan, who has long resisted breaking from the Episcopal Church, now seemed ready to create his own church which, if not replacing ECUSA, would stand alongside it as a separate member of the Communion. To get there, however, would require the breaking of the federation of dioceses that comprises the Episcopal Church. Duncan reminded the gathering that this is what happened when some dioceses left the Church at the time of the Civil War.

The tone of the meeting in Pittsburgh bordered on the apocalyptic and the rhetoric on the hyperbolic. Duncan compared the steps the group were considering to those of the Reformation, the American Revolution, and the U.S. Civil War. He upped the ante as well by suggesting that the true believers are on the edge of martyrdom. "My prayer for us who gathered here is that . . . we will be such a threat to the present order that we will be found worth killing" and if so, he offered, then let it be "the red martyrdom" of death. [89]

Shortly after the Common Cause meeting in Pittsburgh, PB Jefferts Schori wrote to Duncan and Bishop Iker of Fort Worth warning them that if they continue to attempt to withdraw their dioceses from the Episcopal Church (which is not permitted under the Constitution and Canons of the Church, which require that dioceses accede to those canons), she will have no choice but to take the appropriate steps to consider whether they have "abandoned the Communion" of the Church and become subject to disciplinary action. [90] Duncan responded to her letter with a terse, but typically hyperbolic comment, echoing Martin Luther, "Here I stand, I can do no other." [91] Should these bishops be found guilty of abandoning the Communion of the Church and be deposed, a new era will have begun in ECUSA. And in March 2008 the House of Bishops would formally depose Bishop Schofield of San Joaquin for precisely this.

The second major response to the House of Bishops' statement came from the Joint Standing Committee of Primates and the Anglican Consultative Council. [92] The Committee had been formed by the ABC to report to him on the response of the House of Bishops to the questions of the Primates set forth in their Dar Es

Salaam Communiqué. The Committee found, despite what many of the bishops present in New Orleans thought they had said, that the use of any rites for blessing same sex relationships "will not in future have the bishop's authority," even though many bishops are continuing to grant that authority in the context of pastoral concern for same sex couples. The Committee could be interpreting the bishops' response as not officially authorizing the development of public rites but tacitly allowing private blessings. Bishop Robinson himself said in his open letter of October 9 to the LGBT community, that he strongly believes that the Joint Standing Committee

> MISunderstood us when they stated that they understood that the HOB in fact
> "declared a 'moratorium on all such public Rites.' " Neither in our discussions nor
> in our statement did we agree to or declare such a moratorium . . . The General Con-
> vention has stated that such rites are indeed to be considered within the bounds of the
> pastoral ministry of this Church.[93]

At any rate, the Committee concluded that the Bishops had met the request of the Primates both in the area of same sex blessings and by a refusal to consent to the election of openly gay candidates for the episcopate. The bishops have, in short, "given the necessary assurances sought of them." On the issue of delegated pastoral oversight, they urged ECUSA to "consult further" on the matter in conjunction with PB Jefferts Schori's plan for episcopal visitors, which they commend as a "way forward" for the Church. With respect to interventions from foreign bishops, the authors of the report state that they do "not see how certain primates can in good conscience call upon The Episcopal Church to meet the recommendations of the Windsor Report while they find reasons to exempt themselves from paying regard to them. The time is right," they assert, "for a determined effort to bring such interventions to an end." They conclude their report by urging the Communion to "move towards closure" on these issues. While it is inappropriate to proceed to create public rites of blessing same sex unions, nevertheless, "we need to take seriously our ministry to gay and lesbian people inside the Church." Of course, how that ministry can succeed when its recipients are both declared to be full members of the Church and at the same time denied access to ordination and blessing is not made clear and continues to haunt the discussion.

Immediately after its release, the Joint Standing Committee's statement was found "unsatisfactory" by the Council of African Bishops (CAPA), who denounced it in part because it attempted no discipline of ECUSA. What is at stake, in their opinion, is the "very nature of Anglicanism," which ECUSA is threatening to replace "with a religion of cultural conformity." [94]

Less than two weeks later the Canadian Diocese of Ottawa voted to approve same sex blessings and sent a recommendation to that effect to Bishop John Chapman. Chapman acknowledged that the vote was overwhelming (177 to 97) but withheld making a final decision. Nevertheless, he said it was not helpful for the diocese to walk alone (though New Westminster has had an approved public Rite of Blessing since 2002), but if need be "we're not afraid to walk alone."[95]

Property Issues

The issue of the ownership of parish property returned in a significant way in November 2007 when the Diocese of Virginia, with the authorization of the executive council of ECUSA, sued 11 parishes in the diocese which have "departed" from the Episcopal Church to join the Convocation of Anglicans in North America (CANA), under the episcopate of Martyn Minns who had been installed as bishop for CANA by Peter Akinola in May. At the heart of the property dispute are two legal principles and one principle of polity. The legal principles are (a) deference to hierarchical authority in the ecclesiastical body, and (b) neutral principles based on state law regarding property trusts and deeds.[96] Most courts do not want to have to decide property issues on the basis of which group within a divided church adheres more closely to official doctrine. If the body is hierarchical in nature, then whatever the hierarchy determines is dispositive for the settlement. On the neutral principle, the court is primarily concerned with the nature of the trust or deed establishing the property of the congregation in question and often decides by determining what the majority vote in the congregation has been. Circuit Court Judge Randy Bellows ruled that the trial in Virginia would focus on

> whether there has been a division within the Episcopal Church and the Diocese of Virginia, whether the Anglican Communion meets the law's definition of a church or a religious society, whether there is a division in the Anglican Communion and whether the departing churches were attached to the Anglican Communion.[97]

The diocesan and TEC's argument, relying on testimony from Church historian Bruce Mullin and missiologist Ian Douglas was that constitutionally the Anglican Communion is not a church (and, in fact, has no constitution) but is a federation of autonomous provincial churches linked by a common descent from and affiliation with the See of Canterbury. The Communion's members are only these provincial churches. The present divisions are, therefore, not *within* the Episcopal Church but *between* it and those who departed from it. The other side argued that the Anglican Communion is a worldwide body and that the position of the departing parishes is much closer to the majority position within the Communion than it is to the Episcopal Church. These are crucial questions, but the Court decision will probably be rendered only after this manuscript has been put to bed.

One case that would truly test the legal disposition of property and herald a brand new era in the discontent of the Episcopal Church was the action taken by the Diocese of San Joaquin at the beginning of December 2007. There, after the second reading of a resolution to remove all references in the diocesan constitution to affiliation with the Episcopal Church, originally introduced in

2006 at a previous diocesan convention, an overwhelming vote approved the diocese leaving the Episcopal Church. Members would then join the Province of the Southern Cone in South America. This was the first time an entire diocese has voted to depart from the Episcopal Church. Clearly issues of diocesan property will be fought over as the national Church seeks to retain the property. It is expected that the Dioceses of Fort Worth and Pittsburgh will follow San Joaquin's example in the next year. The Presiding Bishop has written the bishops of these three dioceses and warned them that, should they follow through on attempts to remove their dioceses from the Episcopal Church, she would ask a review committee to determine if they have "abandoned communion" with the Church, and, if so, she threatened to ask the House of Bishops to depose them. By the spring of 2008, Bishop Schofield of San Joaquin had been deposed. The action of a diocese in breaking completely from the Episcopal Church is unprecedented and may signal the way in which some other dioceses will seek to resolve their disputes with the Episcopal Church. In effect, they will become or join a different Church, no longer claiming a place in the Episcopal Church. Whether they will be accepted as constituent members of the Anglican Communion is uncertain.

Section Four

Perspectives from the Discontented

—— 7 ——

The Conservative Plea for Moral Certainty and Ecclesiastical Discipline

"Spiritus Mundi troubles my sight"

Although they prefer the word "orthodox," conservatives can truly and appropriately claim the word "conservative" to represent their views. They are deeply opposed to what they believe are misguided actions stripping the Church of those essentials that need to be conserved if it is to remain true to "the faith once delivered to the saints." (This phrase from Jude 1:3 is repeated in virtually every position statement set forth by the conservatives.) This faith is under continual attack by the "world," which seeks to undermine, corrupt, or destroy it.

By "world" most conservatives mean secularism, the absence of God and the Gospel from those structures and principles that shape both contemporary culture and the Church. Secularism has replaced the historic moral teachings, worship, and doctrine of the Church. For them it has substituted "paganizing forces," [1] social justice issues, an idolatrous yearning for "relevance," and indiscriminate "inclusivity" of incompatible beliefs, all motivated by autonomous individualism, subjective judgment, a lack of appreciation for the radical nature of human sin, and a tolerance for ambiguity in thought and interpretation of sacred authorities.[2] The Achilles heel of Episcopalianism is, according to one of its most thoughtful critics, a "penchant for over-adaptation to its environing culture." [3] Philip Turner and Ephraim Radner are among a handful of serious, informed, and rhetorically skilled defenders of the conservative position. Therefore, I have chosen to give somewhat more weight to their reflections than to those of other individuals and groups more directly engaged in the political side of the ecclesiastical struggle.

In attacking the "world," conservatism displays an almost Manichaean understanding of the cosmic conflict between God and the world. Christians are caught between living faithfully in obedience to the demands of the Gospel and whoring after false gods, submission to whom requires abandoning the historic "deposit" of the faith as it has been faithfully received and transmitted through the centuries by the Church. The faith that the conservatives defend is generally regarded as transhistorical, protected from the corruptions and contingencies of humanly manufactured history by the Holy Spirit. There is, in fact, a deep suspicion of the vicissitudes of history when it is in the hands of fallen humanity because they threaten to destabilize the eternal truths on which the Church rests. The Church's unshakable foundation, not subject to the contingencies of history, is, according to Radner, the "trinitarian description of God, the authoritative unity of the scriptural history within this description and the exclusive Christological figure in which this historical unity is embodied." If this is not the case, then the Church becomes "nothing but a prism through which to view the arbitrary shackles imposed by time upon our social consciousness." [4] In short, in true Manichaean fashion, there is truth and goodness on one side (preserved from change and contamination by the Spirit within the historic teachings of the Church), and there is corruption and falsity on the other side, found in the agendas set by "worldly" entities.

History is, however, a double-edged sword for the conservatives. On the one hand, the historical continuity of the Church's teachings is essential for establishing its authority. On the other hand, history in the hands of most historians reveals the ever-present hand of contingency, ambiguity, and ironic reversals because it is history made by fallible human beings, none of whom have absolutely "pure" motives or for whom there are "pure" outcomes. Conservatives are suspicious, for example, of Biblical scholarship that relies too much on the historical context of Biblical writings as a basis for discerning what their authors meant. Christopher Seitz, himself a reputable Biblical scholar, has said that historical criticism should play no positive role whatsoever in determining the meaning of the Bible for Christians today since that should be left to the Church. Scholarship can at best show that the Bible is a multi-author volume. [5] Echoing the principles of the Vincentian Canon, Radner claims that the Church under the guidance of the Spirit, in its collective wisdom, not the individual operating independently of ecclesiastical authority, is the only authoritative interpreter of Scripture. Scripture finds "its authoritative expression only as it is discerned and articulated within the unity of the Body of Christ." The authority of Scripture is always "Scripture-in-communion." [6]

The authority of the Communion that is the Church must always be tied to its being "ordered" and structured, living in faithful obedience to God's word as revealed clearly and without ambiguity in Scripture, the historic creeds and councils of the Church, and the teachings of the bishops who stand as Christ's successors. This is why conservatives generally tend to look to the primates and bishops, not to the laity, for authoritative teaching, and the imposition of ecclesial discipline through the appropriate "ordering" of church relationships. Conservatives maintain that the core beliefs of what the Church teaches as the faith once delivered to the saints are accessible without being relativized, histori-cized, psychologized, or modified to fit contemporary sensibilities as defined by secular individualism and corrupted by the acids of modernity. The only antidote to these secularizing forces is a church that has the "power to regulate, uphold, require, or adjust correct practices, and to condemn, exclude, undermine, or replace *incorrect* ones."[7]

In fact, much of the literature emanating from orthodox or conservative circles continually reverts to language that demands strong discipline be imposed on those who hold incorrect or unorthodox views. Divine judgment on the betrayal of the faith by false teachers who are in thrall to the calculus of the liberals is what has been missing from the Church. The false prophets (most of whom are in the Global North) have a completely unjustified optimism about human nature. They no longer believe that human nature has been radically infected by the prideful arrogance and sinfulness of the Fall and therefore are naively overconfident that social progress will yield only unalloyed benefits. This feeds directly into their attraction to justice agendas, especially for those they take to be oppressed and marginalized. They issue their calls for justice on the basis of a high view of the autonomous self, making judgments according to selfish pref-erence with little or no attention to the collective judgment of the community as a whole, especially as it stands in historical continuity with the Church under the guidance of the Holy Spirit. As Philip Turner puts it, the secular Church has opened the door to the "subversion of Christian belief and practice by the logic of autonomous individualism."[8] The only antidote, for many conservatives, is the exercise of godly discipline, emanating primarily from the top of the Angli-can hierarchy (bishops and primates), on those below them who are betraying the faith even though they think they are advancing God's kingdom. One way in which true discipline could be restored to the practice of the wayward Church is through alliances with other conservatives and evangelicals outside ECUSA, especially those from the Global South.

Discipline plays a large role in conservative thinking because of the stress it places on the ordered structure of the Church, which, precisely because it is ordered, has a means for correcting wayward members. Liberalism can only be overcome by a united, purified Church, not one broken into fragments character-ized by separate congregational, provincial, and diocesan "agendas." Fortu-nately, the conservatives believe, the liberal penchant for individualism will eventually make it unable to resist the collective force of the ordered structures of the true Church, which are grounded in the eternal truths on which it rests. We must choose, Turner argues, between a "moral universe with an order . . . to which we are required to conform" or live in a social world "created by preference-pursuing individuals."[9] The God of the liberals is "in the end, no more than the affirmer of [private, individual] preferences."[10] To restrain such self-seeking with its mantra of freedom of choice and the right to modify long-established moral practices, the Church must lift up the authority of the teachers of Scripture (almost always the bishops) and recall Paul's willingness to administer "severe discipline in the case of scandalous behavior." In fact, the Windsor Report is faulted by Turner for not saying enough about the need for the imposition of discipline.[11] The alternative to imposing discipline would be "schism, legal chaos, disintegration, the public scandal of Anglicanism in this part of the world [the United States], and finally the disappearance of American Anglicanism as a viable Christian church altogether."[12] This means, at least in part, that the "American" church has failed to submit itself to the judgment of the Communion that today represents the true Church. Apart from the intrinsic merits of their argument against homosexuality, the main attack the conservatives make on the liberals is that the latter are not willing to wait for a common mind to develop in the Communion (presumably within the constraints of historic orthodox teaching) before launching new initiatives.

In fact, many conservatives believe that not only does the Church possess the true faith but that it is clear and unambiguous, even though it can be grasped only through and within the worship and teachings of the Church as they have been preserved and transmitted by its authoritative teachers. God's revelation in Christ "is both clear and continuously available to the church, whatever the circumstances."[13] Scripture's clear meaning, the conservatives insist, "is given through the accountability of interpretation to that teaching that is 'delivered' apostolically,"[14] i.e., through the bishops.

It is not always clear why the conservatives pick out certain doctrines as more central than others except that this is what the Church has done from the beginning. The Church's authority through the continuity of its teachings must necessarily trump individual, local, and provincial challenges to or experiments in modifying those teachings. At the foundation of conservative thinking is the claim that

> there is a discernible pattern of Christian truth, a pattern derived from the apostolic witness across time as the *depositum fidei,* or what the New Testament calls "the faith once delivered to the saints." This pattern is embedded, like a genetic code, in the inspired text of Scripture itself.[15]

There is clearly here an echo of the ancient Vincentian canon. As noted earlier in this book the earliest Christian Church, faced with a variety of different and sometimes conflicting interpretations of Scripture and practice, felt a "great need for the laying down of a rule for the exposition of Prophets and Apostles in accordance with the standard of the interpretation of the Church Catholic."[16] It was the collective voice of the Church, enunciated with authority by the bishops, that must serve as the interpreter of last resort because only through its collective judgment can the subjectivity (and potential destabilization) ingredient in private interpretations be checked. This appeal to a doctrinally pure primitive church becomes the criterion by which to reject any ideas that either have no support in the early church or which cannot be reconciled with the teachings of that church.

If there is to be change in the Church it will require "changing only through orderliness, and tying the church to the past." [17] This means subordinating the felt imperatives at the provincial or diocesan level to the authority of the Communion as a whole as determined and administered by the bishops and Primates. The heresies espoused by some provincial churches (ECUSA and Canada in particular) are almost by definition "an embrace of the local as a definitive discernment" [18] rather than a submission to the mind of the whole, the Anglican Communion in its entirety. Clearly, without the authority of the Communion to rein them in, these provincial bodies are running amuck trying to appease secular voices demanding the replacement of tried, true, and eternal virtues with new and variable political agendas (or "historically aberrant ethical innovation[s]") [19] driven by worldly concerns, not by Gospel imperatives as mediated by the Church. That this ecclesial understanding virtually mirrors that of political conservatives is neither accidental nor insignificant.

Conservatives have a strong, if implicit, streak of communitarianism. There is no discourse, they would argue, outside a community shaped and defined by its historical traditions. Liberals, unfortunately, think they can transcend their communities and speak for larger, more inclusive, less time-bound, and more universal issues such as justice, freedom from oppression, and human rights. But truth, according to the communitarian position, which I believe the Church conservatives share, is what is found arising from *within* the community and its traditions, not coming to it from the outside (an outside already complicit with the impure secular world). This communitarianism limits how much the conservatives are willing to speak the language of the world or to share its agenda, even when issues of social justice are at stake. The fact that the world outside the Church actually addressed the issue of racial and gender discrimination before the Church did seems not to trouble most conservatives.

In today's climate the central doctrine of the Church that conservatives appeal to is that of the Trinity, oddly, a doctrine not actually formulated in the Bible but interpreted historically by the Church as implicit within it. Internal to the community of the Church the selection of the doctrine of the Trinity is not the only doctrine for inclusion in the "core" that the conservatives fail to fully justify. It is not clear, for example, what criterion, other than the fact that Christians have believed them, determines which doctrines are central and which, over time, prove to be peripheral. Revealingly, Turner himself confesses in passing that the notion of "core doctrine" has proven again and again "impossibly vague and unstable." [20] The fact that slavery and discrimination against women had long established church support is no longer sufficient to give those practices current approval, though not even conservatives would claim that they were "core" at any time. But they seem to think the teaching on homosexuality *is* core, even though the doctrinal record of Church teaching fails to bear out this claim. The conservatives also generally elide the question of by whom and how the decisions of what counts as core are made. Once again it is a question of interpretation. Someone, some body, has had to interpret the doctrinal and moral teachings of the Church, as well as its practice, in deciding what is binding today and forever and what can be relegated, with respect perhaps, to an earlier period in the development of the Church. The very fact that the Church today is torn over how to interpret parts of its own history is enough to belie the claim that what the Church taught at all times and places is unambiguous and forever binding. This is why the study of the history of the Church can be so threatening to many conservatives: it might reveal the actual contingencies by which doctrine was made. There may be no seamless thread of pure belief and practice that links all the generations of the Church. This does not mean that the Church's history is irrelevant even for liberals: far from it. For liberals it reveals how much God's involvement with the world is subject to the fragility of human interpretation and judgment. It is a history of the risk God took in creating the world and its human inhabitants as both finite and free, with the capacity to undercut or confound the divine intentions. It is also a history of what it means for God to take seriously his own incarnation into the vicissitudes and contingencies of human history. But even the history of the Church, no matter how much God intends it to be the bearer and preserver of the Good News, needs to be contextualized if it is to be properly understood. As fallible, finite beings ourselves, we know that our own decisions are contingent and shot through with ambiguity no matter how pure our intentions. Liberals tend to be people who can live in that place of uncertainty and precariousness, believing that somehow God will be present even in the fragility and tension of those moments. Conservatives tend to be people who fear believing and acting upon that which is less than absolute and certain, believing instead that God has already spoken unambiguously once and for all. For them, at least within the Church, there is nothing new under the sun.

But it is not clear how the conservatives square their belief that the true faith was laid down in the first few centuries and is now unchangeable, especially on the issue of homosexuality, with their frequently stated appeal to the mind of the Church, which they believe the liberals have failed to heed, but which, presumably, over time can change. What if, over time, through reception, listening, and responding to the experiences of gay and lesbian persons, the mind of the Church comes to accept homosexuality as perfectly consistent with a Christian ethic of love? Would the appeal to the tradition be nullified? You cannot have it both ways: if you believe that something is true for all time and unchangeable no matter how many people believe otherwise, then you cannot believe that same thing can be changed through a new consensus. But the conservatives believe that the teaching of the Bible on homosexuality is "universally consistent and, as we know, consistently negative." [21] And they criticize the Episcopal Church for not waiting for the mind of the Church to change on the issue. These dual claims are fundamentally inconsistent with each other. In the end, if the mind of the Church accepts what the conservatives now believe to be immutably wrong, they will have to choose between the mind of the Church and their particular reading of Scripture. Either the mind of the Church trumps the present claims to absoluteness or the claims to absoluteness trump all contrary opinions no matter how many of the "faithful" hold them.

The Emergence of Organized Conservative Opposition

The history of the conservative groups that come into being out of frustration, anger, and dissatisfaction with the mainstream and majority members of the Episcopal Church is complex and confusing. In reaction to or dissent from the majority in the Church, groups begin, morph into newer groups, merge with each other, go out of existence, and begin again in new forms or coalitions. Miranda Hassett has helpfully schematized the growth of conservative organizations at least up until 2006.[22] Feeling "alarmed and frustrated," [23] and powerless within the mainstream of the Church, a number of self-described evangelicals began to form organizations to recapture orthodoxy from the liberals in the early 1980s. It is simply not possible to trace the history of each and every group that came into existence in opposition to what it saw as the decline in orthodoxy among mainstream Episcopalians. However, some of the highlights of that history can be identified.[24]

If evangelicals believe strongly in the absolute authority of scripture and in using Biblical authority to attack "secular" values affirming homosexuality and women in church leadership, and attacking "moral relativism," then conservative Episcopalians are evangelicals. If evangelicals are all born again, then many conservative Episcopalians do not fit the bill. If evangelicals tend to locate ecclesial authority in the local congregation and its pastor, most Episcopal conservatives would demur, since they are generally attracted to a high view of episcopal authority, apostolic succession, and an affiliation with the Anglican Communion under the leadership of bishops and primates. Most evangelicals are less concerned about strict fidelity to historic church teachings (as found in the earliest ecumenical councils and, in particular, in the historic reference points of the Anglican tradition such as the Archbishop of Canterbury, the Chicago-Lambeth Quadrilateral, the 39 Articles, and the resolutions of the Lambeth Conference), reaching back instead to the uninterpreted words of Scripture alone. If a willingness to downplay set liturgies and the privileges of priesthood common to Episcopalians in favor of a free-flowing, spirit-filled form of worship is common to evangelicals, then conservative Episcopalians are not core evangelicals. Episcopalians are also more comfortable with a higher doctrine of the Trinity and a higher Christology than would be the case among most non-Episcopal evangelicals. To my knowledge no full-length study has been done on the points of similarity and difference between Episcopal evangelicals and non-Episcopal ones. But the topic is one that deserves further study because much of contemporary evangelicalism in America is closely tied to the same rejection of homosexuality (and in many cases the rejection of women from ordained ministry) on the same moral and Biblical grounds on which their Episcopal counterparts base their rejection of what they consider the heretical teachings of mainstream Episcopal leaders in the United States.

There had, of course, been deep dissatisfaction among some Episcopalians at the revision of the *Book of Common Prayer* in 1979. They believed that this revision was a capitulation to the secularizing trends of the time, seeking to replace the elegance of the 1928 version of the BCP with more colloquial, less refined language. The issue of women's ordination, traced earlier in this study, also discomfited many. By the 1980s the breaking point for many conservatives came with explorations into reconceiving historic teachings on sexuality, culminating in the exoneration of Bishop Walter Righter in 1995 (on charges that he had committed heresy in ordaining an openly gay man to the priesthood), the election of Gene Robinson in 2003, and the openness on the part of some bishops to permit the blessing of same sex relationships and to ordain openly gay and lesbian persons to the priesthood. The way was now open for the creation of numerous dissenting groups by those who had identified sexual deviancy as the Achilles' heel of contemporary Episcopalianism.

By the mid-1970s, and certainly by the early 1980s and 1990s, a number of organizations arose to combat these trends and to defend what they regarded as the "orthodox" position of the Church. The Ekklesia Society was one of the first, coming into existence in 1995, through the work of the Reverend Bill Atwood of Texas (who in 2007 was consecrated a bishop in the Church of Kenya). It is primarily focused on supporting the authority of the Primates and regards itself as a support network for Episcopalians who are distressed at the direction their national Church has taken. Hassett believes that a "central role in the development of conservative Anglican global relationships" was played by Atwood, who linked bishops from the Global South with conservatives in the North.[25] This linkage would play an important role in Lambeth 1998 where, for the first time, the Global South bishops were able to muster a majority of votes, particularly on the infamous 1.10 resolution on homosexuality.

A selection of statements of purpose indicates the thrust of these groups: First Promise:

> As evangelicals and Episcopalians, we are witnessing the Episcopal Church embracing a secular humanism that refuses to acknowledge the meaning and authority of the Word of God as spoken through the person of Jesus Christ and revealed to us in Holy Scripture. Recent events have forced us to a dismal realization—that we are a Church in disarray. We have become a Church which contradicts its own doctrine and teaching.[26]

Concerned Clergy and Laity in the Episcopal Church (CCLEC): "Today, there are two religions in the Episcopal Church. One remains faithful to the biblical truth and received teachings of the Church, while the other rejects them."[27]

Anglican Mission in America: This group represents what would become an increasingly popular approach by the conservatives, namely, to ordain

Americans as bishops under the authority of African Primates for service in the United States as a way of gathering up those who were disaffected but keeping them under the Anglican umbrella. This practice of "intervention" in the affairs of the Episcopal Church in America would become one of the most volatile and contentious aspects of the current crisis. AMiA began in 2000 with the consecration in Singapore of two American priests as bishops under the authority of Archbishops Emmanuel Kolini of Rwanda and Datuk Yong of South East Asia. It claimed to be the vehicle through which congregations and clergy could be "fully Anglican—connected to the worldwide Anglican Communion through the leadership of Rwanda and South East Asia—while at the same time, being free of the crises of faith, leadership and mission in the Episcopal Church USA." Its specific mission would be "planting new Anglican congregations from coast to coast." [28]

Perhaps the most important continuing "orthodox" organization is the American Anglican Council. Beginning in 1996 out of a conviction that the Church under its present leadership was as if "locked in a downward spiraling dance of death with postmodern Western culture," a group of nine bishops and over 60 laypersons and priests met to form the AAC. They originally were candid enough to say that their founding group represented a variety of different views and that the AAC would hold these "in tension." [29] They are composed of persons who "affirm Biblical authority and Christian orthodoxy within the Anglican Communion." They intend to "present to secular society a coherent demonstration of God's kingdom in an expression that is faithful to Anglican tradition" based on a conviction that Biblical authority is based on "unchanging biblical revelation." Its most well-known statement of faith, issued shortly after the 2003 General Convention, was called "A Place to Stand, A Call to Action." [30] It calls on ECUSA "to repent of and reverse the unbiblical and schismatic actions" of the Convention. The supporters of the statement commit themselves to the 1998 Lambeth resolutions on sexuality and marriage for everyone "seeking sexual purity and wholeness." And they call for the Primates to intervene in the Episcopal Church and to discipline its deviant bishops.

In June 2004 a coalition of conservative groups was created, calling itself Common Cause Partners, claiming to represent and provide pastoral oversight for more than 200,000 American Christians in the Anglican tradition. One of their objectives is to "ensure an orthodox Anglican Province in North America that remains connected to a faithful global Communion." [31] In their "covenant declaration" they reaffirm the view that the Church has no authority to "innovate: it is obliged continually . . . to return to 'the faith once delivered to the saints.' "

Growing out of the AAC in early January 2004 was another movement calling itself the Network of Anglican Communion Dioceses and Parishes. It claims to have started at the direct suggestion of Archbishop Rowan Williams, though this has not been confirmed. The parishes joining the Network were audacious enough to compare themselves to the Confessing Churches of Germany under the brutality of the Nazis, even promising that they will "lay down their lives for one another in the face of risk and oppression." (It is not clear what specific threats of violence against members of the Network have been received or from whom, though one report suggests that Bishop Duncan has been the object of at least one crude protest.) They also see themselves as living in a diaspora in North America.[32] By mid-summer of 2007 the Network was claiming ten dioceses as affiliated members (though there was some confusion as to whether a diocese could join the Network solely at its bishop's discretion or whether it required a vote by the diocesan convention). Bishop Duncan of Pittsburgh was elected moderator of the Network. Its core purpose is to be a "united missionary movement of Anglicans in fellowship with global Anglicanism, planting churches that plant churches in North America and to the ends of the earth." They commit themselves to both evangelical faith and catholic order, and, as is typical of most conservative groups, they believe that order is to be administered by the episcopal hierarchy. They identify the Primates' Meeting and the Lambeth Conference as the "moral and teaching authority" of the Church to which they will submit. If a diocese will not join the Network, then a convocation of individual parishes and congregations will be able to do so. Some of these will be geographical and others (to be known as Forward in Faith North America [FiFNA]) will be nongeographical. The Network lays down a rule that when at least six worshipping congregations have joined they will constitute a convocation. It is significant that in the Diocese of Connecticut the first organized opposition to the actions of its bishop, Andrew Smith, began when six like-minded congregations and their priests came together to form what they called the Connecticut Six.[33] It is also part of the Network's agenda to press for "adequate episcopal oversight" as called for by the Primates. Although homosexuality is clearly a major issue for the Network, in their founding document they make the curious claim that "local faith communities are operating within the bounds of our common life as they explore and experience liturgies celebrating and blessing same-sex unions." Unless this is a misprint, there is a curious disconnect between the "orthodox" position on homosexual relations and the position of the Network on this point.

It should be noted that the Network, at least to date, is not talking about splitting from the Episcopal Church. Instead, they hope to reform it from within. One of the major divisions that is beginning to emerge among the conservatives is between those who remain committed to preserving the Episcopal Church, no matter how deviant its present policies and practices are, and those who are willing to abandon it entirely and join more orthodox churches around the world or form their own distinct Anglican province. Part of this division includes the question of how far American Episcopalians are willing to place themselves in the hands of specific African bishops, the culture of whose peoples is often rather different from those in the Global North. It is not clear how far they are willing to go in ceding authority to bishops whose experience and training in impoverished and conflicted nations have little in common with prosperous middle and upper class Americans. How much "local autonomy" will the African bishops be willing to give to their American congregations? These questions are only now beginning to arise and the answers are not yet clear.

It would be tedious to pile up a complete list of all the organizations, convocations, conferences, and councils that presently dot the conservative landscape. But it would not be inappropriate to pay some attention to how these groups are being funded. I want to say immediately that the issue of funding is, technically, irrelevant to the truth or falsity of the theological and ecclesiastical positions taken by conservative groups. My examination of their teachings has attempted to take their arguments in their own terms. While some criticize what they call the "life-choices" Gene Robinson has made, for example, their opposition is not to him as a person but to a church that finds his way of life compatible with its moral teaching and its assignment of episcopal responsibilities to persons who are openly gay and living in same sex relationships. That is a principled argument (though not necessarily one that is supported by reason, Scripture, experience, or tradition): it is not for the most part an *ad hominem* argument. But in a climate where financing is important for the propagation of ideas, and where charges of being too complicit with the prevailing culture have been leveled against the liberals, it is not out of line to see if the conservatives within the Church have made common cause with political and social conservatives who obviously have their own cultural "agenda" to promote. When funding is generous, it gives the voices being funded a much more influential platform from which to speak. Whether this is a kind of "cultural captivity" of the religious conservatives by right-wing politics is an issue that they still need to address.

It should also be noted that the House of Bishops received on April 9, 2007, a memorandum from a task force it had appointed in 2006 on "property disputes" in the Church.[34] In the document, significantly subtitled "connecting the dots," the bishops themselves reported that TEC "is dealing with a well-thought-out, well-organized, and well-funded strategy designed to enable and justify the removal of assets from use for the Church's mission and ministry in the world." They charged those seeking to remove property from the Church with hoping "to create confusion as to the nature of the hierarchy of TEC." They would do this, the task force claimed, by asserting that the authority of TEC is subservient to the Anglican Communion, despite the fact that no basis can be found for such an assertion. And they locate the beginnings of this attack on the established authority structure of the Church soon after the close of the 2003 General Convention and the formation of the Anglican Communion Network. Among the many documents they assemble to make their case, the Chapman Memo has pride of place. Therefore, it is not amiss to follow the trail the bishops have examined by looking into funding issues.

An important organization involved in funding conservative religious groups is the Institute on Religion and Democracy (IRD). It was founded in 1981 by conservative religious scholar Michael Novak and soon-to-be Roman Catholic priest (and former Lutheran) Richard John Neuhaus. It attacks what it considers to be "bureaucrats and elites in the churches which have championed leftist secular and political agendas along with outdated liberal theologies over against (and often behind the backs of) the faithful men and women in the pews." [35] While condemning actions called prophetic by liberals, such as electing gay persons to the episcopate and blessing same sex relationships, IRD says it has found it necessary to be a "prophetic" voice in the churches. It claims to hold, in the words of IRD board member Thomas Oden, "firmly to apostolic teaching. . . . The theology is orthodox, reliable, stable, beautiful, familiar, and glorious. By it the Church has been blessed by God for two thousand years." In a 2000 fundraising venture it announced that it was seeking to "restructure the permanent governing structure" of "theologically flawed" Protestant denominations.[36]

According to Group Watch, IRD is heavily funded by groups that are associated with right-wing political causes. Its

> income for 1982 totaled $352,659. Of this, $200,000 came from Scaife Family Charitable Trusts/Scaife Foundations and $81,000 from the Smith Richardson Foundation. IRD also received a $44,000 grant from USIA in 1985. In 1985, IRD received grants of $5,000 from the Adolph Coors Foundation, $64,000 from the John M. Olin Foundation, and $90,000 from the Smith Richardson Foundation. In 1986, it received grants of $75,000 from the John M. Olin Foundation, $45,000 from the Smith Richardson Foundation, and $100,000 from the Lynde and Harry Bradley Foundation.[37]

IRD's 1987 budget—as listed in a 1988 publication on organizations in Washington, D.C.—was given at $450,000 annually. IRD had a budget of $613,000 in 1988, 85 percent of which came from ten politically right-wing foundations. In its first 26 months of operation, 89 percent of its funding came from the same foundations. All of these organizations are heavily involved in financing right-wing political organizations. The Scaife and Ahmanson families, whose money comes primarily from banking fortunes, are particularly generous in their financing of conservative causes. Richard Mellon Scaife also funds the politically conservative Heritage Foundation. Religious conservatives have obviously found the religious right's agenda, including that of many of the conservative Episcopalians, compatible with their own. It is not without significance that the American Anglican Council at one time shared office space in Washington, D.C., with IRD. Howard Ahmanson, Jr. is reported to have given at least $200,000 annually to the AAC and was (for a time) a donor to a group known as the Chalcedon Foundation, which advocates a theocratic state enforcing Biblical law in the United States. He claims to no longer hold this view. He is reputed to give $10 million a year to conservative causes. His rector at one time was David C. Anderson, first president of the American Anglican Council.[38] Ahmanson's wife sits on the IRD Board of Directors. Diane Knippers, who was a member of the arch-conservative Truro Church in Fairfax, Virginia, ran the daily operations of IRD and simultaneously sat on the AAC's board and was, before her untimely death, a strong critic of the actions of the Episcopal Church.

Now none of this suggests that the conservatives in the Church have adopted their views because of funding from conservative political sources. In fact, I am convinced that their views are serious, sincere, and held with conviction. But their influence on the "politics" of the Church would not be nearly as strong were it not for the financing many of their groups receive from those who are politically and financially connected to other forms of conservatism. In this respect, the question of the relationship between culture and religion is as complicated and murky on the conservative side as they claim it is on the liberal side.

—— 8 ——

The Communion in Africa: From Imperially Colonized to Moral Colonizers

"Somewhere in the sands of the desert"

It is impossible to understand the crisis in the Anglican Communion without at least a brief look at Anglicanism in Africa. African bishops (with the notable exception of those in South Africa where, because of its struggle against apartheid, its Anglican churches are far more sympathetic to the struggles of other oppressed groups, such as gays and lesbians) are among the most conservative in the entire Communion on the issue of homosexuality. How did that come to be the case? To answer that question requires some contextual history (an approach that, ironically, conservative African bishops would not want applied to the Bible whose truth, they believe, is independent of the historical and religious contexts in which its various parts were written).

Obviously, no history of Anglicanism in Africa is possible without understanding its colonialist roots. Anglicanism was brought to Africa by missionaries accompanying persons sent by Great Britain to colonize as much of Africa as possible in pursuit of increasing British wealth. In 1799 the Society for Mission to Africa and the East, inspired by reports from the Societies for Propagating the Gospel and for Promoting Christian Knowledge, lamented that "there seems to be still wanting in the Established Church a society for sending missionaries to the Continent of Africa, or the other parts of the heathen world." [1] Soon thereafter the Church Mission Society (CMS) was founded by people inclined toward evangelicalism and particularly critical of polygamy in Africa. This is not the place to rehearse the often sad and racist history of missionary activity in Africa. But it was clear that the interests of Great Britain in expanding its commercial concerns coincided with the interests of the Church in expanding the outreach of the Gospel.

The first native Anglican bishop in Africa was Samuel Crowther (ordained to the episcopate in 1864), a man from Sierra Leone of the Yoruba tribe.[2] According to Church historian William Sachs, Anglican bishops like Crowther understood the role of the Church to be that of providing a public religion, instilling a sense of national identity, into non-Western cultures.[3] Crowther fully accepted the idea that expansion of the trade network would encourage conversion. Later, as Great Britain moved toward a commonwealth of nations, the Church moved toward the idea of a confederation of national churches, and thus the beginning of the Anglican Communion mirrored that of the growth of the Commonwealth of Great Britain.

Two of the early moral issues faced by the Church in Africa were that of polygamy and the participation of Africans in the slave trade. Many missionaries put more emphasis on weaning converts from polygamy than they did on eradicating slavery. Adherence to polygamy, according to African historian J. F. Ade Ajayi, was one of the strongest obstacles to getting African rulers to convert to Christianity. As he puts it, the rejection of polygamy by the missionaries "became, as it were, the most essential dogma of mid-nineteenth century Christianity in Africa." Polygamy was seen as an absolute moral wrong with which there could be no compromise.[4] As Ajayi interprets this position, for Africans polygamy was essential to the notion of family and tribal unity, and to give it up would be to succumb to a culturally conditioned adherence among the British to a strong form of individualism, which is not entirely consonant with African tribal customs that focus far more on the community, the tribe, and the extended family. Ironically, today in Nigeria polygamy remains widespread among "traditionalists" and Muslims.[5] (It is ironic that issues of sexuality seem to have been introduced into the African Church from the very beginning of the missionary movement. It is no wonder that sex issues continue to inform and characterize the Church's views there even though the tables have turned and many African leaders regard the West as having succumbed to the corruption of degrading sexual practices while Africa holds on to the "purity" of sexual values scented by a strong whiff of the Victorian morality originally introduced by the Western churches.)

The reason slavery was not initially treated by the missionaries with as much moral seriousness as polygamy was the belief that slavery was a "social evil," an historical variable that would be reformed over time (and they expected that the "owners" of slaves in the United States would eventually come to treat them as "servants," not as property, thus lessening slavery's moral stigma).[6] In light of contemporary issues of Biblical authority, it is significant that the issue was fought out, at least in part, on Biblical grounds. Missioner John Venn of the CMS wrote to the Committee to which he reported that slavery is "directly contrary to Scripture." The Committee responded by saying that "the Word of God has not forbidden the holding of slaves ... [but over time] Christianity will ameliorate the relationship between master and slave; polygamy [however] is an offence against the law of God, and therefore is incapable of amelioration." [7]

It will be remembered, perhaps, that Lambeth 1988 (and before it, Lambeth 1968) expressed a degree of tolerance toward the current practice of polygamy in parts of Africa while having long since condemned the moral odiousness of slavery. While not explicitly permitting polygamy and while clearly reaffirming the traditional view that "monogamous life-long marriage [is] God's will for mankind," Lambeth '88 nevertheless accepted the practice of allowing polyga- mists to enter the local churches provided that such action had the consent of the local community; and it acknowledged the social harm that would follow from the "putting away" of all but one wife. All of this suggests both that the Communion was willing to accept polygamy in the context of a particular culture and context, and that, at the very least, what one generation regards as "absolutely" morally wrong on Biblical grounds a later generation can make its peace with. Perhaps this will be true, over time, with the issue of same sex relationships.

There were other events in African church history that hover in the back- ground of the contemporary debate. One has to do with what came to be inter- preted as the martyrdom of a number of Christian converts as well as Anglican and Roman Catholic priests in Buganda (present-day Uganda). The story is that in 1884 Mwanga II came to power as the new king of Buganda. Suspicious of the power being exercised by the newly arrived Christian missionaries and their converts, Mwanga began to persecute Christians. He is reported to have demanded of some of his newly converted male servants that they have sex with him. Because they refused his demand (thus failing to recognize his power over them), they were executed and became the first Ugandan martyrs. Naturally this story, in today's context, is interpreted by conservatives as demonstrating that a true Christian would prefer death rather than engage in a homosexual act. Others would argue that the martyrdom was for refusing to accept a temporal authority rather than God. They argue that this is not a story about homosexuality but about the abuse of power. Forced nonconsensual homosexual acts imply nothing about homosexuality as a natural orientation to another of the same sex. The story may be a condemnation, instead, of using force (through sexual violence) to have one's way and in the process violating the personal dignity of the victim (just as rape says nothing about sexuality but everything about coercive power in which a sexual act is only a means of domination and control).[8]

The issue of episcopal authority and the authority of the Church and the Bible also has a history in Africa. It was at the heart of what was called the Kikuyu controversy. Kikuyu is a region of East Africa. The question was whether Angli- cans should permit non-Anglicans to participate in a common Eucharist. Anglo- Catholics feared such an action would be a threat to the indispensability of the episcopacy since most non-Anglicans did not recognize its ecclesiastical and authoritative claims. To allow such ecumenical services, according to Anglican Bishop Frank Weston of Zanzibar, would eventually allow "any priest to deny the Trustworthiness of the Bible, the Authority of the Church, and the Infallibil- ity of Christ." [9] Thus episcopal power and the authority of the Bible and the

Church were inextricably linked in a way that is still reflected in the positions taken by a number of conservative African bishops today. But episcopal power, once unleashed, could also be exercised in ways that, to some, threatened the historic teaching of the Church. The so-called Colenso affair also reveals this dramatically.[10] This does suggest that issues of episcopal authority are not new to Africa.

Another factor in the rise of the current exercise of authority in the Anglican churches in Africa and their commitment to the near-literal truth of the Bible was the East African Revival or Balokole movement in the 1930s and 1940s. This revival began through the missionary work of English Anglicans who brought with them a rather strong conservative understanding of the authority of the Bible. Influenced by the Keswick Holiness movement, which emphasized the need for personal purity in the eyes of God, it inculcated a view of Scripture as absolutely true and submission to whose authority was necessary for holiness.[11] Some of that concern for holiness coupled with accepting a conservative view of the authority of the Bible has continued to the present day in some African churches and may account for the influence of the Leviticus passages that are at the center of much of the interpretive wars over homosexuality. In ancient Israel separation from the pollutions of the world accounted, to a large extent, for the Levitical prohibitions on certain actions that were common to Israel's pagan neighbors.[12]

The cultural context of African life is also important for understanding how ecclesiastical power is exercised in the Anglican Church there today. John Pobee, one of the leading Anglican African experts on the topic, has written that there is a long tradition in African society of authority being vested in the ruler, or chief of a tribe (often understood as an extended family). His authority derives from special gifts he is thought to possess in connection with his ability to work in service to the whole community. He is, in Pobee's words, "the zenith of power . . . at once judge, commander-in-chief, legislator, the executive, and administrative head of the community." He is both the political leader of the tribe as well as its "centre of ritual expression." [13] He combines both political and religious power, mediating the sacred as well as holding the community together politically. If the Bible is humankind's access to the Divine, then the clerical leadership must mediate its truth and meaning to the religious community through the voice of authoritative teaching. Present Archbishop of Uganda Henry Orombi has said that his authority rests on the reassertion of Scripture as "the central authority in our communion. . . . [T]o compromise God's call of obedience to the Scriptures would be the undoing of more than 125 years of Christianity through which African life and society have been transformed." In addition, doctrine based on Scripture "transcends all cultural distinctions." [14] This is clearly a view of episcopal power based on the one document many believe contains absolute unchangeable truth in order to preserve the purity and unity of the community. To allow the Bible to be "relativized" by contextual or historical readings (common among many "Western" Biblical scholars) would be tantamount to threatening the authority of the religious tribal chief who is the mediator of the Bible's authority for the community for which he is morally and spiritually responsible.

Simon E. Chiwanga, himself an Anglican Bishop in Tanzania, has raised some questions about the notion of the monarch or chief that has influenced much of African church leadership. He was, in fact, the chief of his tribe for three years and knows the role from the inside. The problem with the chief model of church authority, he argues, is that it creates an undue sense of dependency on the leader. In the colonial period this played into the hands of the colonial administrators who could rely on the chiefs to keep their communities in line. Chiwanga wants to replace the older chief model with one in which the leader gains authority through his service to the community as part of a team. This is a much more organic model that stands in contrast with the traditional hierarchical one imported from the Church in England, a model that fit well with the chief model.[15] As a result of his reinterpretation of the chief model, Chiwanga is far more open to a tolerant acceptance of practices in other parts of the Communion if they genuinely reflect the experiences of those communities. In a sermon he preached at Lambeth 1998, he asked for an "interpretive charity in our Christian dialogues" and for the application of the "most loving interpretation to [the] actions and opinions of others." Leave the final judgment to God, he pleads. "Forcing your point of view by excluding from your circle those who disagree with you, or by compelling acceptance, is to usurp the place of God." [16]

It is significant that Africa has not had a single monolithic view of sexuality through the centuries. It has known different sexual practices over the course of its history. Miranda Hassett points out that contemporary scholarship is revealing the "elusive contours of diverse African sexual identities and desires, past and present." [17] Some scholars have been struck by the relative silence on same sex relations in most of African history, though the existence of same sex relationships has been present in all African societies (not, in the eyes of Africans, as indicative of a permanent or natural "orientation" on the part of the partners, but as part of one's progress through the various stages of life; a temporary form of "experimentation" by people during their growing up years). The silence on the issue has led some in Africa, however, to argue that therefore homosexuality is "not African." [18] In Uganda, according to Hassett, discussion of homosexuality only began in earnest in the late 1990s, due mainly, she argues, to the influence of forces outside Africa, among which were sensationalist media portrayals of sexuality in the West, and evangelicals preaching against sexual liberation and homosexual practices.[19] Her research led her to the conclusion that for many Africans homosexuality is a problem mainly originating in the former colonizing powers that is now causing them to implode morally, an implosion from which Africa must steer clear. To attack homosexuality in Africa, therefore, is to protect the purity of the community from the contamination spreading from the secularized morally corrupt cultures of the West.[20] Other scholars have remarked on the fact that homosexuality, until very recently, has not been of overwhelming importance to African societies. Lecturer in African Studies Kevin Ward has observed that not only have same sex relations been present in African societies but they "exist in a wide variety of contexts and situations, with varying degrees of approbation or disapprobation, but without the essentialising of sexual identity which has been a characteristic of western constructions of homosexuality . . ."[21]

The concern for keeping the community "pure" in contrast to its neighbors in the Communion would make the passages from Leviticus, in which Israel was trying to protect its purity from its pagan neighbors, extremely relevant to many African bishops. When a community believes its practices are under threat, it will often attempt to set clear boundaries between it and its threatening (morally impure) neighbors. Many scholars argue, as we shall see, that this desire for protection and boundary setting explains the origin of the purity codes in the Old Testament, among which are prominently included those dealing with homosexual acts. By implication, if that threat is no longer present, or other or different forms of protection are available, purity codes can be set aside, as many argue happened to the earliest Christians who felt free to set aside many purity practices such as not eating food offered to idols or eating with Gentiles.

In a seminal article on this issue scholar of religion Mary-Jayne Rubenstein has argued that underlying the issue of homosexuality for some African bishops is the issue of women. Not all African bishops have accepted the right of women in the Church to ordination, let alone to the episcopate.[22] Nevertheless, she points out that women in African history did have power that, after the introduction of Christianity and Islam, they no longer were permitted to exercise. In the area of sexual practice she discovered that there were woman-to-woman "marriages" in the precolonial societies of Nigeria. There were also cases of what we might call gender-bending in which women could take on traditionally male roles and vice versa.[23] Before the imposition of the English Victorian morality carried by the missionaries, the Yoruba religion had a notion of the genderlessness of the priesthood such that there was no distinction between males and females. (This is particularly ironic because the most powerful voice among African Anglicans belongs to the Archbishop of Nigeria, Peter Akinola, who is himself of Yoruba descent.[24]) This openness to women serving in positions of authority came to an end with the arrival of the colonizing missionaries. According to African scholar Ifi Amadiume, on whom Rubenstein draws extensively, "Christianity domesticated Igbo [another Nigerian ethnic group] women by cutting off their direct access to the divine and by fixing their gender to their sex."[25] Rubenstein believes that Akinola is continuing the practice of limiting the authority of women in the Church. He is reported to have said that God did not make a mistake in assigning different roles to men and women and is also reported to believe that a woman has no right to refuse intercourse with her husband for any reason.[26] In this respect Akinola is not only exercising his authority as Archbishop in a way that reflects early tribal customs and the chief model, but also in a way that selectively reads out of African tradition diverse notions of sexuality in favor of one that was largely imported from the West by colonizers driven by a Victorian morality that itself selectively drew upon certain parts of the Bible and not others. It is significant that the original home of the missionaries, England, was among the last countries in the Global North to recognize the validity of women's ordination to the priesthood. Today scholars agree Nigeria is still "a man's country" in which "in general women are not trusted with leadership." [27] The opposition to homosexuality may be simply an extension of opposition to authority resting in anyone other than a heterosexual man.

The attempt to force their episcopal voices on others (to use Chiwanga's phrase) has been characteristic of many of the African bishops who operate on the chief model of authority. That authority is both cultic and political and in service to the community. Thus, when contemporary episcopal leaders in Africa speak on theological, moral, and Biblical issues, their voices carry a great deal more weight than would the voices of their counterparts in the United States, Canada, or Great Britain where episcopal authority has been modified by democratic and congregational forces. They are expected to protect the members of the communities that they serve (as chiefs or leaders) from threats to the unity and purity of the tribe. In the issue of marriage, it is often the power of communal unity operating as a strong moral force against divorce that helps to keep the divorce rate low.[28] This sense of the community as a family is quite strong in Africa. As Kenneth Skelton, Bishop of Matabeleland has said, the conception of "the family underlies all the African's ideas about life and society. . . . There is no place in the African system for an 'opposition' after the western model." [29] Clearly many African bishops see the practice of homosexuality as a threat to the moral integrity of the Church, especially as it stands in tense relationship with Islam and its strict moral teachings against homosexuality. Their sense of responsibility to the larger community, and their sense that its voice may not be as authoritative as their own, might help to explain why there is a tendency among many African bishops to look to the episcopate alone as the source of authoritative teaching on matters of sexuality. They would, therefore, be more inclined to accept an ecclesiastical arrangement in the Communion in which bishops play the central roles. This, of course, would reinforce three of the already existing four Instruments of Unity to which the Communion presently looks for guidance: the Archbishop of Canterbury, the bishops-only Lambeth Meetings, and the Primates' Meetings.

In this respect, it is not surprising that many African bishops today would appropriate the titles of power that once characterized prelates in the Church of England. Anglicanism informed by English traditions and Anglicanism conforming to African culture were not always smoothly integrated. Pobee observes that many African bishops like to be called "Lord Bishop," a title that, in his opinion, "reflects an English culture and social structure which are irrelevant to the African situation." [30] Other Africans have also criticized the monolithic, even dogmatic, exercise of authority by many bishops in Africa focusing on their power to instruct their people from single authoritative teachings in Scripture. Bishop

Prince E. S. Thompson of Sierra Leone believes that the appeal to a single interpretation of Scripture by many African bishops is not particularly Anglican. It is
important, he argues, to "emphasize that there is no one tradition to which all
Anglicans must conform. You need only refer to . . . different approaches to the
Bible (from rabid fundamentalism to excellent scientific study) to be convinced
that there is in fact no one tradition." He suggests that Scripture should be read
"through the African spectacles [which] bear the marks of culture and poverty"
(not, incidentally, the marks of sexuality).[31]

Bishop Njongonkulu Ndungane, the retiring Archbishop of Capetown (and in
African terms a "liberal") has also addressed the question of the authority and
meaning of Scripture for Africans. For him these "have to be worked out by
the local Christian community. In this sense the authority of the church and that
of the Bible go hand in hand, and their authority have [sic] to be freely
accepted." [32] (To be sure, Ndungane does not speak for the majority of African
bishops but they, it appears, do not speak for all African bishops as long as South
Africa is still considered part of the Council of Anglican Provinces of Africa
[CAPA].) He makes the point that this notion of authority rules out giving
authoritative power to someone who is removed, either geographically or rela-
tionally, from the local context. What is even more unacceptable, he claims, is
the notion that the Bible's authority can be separated from the culture in which
it is interpreted and lived and "therefore has authority over African traditions
and values." [33] (This claim, of course, cuts two ways: the Global North should
not assume that its reading of Scripture can be applied to Africa without attention
to the local context, but nor should a reading relevant to the African context be
assumed to bind communities in the Global North.)

Archbishop Ndungane also notes that power in the African church resides
almost exclusively in the hands of men and their request for more tolerance of
polygamy was made without listening seriously to the voices of African women.
Even the Bishop of Ghana's wife has been bold enough to assert that her country's problem with AIDS is due to the "unlimited matrimonial powers that husbands generally wield over their wives. . . . [T]he fact that only the male
condom is widely available in itself gives a promiscuous man power to sentence
a woman to death if he will not use a condom." [34] This point reinforces Rubenstein's claim that the issue of men's power over women may well underlie the
entire debate over homosexuality in much of Africa. It should be remembered
that the Leviticus prohibition on a man lying with another includes the phrase
"as if with a woman." A man acting as a woman (submitting passively to the sexual overture of another man) has degraded himself by occupying, however
briefly, the position of an inferior. This would have particular resonance in African culture.

It is not without significance that some of the loudest voices against homosexuality belong to men representing churches that were complicit with the
genocide in Rwanda. This is not to suggest that the present leadership was complicit, though it is clear that final investigations into who did what from within

the churches have not been completed and may never be. In Rwanda, for example, the Anglican Church leadership was exclusively Hutu, and no one in authority within the Church at the time spoke out against the Hutu-led government.[35] Scholar Roger Bowen traces this reluctance to criticize the government in part back to the East African Revival and its emphasis on personal holiness (and less emphasis, consequently, on social justice or on the need of the religious community to address "political" issues), and in part to an ingrained sense of a duty to obey established leadership, both political and religious. "Obedience to authority is inculcated within African culture." Carried over to the Church, this means that it would be considered prudent to obey the bishop and not engage in much critical thinking or questioning.[36] Some of the most evangelized countries were those in which "many Christians clearly believed that in participating in the massacre of Tutsi, they were doing the will of the church." [37] One aspect of the Church's participation in the genocide (or more charitably, its refusal to challenge the genocidal actions at the time they were occurring) is the tendency many of its leaders fell into of demonizing the "other" (e.g., the Tutsi if one were Hutu). This tribal or ethnic demonization, the labeling of a group of people as a whole as impure, dirty, contaminated, etc., can be seen, perhaps, repeated in the way in which homosexuals are demonized by many African bishops today.

This is not the place to determine the guilt or innocence of individual Anglican leaders and parishioners during the genocide. But the point needs to be made that the atrocities of that event ought to make the consensual acts between loving persons of the same sex pale into insignificance. But so far that has not happened, and one hears very little from the Anglican leadership in Africa about the genocide and the part they and other Anglicans may have played in it or the degree to which their silence, if not their complicity, made it possible for murderous regimes to carry out their horrific acts without overt moral condemnation from the churches. Until they can come clean on the issue of genocide, their pronouncements on consensual sex among persons of the same sex lack a degree of moral consistency and seriousness.

Demonization is also common in the rhetoric of some African leaders toward those in the Global North who have been "permissive" of homosexuality. "The devil has entered our church" (Archbishop Benjamin Nzimbi of Kenya, November 3, 2003); homosexual behavior is "obnoxious . . . devilish and satanic. It comes directly from the pit of hell" (Church of Nigeria statement).[38] On the nomination of Jeffrey John to the bishopric of Reading, Archbishop Akinola said it was "barbaric." [39] He has called the Episcopal Church a "cancerous lump" that "should be excised" from the Anglican Communion. Akinola's is, of course, the voice most well known to the Global North. As Archbishop of Nigeria he carries a great deal more weight (or at least his utterances are given a great deal more media attention) than other bishops and Primates in Africa. He was even listed in *Time* magazine in 2006 as one of the 100 most important persons in the world today. He is reported to support outlawing wedding ceremonies for same sex couples in Nigeria (it already has a law prohibiting homosexual acts between

consenting adults) and even the public display of affection between persons of
the same sex.[40] Given the importance accorded to him, it is important to know
a little bit about him. Calling himself a "low church" evangelical, he was born
in 1944 to a Yoruba family and studied at a Nigerian Anglican seminary. Later
he studied at Virginia Theological Seminary. He did not accept the Windsor
Report, especially those parts criticizing interventions into ECUSA by overseas
bishops. Referring to the imperialistic past he said, "When England takes the
Gospel to another country, it is mission. When Nigeria takes it to America it is
an intrusion. All this imperialistic mentality, it is not fair."[41] Nor is he particularly enamored of the present Archbishop of Canterbury or of the office itself.
"You do not have to go through Canterbury to get to Christ." The Anglican
Church of Nigeria has actually deleted from its constitution the requirement that
it ought to be in communion with the See of Canterbury and with all dioceses and
provinces that are in full communion with it. Instead, the Nigerian Church says it
will be in communion only with those Anglican churches, dioceses, and provinces that

> hold and maintain the historic faith, doctrine, sacrament [*sic*] and discipline of the
> one Holy, Catholic and Apostolic Church as the Lord has commanded in His holy
> Word and as the same are received as taught in the Book of Common Prayer and
> the ordinal of 1662 and in the Thirty-Nine Articles of Religion.

It also passed legislation permitting it to directly minister to Anglicans in North
America who have dissented from the present Church's teachings on sexuality.[42]
On homosexuality, of course, he is clear and insistent: "if the Bible says it is an
aberration, it is an aberration." At the heart of his theology is his conviction that
he is protecting, as any tribal or religious chief would, what the conservatives
call time and again, "the faith that was once delivered to the saints."

In a remarkable interview in late July 2007,[43] Akinola was particularly forceful in his comments on homosexuality. While admitting the existence of homosexual persons in Nigeria, he insisted that the Church not celebrate that fact,
"for God's sake." If they claim that they were "made" homosexual by God, we
have to say "no to that. God did not make a mistake in creation." When asked
whether the issue of homosexuality was more important than poverty or AIDS,
Akinola was quite clear that these problems "come and go." (Jesus said the poor
you shall always have with you.) "But the matter of faith is eternity." And homosexuality is a matter of faith, and thus its importance transcends moral issues that
are mundane and transient. He was also quite vociferous on three other issues:
colonialism, the influence of Western money, and his response to the attacks
being made on him. He said, rather eloquently, that under colonial powers Africans have suffered political slavery and economic slavery. But now these powers
"want to come for spiritual slaves. Now we won't accept it." The Western
powers want to read into the Bible what they think their culture wants to find
there. He is standing against that cultural imprisonment of Biblical truth. On

the issue of money from the West, he says there is "no price tag on Akinola's head. . . . what we are fighting is not about money but about God's kingdom, His authority and his word." So reversing colonial practice, he is sending bishops from Nigeria (e.g., Martyn Minns) to serve true Anglicans in those countries where there is presently no true church to serve them. Ironically, as Mary Jayne Rubenstein points out, Akinola is not completely opposed to colonialism or imperialism "so much as defending his own right to exercise it alongside everyone else."[44] On being the victim of vicious attack, he says, "I celebrate and rejoice that I'm counted worthy of being demonised [sic] by the world."

Akinola is expected to retire in the next few years. And there are signs that his influence is already waning. In the summer of 2007 Nigerians voted to remove him from the presidency of an umbrella group representing all Nigerian Christians, citing his rigidity and intransigence against Muslims.[45] Whether his departure from his episcopal office will significantly alter the voice of the African bishops is hard to say. Episcopal News Service writer Frederick Quinn also claims that the image of the "Global South" as a unified block is rather misleading. Instead, he argues, its membership "appears to be porous, driven by a small number of special interest advocates" from a region in which there is, in fact, "an amazing diversity of religious expressions."[46] Missiologist Ian Douglas, a member of the Anglican Consultative Council, agrees, and argues that the Western press's attention to Africa overlooks its vast plurality of opinions and experiences. They seem fixated on the actions of the Primates without sufficient awareness of the diversity of views among the bishops and laity who constitute the churches in Africa.[47]

One possible indicator of the future is a comment made in late August 2007 by Anglican Bishop Trevor Mwamba of Botswana and the new dean of the Anglican Church of the Province of Central Africa. Bishop Mwamba claimed that the Anglican churches of Africa will "soon return to their mission to alleviate poverty, disease and injustice and abandon a 'fixation' with homosexuality." He went on to say that "very few of us take the homosexual debate as a top priority issue because there are more pressing issues facing the African church." He even expressed a hope that there could be a "breakthrough" on this issue at the October 2007 meeting of CAPA.[48] There was, in fact, at that meeting attention given to issues of economic empowerment. Nevertheless, the Global South Primates released a communiqué from their meeting on October 30 reasserting their belief that the Communion was in crisis over the very nature of Anglicanism.[49] They condemned the call for greater inclusivity as a "grave mistake." They called for an urgent meeting of the Primates in order to conclude a draft of the Anglican Covenant and set a deadline for its ratification. They also asked for a postponement of the next Lambeth Conference because, given the current disagreements, hundreds of bishops would refuse to attend and that would be "an end to the Communion, as we know it." These are not the words of those prepared for a breakthrough. Nevertheless, Douglas has suggested that bishops may decide to assert their own authority over against that of their Primates and come to Lambeth anyway. The Archbishop of Canterbury has recently been reported as saying that "the organ of union with the wider Church is the Bishop and the Diocese rather than the Provincial structure as such . . . as the primary locus of ecclesial identity rather than the abstract reality of the 'National Church.' " [50]

Section Five

Biblical Perspectives on Slavery
and Homosexuality

—— 9 ——

Reconciling Natural Law, Biblical Truth, and the Moral Abomination of Slavery

"Twenty centuries of stony sleep"

And who are we that, in our modern wisdom, we presume to set aside the Word of God . . . and invent for ourselves a "higher law" than . . . Holy Scriptures? Who are we that virtually blot out the language of the sacred record, and dictate to the majesty of heaven what He shall regard as sin and reward as duty? Who are we that are ready to trample on the doctrines of the Bible . . . ?[1]

One might think that this quotation is from a contemporary conservative arguing against the attempt by liberals to "hijack" Scripture in support of a higher moral law condoning gay ordinations and to do so by trampling the clear Biblical prohibition on homosexual acts. What is at stake for the author of this quotation rests on his sense of what is clearly proscribed by the "doctrines of the Bible." In fact, what was at stake for the writer in 1861 was a ringing defense of slavery against antislavery "modernists" who were distorting the Bible in support of slavery's abolition.

The author was the Right Reverend John Henry Hopkins, bishop of Vermont, and later Presiding Bishop of the Episcopal Church. He was decrying the sorry state of affairs in the mid-nineteenth century resulting from the unwarranted moralizing of those who would in the name of the secular morality of antislavery not only trample on the doctrines of the Bible but also would "tear to shreds the Constitution of our country." [2] While the Bible's defense of slavery is, in fact, rejected by today's defenders of what they take to be the "clear" message of the Bible regarding homosexuality, what is clear to them was equally clear to the supporters of slavery who used the Bible in its defense.

It is also important to point out that in the process of defending slavery on Biblical and natural law grounds, some of its defenders in the South were willing to risk the unity of the Church in order to protect the Biblical sanction for slavery. Episcopalians in the North, on the other hand, were more desirous of maintaining the unity of the Church than in confronting the evil of slavery. As Bruce Mullin has nicely put it, in referring to the high church advocates, the emphasis upon "the sacred nature of the church, its fear of schism, and its concern with unity as a mark of the spirit of God retarded any radical action on the question of slavery."[3] The price of this insistence upon unity above all, according to Mullin, was "a willingness to abandon any elevated moral vision for the church, an abandonment which all too often appeared to stem more from a desire to avoid debate than from any established principle."[4] While northern Episcopalians continued to read the list of southern bishops and delegates at the General Convention, the southerners broke off in 1861 to form their own Protestant Episcopal Church in the Confederate States of America "as independent as the Confederate States themselves."[5] They justified this action, in part, on the way in which Episcopalians in the United States formally separated from the Church of England following the Revolutionary War.[6]

On the Biblical defense of slavery, Bishop Hopkins observed that in the Bible slavery is manifestly authorized by God, and he attacks the arrogance of the abolitionists for claiming a moral position at odds with the explicit language of the Bible. Hopkins's defense of slavery rested on what he called "the unanimous voice of the Universal Church" and the "manifest sense of Scripture." And antislavery was criticized for being a "recent" notion spurred on mainly by secular opponents of slavery and thus beyond the reach or concern of the Church.[7] As another Episcopalian put it, Christian feeling must be on guard "against its being diverted by wayward impulse and wasted on worldly and ephemeral projects" such as antislavery, too much "inebriated by too copious draughts of the spirit of the age."[8] The so-called primitive church had not addressed the issue of slavery except by not rejecting the Biblical support for it, especially in 1 Peter 2:18–25, in which Peter tells slaves to accept the authority of their masters with all deference, and not just of those who are kind but also those who are harsh, because by so doing they will imitate Christ's suffering. At the same time, the appeal to individual conscience on matters of justice could be countered by a "defense of subordination and tradition." All the elements of the current opposition to treating homosexuality as an issue of justice had already been rehearsed in the debate, not so much over slavery, but over the arguments for treating it with moral seriousness. We find the appeal to the early church (George Templeton Strong, a prominent Episcopalian layman, said that if there were moral guilt in slaveholding "the primitive church would have entered its protest against it and overthrown it with the overt corruptions of the old world"),[9] to the plain sense of Scripture, to tradition, and to an attack upon the spirit of the age (today that would read the spirit of secularism having taken liberals captive).

Hopkins was hardly alone in providing a Biblical defense of slavery. His work was preceded by numerous southern "divines" who mined the Biblical texts (and it was not difficult to do) for passages showing that faithful adherence to God's will did not and was not intended to lead to the abolition of slavery. Twenty years before Hopkins penned his thoughts on the topic, a Virginia Baptist, Thornton Stringfellow, wrote a piece entitled "A Brief Examination of Scripture Testimony on the Institution of Slavery," which succinctly summarizes the Biblical argument. Stringfellow is aware that northern abolitionists are using the Bible to condemn slavery as a "great sin." But Stringfellow believes he has a truer insight into the plain meaning of the Biblical text: "we shall be seen cleaving to the Bible and taking all our decisions about this matter from its inspired pages."[10] Stringfellow's commitment to Biblical authority is reflected in the thought of most of his fellow clergymen. Alexander Campbell, founder of the Disciples of Christ, said in response to those "liberals" who would question the Biblical sanction for slavery, that

> such is their faith in their own reason . . . that if any sacrifice is to be made, they will sacrifice the Bible to their theory rather than their theory to the Bible. I have nothing to say at this time to such Christians as these![11]

Pastor Ferdinand Jacobs said, "If the scriptures do not justify slavery, I know not what they justify."[12] And Methodist clergyman William A. Smith declared that to the South especially "is given the high and holy keeping . . . of the whole Bible, and nothing but the Bible . . . free from the doctrines and commandments of men."[13]

In citing Biblical passages in defense of slavery, Stringfellow makes particularly strong use of sections from the Book of Leviticus, the same text, of course, that is used today to condemn homosexuality. His defense of slavery begins by noting that in the patriarchal age the very persons God had chosen for divine favor held slaves. In fact, God "decrees" slavery, giving it his legal blessing. So if slavery is a sin, as the abolitionists claim, then it has become sinful *after* God instituted it for the patriarchs. And if its moral status can change from being good to becoming sinful, then its sinfulness is not intrinsic to it as such. Perhaps, then, if slavery is now wrong when once it was right, it is because God has changed his mind about it. But we find no evidence in Scripture that God has altered his initial decree. God wrote slavery into the laws of ancient Israel and those laws even Jesus concedes to be still binding. (He did not come to change one jot or tittle of the law.) Most importantly, the laws of slavery authorize "chastising them with the rod, with a severity that terminates in death." And to drive his point home, Stringfellow reminds his readers that "he who believes the Bible to be of divine authority, believes these laws were given by the Holy Ghost to Moses."[14]

When we turn to the New Testament, it is quite clear to Stringfellow that Jesus found no fault with the divine decree instituting slavery. Nor does St. Paul call for the abolition of slavery. He tells servants, "be subject to your masters with all fear whether good or bad." Slavery is a governmentally sanctioned institution and Christians are required to obey the governments that are placed over them for their own good ("be subject to the governing authorities. . . . Whoever resists authority resists what God has appointed." Romans 13:1–4).

Finally, Stringfellow engages in a defense of slavery as an institution that does great good to the slave, the master, and the social order. If it were not for slavery, the descendants of Ham (believed by most defenders of slavery to be Africans) would have "sunk down to eternal ruin" because they would not have known God and would not have been prepared to live in a civilized society, such as the one their masters had built. Therefore, abolitionists, appealing to a purported higher morality that is not the consensus view among Biblically based Christians (as liberal views today on homosexuality are also declared not to be), are engaged in an "officious meddling with the institution [of slavery] from feelings and sentiments unknown to the Bible." [15]

Civil rights (or their absence) for slaves have nothing to do with God's judgment of the moral character of their persons. To think otherwise, as today's liberals tend to do when they insist that the civil and moral rights of gay persons should be identical to those of heterosexual persons is to confound two distinct realms of life and morals. This point is forcefully made by James Henley Thornwell, a Presbyterian minister, in a sermon given in 1850 at a church in Charleston, South Carolina, erected "for the Benefit and Instruction of the Coloured Population." It was later published as "The Rights and Duties of Masters." To deny the slave what we would call civil rights in no way denies him the right to be a fully accountable moral being in the eyes of God. (To insist, he says, that civil and moral rights are identical would, if fully carried out, "condemn every arrangement of society, which did not secure to all its members an absolute equality of position; it is the very spirit of socialism and communism." [16]) One can clearly see a foreshadowing here of the present argument against granting gay persons (and, for some, women) the rights of heterosexual men in the area of ordination. Gay persons and women still have the capacity and moral duty to obey God—and presumably to be in a fulfilled spiritual relationship with God —even though they do not have the right to ordination or, for gay people, to marriage. They must learn to live with their created condition, which unfortunately entails fewer ecclesiastical rights than those available to heterosexual men, but God will not hold their condition against them as long as they use it to develop their spiritual and moral capacities for a deeper relationship with God. Women and gay persons are not prevented from achieving a robust spiritual and moral life as long as they do not insist upon possessing the same contingent, civil, or ecclesiastical rights as heterosexual men.

Another important argument in defense of slavery was predicated on the need for a structured, organic, hierarchical arrangement for the social order. It is this argument that Samuel Seabury (the eponymously named grandson of the first bishop in the Episcopal Church in the United States) takes up in his 1861 book *American Slavery, Distinguished from the Slavery of English theorists, and*

Justified by the Law of Nature.[17] Seabury draws, I believe, at least implicitly, upon his grandfather's reliance upon a strongly organic, hierarchical view of society in which the interests of individuals must be subordinated to the interests of the organic whole. In the South, according to historians Elizabeth Fox and Eugene Genovese, slavery was already part of a "hierarchical, organic social order—as a special case of the historical pattern of the mutual dependence of human beings of differing social stations."[18] Slaveholders defended slavery "as a system of organic social relations that . . . created a bond of interest that encouraged Christian behavior."[19] This reliance upon an organic/hierarchical view was seen as a defense against the dangers of democracy, which would have allowed every individual, regardless of background or breeding, to have an equal say in the determination of the values and laws of his or her culture. Rampant democracy, individualism, and personal autonomy threatened the "social bonds that nurtured human social relations."[20]

The younger Seabury clearly has this organic/hierarchical view in mind when he claims that slavery is related to a law of nature applicable to nations or societies. He simply assumes that slavery is not forbidden by Scripture (he does not go as far as Stringfellow in claiming that it is decreed in Scripture), but his real argument is that slavery is a "legitimate and often necessary object of municipal legislation" and is to be treated only on economical and political grounds.[21] Seabury even suggests that slavery is "founded on mutual consent and productive of mutual benefit" with the parties to it bound together "with the ties of a moral union."[22] Slavery defines a particular relation in which the slave stands to others. It does not define his essential self. All men are essentially equal in possessing natural rights, but "considered as male and female, adults and children, rich and poor . . . master and servant . . . they are infinitely unequal."[23] And given this unequal social state, the slave owes his labor for life to his master. In return he is owed the support and protection of the master. Fortunately, Seabury believes, Christian masters in the South will do all that they can to mitigate the rigors of slavery because they are essentially moral people. In the end Seabury accepts slavery and rejects the North's claim to abolish it, if need be by violence, in order to preserve the Union. Those who would defend slavery would be doing battle with the Antichrist for the survival of Christian civilization.[24]

It is significant, of course, that presumably neither Seabury, Thornwell, Stringfellow, nor Hopkins ever "listened" to the experience of the slaves themselves (just as the voices of gay and lesbian persons do not seem in practice, despite injunctions to do so, to be listened to by those who oppose granting them ordination or the blessing of their relationships).

Lest it be thought that the pro-slavery advocates had a monopoly on Biblical interpretation, we must note that the strongest and most fervent abolitionists also appealed to the same document. And they did so while claiming the mantle of evangelicals. As evangelicals, these crusaders for ending slavery, in the words of historian Donald Scott, had been reborn and adopted a "compelling need for continuing moral activism . . . Rebirth had created intense hatred of [sin] as the horrendous bondage from which they had been delivered and against which they had been called to wage unrelenting war." [25] And the war that they felt called to wage was against the insidious evil of slavery. In this fight many of the abolitionists took the Bible as their ultimate inspiration and authority. Angelina Grimke, in her antislavery tract *An Appeal to the Christian Women of the South,* said, "the Bible is my ultimate appeal in all matters of faith and practice." [26] Nevertheless, she read the Bible quite differently from her pro-slavery opponents. The kind of slavery (or servanthood), for example, mentioned without condemnation in the Bible was radically different from the chattel slavery of the Southern states. She and her sister, Sarah Grimke, stressed those parts of Scripture that demand liberation of the "poor and the needy, the despised and the oppressed" [27] such as those in a state of abject bondage. At the core of the sisters' Biblically based attack on slavery is their conviction that the rebirth in Jesus overthrows all human forms of domination, especially that between master and slave, but also between men and women, husband and wife. One is free only in and through subservience to the Lordship of Jesus Christ. All other human forms of subservience or subordination are idolatrous and evil and are the result of a sinful lust for arbitrary domination over others. Slavery exemplifies this lust in its most hideous and brutal form.

The exercise of arbitrary power to which Angelina Grimke refers was also the basis of another attack on slavery and slaveholders by evangelicals in other parts of the South. Slaveholding was a form of tyranny that Christ had come to destroy. Even though Americans had overturned the tyranny of the monarchy in England, they had not completed the job because, as David Barrow, a southern Baptist abolitionist, put it "every *slave-holder,* (in his little dominion) certainly is as *absolute, uncontroulable,* and *arbitrary,* as were more of the *ancient* or *modern monarchs*." [28] In addition to the sin of unjust domination, these sins also led the evangelical reformers to attack both slavery and the sinful lives into which it tempted slaveholders. "Slavery produces idleness; and idleness is the nurse of vice." [29] The sin of covetousness was also endemic to slavery. It leads Christians, according to Baptist minister David Barrow, "to hold and retain in *abject slavery,* a set of our poor fellow creatures, *contrary to the laws of God and nature*." [30] Many of these southern evangelical reformers also anticipated the Grimkes' argument that slaves had the same moral rights as all other human beings. By keeping slaves, Presbyterian minister David Rice argued, Americans were destroying "God's creatures whom he has made free moral agents, and accountable human beings; creatures who still belong to him, and are not left to us to ruin at our pleasure." As historian James Essig goes on to paraphrase Rice, "The fact that whites enslaved blacks to cater to their 'ease, luxury, lust, pride, or avarice' only deepened his [Rice's] conviction that there was nothing benevolent about the practice." [31]

The Biblical and civil defense of slavery is a paradigm of how the attack on homosexuality is being conducted today by those who tend to rely on the "plain" meaning of Scripture and on what they take to be the "natural law" revealing homosexuality as disordered or defective. Conservatives have yet to address satisfactorily the question of why their reading of the Bible with regard to homosexual acts is any more definitive than the reading of the Bible by its pro-slavery "orthodox" defenders.

—— 10 ——

The Bible, Sex, and the Contest
of Interpretations

"A gaze blank and pitiless as the sun"

Various and continuing resolutions from Lambeth Conferences, the ACC, and the Primates urge Anglicans to take Biblical scholarship seriously. All agree that the Bible is the supreme authority for Christian belief and practice. Nevertheless, what it means for the Bible to *be* an authority is not always clear. The Bible is a compilation of different texts written by human beings over time. Some argue that the words in the texts were dictated by God, others that God inspired them in some strong sense, and still others that they were written by human beings, inspired by God in a weaker sense, who were trying to express their understanding of experiences in which they believed God had been present.

Biblical Authority

However divine speech is understood, human beings are an indispensable medium through whom God communicates. And the texts they write will inevitably bear the marks of human filtration, editing, and interpretation. For the mainstream of Anglican scholars, the Biblical writers are not simply automatons repeating verbatim through oral tradition or transcribing onto papyrus words uttered in their ears by God without any mediation on their part. Therefore, if the texts they write have authority, it must be because those texts are *given* authority by the people who receive them. The texts do not carry their authority on their face, as it were. It is the *reception* of those texts by a believing community that gives the texts authority for that community. The community consists of those whose life experiences have been informed and shaped by the Biblical narrative and have found the Bible instructive, inspiring, and revelatory of deep truths about themselves and their world. The basis for receiving the text as authoritative is one's experience in community and in one's life.

Since the Bible is about God and humankind (and some would add nature) in relation to each other, then the ultimate authority of the Bible must rest in the authority of God as *experienced* by humankind at different times in its history. So at one level the granting of authority to the Bible is an act of faith. It is an act of trust or confidence (a far better interpretation of the word "faith" than an ability to believe what is rationally impossible or contradictory) that what one has read or heard in the text is not only life transforming now but will remain so in the future. One stakes one's life on the faith that this text will reveal the truths necessary for living a fulfilling and flourishing life. It is not irrational to believe that the Bible will provide this revelation, but it is not, strictly speaking, the logical conclusion of a syllogism that necessarily excludes the authority of other texts for other people.

Once having made the commitment to trust the Bible as an authoritative source of meaning, one has to decide how to approach its interpretation. And this is where the line between the more traditionalist and more "liberal" approaches gets most clearly drawn. The fundamentalist approach to Scripture means accepting as true what appear on the surface as contradictions and historical impossibilities because one has decided ahead of time that the Bible is not only God's word but is so because God dictated verbatim or inspired infallibly everything that is in the Bible. This fundamentalist position cannot be argued with. It is beyond criticism because it trumps the rational criteria for criticism by an appeal to a faith that is inured to rational scrutiny. One irony here is that most fundamentalists insist that because of our fallibility and fallenness we cannot know the mind of God, which so greatly transcends us. But they also insist that in the Bible we know *exactly* what God has prescribed.[1] Biblical scholar Raymond Brown is right when he argues that

> we have spent too much time protecting the God who inspired the Scriptures from limitations that He seems not to have been concerned about. The impassioned debate about inerrancy tells us less about divine omnipotence (which presumably allows God to be relaxed) than about our own insecurity in looking for absolute answers.[2]

Most Anglicans are not fundamentalists. They have accepted the position that the Bible is a human response to what human beings took to be God's actions and initiatives in their lives. Thus there are multiple authors, reflecting their own particular cultures, psyches, backgrounds, orientations, dispositions, and situations. (That out of these multiple voices and settings there emerges a coherent, unifying narrative of God's work in the world that also reflects one's own experience is truly remarkable and one of the reasons why people are willing to grant the Bible authority for them.)

Apart from Biblical fundamentalists, the principle of Biblical authority presumes the role of interpretation. The Bible does not interpret itself. Those who read it, those who wrote, edited, translated, and redacted it, engaged in interpretation. That is, they picked out from the narratives those parts that they deemed more important than other parts. Some interpretation is necessary to discriminate the more from the lesser important Biblical commands and prohibitions. The text itself does not do this for us.

Scripture alone cannot decide what is abiding and what is transitory in its depiction of living in relation to God. Scripture itself does not make the decision as to what remains valid and what does not. Those who might argue that there is, in effect, a canon within the canon, that some parts of Scripture are more authoritative than others, have given the game away. They are recognizing that Scripture does not always interpret itself. Someone other than the writers of Scripture is deciding what parts carry greater authority than other parts, and thus not all of Scripture is equally binding. Even Jesus critiqued the canon of his time by saying that what was said by the scribes was one thing, "but I say unto you."

The Bible and Homosexual Acts

We now come to what most people would regard as the heart of the matter today: the moral standing of homosexuality in the light of Biblical authority. For the conservatives the Bible's "plain and obvious" teaching is that homosexual acts are morally illegitimate (and depending on the individual commentator, range from disordered to abominable and depraved). For the liberals, the Bible's meaning for today is much more ambiguous regarding the moral status of homosexual acts, especially in light of the historical and cultural contexts in which the few Biblical texts mentioning homosexual acts were written.

I think most scholars, both conservative and liberal, would accept the view that what many today call *homosexuality* was a phenomenon not known to the Biblical writers. For many people today homosexuality is a sexual "orientation" within some persons toward other persons of the same sex as themselves. It is constitutive of a part of their created nature. Homosexual persons would claim that insofar as fulfilling their nature through an expression of their sexuality is part of what constitutes their overall fulfillment and flourishing, then same sex relationships, as long as they meet the same tests of mutual love, fidelity, and commitment that heterosexual relationships are expected to meet, should be regarded as moral and fitting for them. The liberal's argument is that such same sex relationships were not contemplated by the Biblical writers (with the possible exception of the loving relationship between Jonathan and David, which some have argued went beyond mere friendship). The conservatives reply that even if there are cases of mutual love between persons of the same sex, that fact is not sufficient to justify a fundamentally disordered or defective relationship never intended by God and inconsistent with the division and complementarity of the sexes.

It is best, therefore, in speaking of the Bible and homosexuality, not to refer to its views on homosexuality as such. It would be more accurate to refer to its position on sexual acts (mostly coerced and involuntary) between persons of the same sex. Much of what the Bible has to say about such acts is that they are not natural or in accord with the divinely created nature of the persons who engage in them. Both the man who submits to a sexual action (almost always anal penetration) is acting like a woman and the man who initiates the action is treating the other as a woman, and both are thereby confusing or violating the divinely created distinction between men and women. If it is assumed, as much of the Bible does, that it cannot be in accord with the divine intention for the created order for men to desire other men in the context of a loving lifelong relationship, then homosexual acts must be regarded as intrinsically wrong.

Assuming that context and the intent of its authors do make a difference to one's interpretation of Biblical texts, then the key passages dealing with same sex relationships are to be found in the story of Sodom, in the Levitical prohibitions on impurity, and in some passages in Paul's letters. Conservatives also, of course, argue that the creation story makes it clear that God intended for man and woman to form a partnership in which a man clings to his wife and they become one flesh. No sanction is provided for nonmonogamous nonheterosexual unions. Those in heterosexual unions are commanded to be fruitful and multiply, a command that homosexual acts cannot fulfill. Sexual relationships between persons of the same sex frustrate or undermine God's intention. He created, as some conservatives are fond of saying, Adam and Eve, not Adam and Steve, for relationship and procreation. It should, of course, be noted that in the creation story there is no explicit prohibition on same sex relationships since they are simply not mentioned at all. Conservatives assume that silence on this possibility automatically means rejection. Two questions that need to be addressed in the current debate are whether, in the light of the overpopulation of the world it is still mandatory for Christians to intend procreation as the chief purpose of sexuality, and, even if some would continue to say yes, whether same sex relationships (estimated by some to be around 10% of the population) threaten or endanger heterosexual relationships that do continue to produce children. And in a world where in vitro fertilization is possible, the bearing and raising of children does not need to depend solely upon sexual acts between a man and a woman.

Moving to those Biblical passages in which homosexual acts are either regarded with suspicion or actually proscribed, we come first to the story of Sodom in Genesis 19. The story is well known. Two angels appear to Lot. He offers them hospitality. The men of Sodom demand to know who these visitors are and tell Lot to bring them outside "so that we may know them." A conservative reading of this passage is that the word "know" means to have sexual relations with them. A more common reading is that to know means literally to find out who they are. Lot, adhering to the principle of hospitality, refuses the men's request and even goes so far as to offer his daughters to the men to do with as they please. (This suggests that, whatever the men in the town were, they were not strictly homosexuals for whom women would have no allure. It is interesting that the willingness of Lot to allow his daughters to be gang-raped is rarely commented upon by conservative interpreters.) God then brings destruction to Sodom. Now the question is whether God's anger is directed against the desire for homosexual acts with the visitors by the men of Sodom or, as some interpreters have suggested, against the blatant lack of hospitality by the town toward the visitors. Biblical scholar Walter Wink suggests the basic sin here was the intended rape of the visitors (for whom Lot is willing to substitute his daughters), a clear violation of the duty of hospitality.[3] When Sodom is referred to in later Biblical texts, the issue of homosexual acts is not mentioned. Rather the references are almost always to Sodom's failure to extend hospitality to strangers. The prophet Ezekiel (16:48–50) is quite specific as to the sin of Sodom: "she and her daughters had pride, excess of food, and prosperous ease, but did not aid the poor and needy." Even Jesus, in the one reference he makes to Sodom, condemns it for its inhospitality (Matthew 10:15). Within the context of the Bible, therefore, the very least one can say is that the later Biblical writers did not see the sin of Sodom as having anything to do with sexuality. Rape is not a sexual act but one of violence and cannot be spoken of in sexual terms.

The second set of Biblical references to homosexual acts occurs in the Book of Leviticus. Leviticus is essentially a set of ritual and cultic laws helping Israel define itself over against its pagan neighbors. At the heart of those laws is the desire to keep the people of Israel from falling prey to the corruptions of the surrounding cults and peoples. This desire is reflected in what is known as the Holiness or purity code which, in Christian ethicist William Countryman's words, "holds up the ideal of an absolute separation between Israel and all that is unclean and utters a 'No' to uncleanness so absolute that it is often enforced through the execution or the 'cutting off' of the polluted."[4] Countryman argues that the ideal of what constitutes a "whole" man or woman, or a member of any species, must be reflected by placing them in appropriate categories and keeping them separate from things that do not belong in those categories. The dietary laws that detail what can be mixed with what in the preparation of food are a clear example of this. In the context of maintaining ritual purity and the separation of "kinds," men belonged to one category and women to another. To mix them was a violation of purity separation and would produce corruption and defilement. In this context men who act like women are violating their category and attempting to mix what should not be mixed. Biblical scholar Jerome Walsh has argued that the purity of the people "is threatened by any act that mixes two separate, potentially defiling bodily fluids in the same receptacle," such as the semen of two different men.[5] A man having sex with an animal is a perfect example of this impure mixing. And so "if a man lies with a male *as with a woman* [emphasis added], both of them have committed an abomination." (Leviticus 20:13.) The same undermining of the purity code is committed when a man lies with his wife and with her mother. In all these cases, the perpetrator is to be put to death. Implicit in many of these passages is the notion that women are filthier (e.g., they menstruate), weaker, and less valued than men. (They are also the property of either their fathers or their husbands, a condition clearly emblematic of their devalued social status.) Even if one takes the passages as still binding today, it would seem that the worst one could say of homosexual acts is that they are filthy, disgusting, and impure. But does that make their commission as morally horrible as war, adultery, economic oppression, and, above all, idolatry and the rejection of God? What moral condemnation awaits someone who engages in other filthy actions such as eating dirt?[6] Not, to be sure, an act that one would want others to do, but is it worthy of being regarded as morally abominable, on the same scale as slavery or rape? Conservatives are not always clear about why homosexual acts are singled out for particular opprobrium when other (to some) disgusting acts are not even considered immoral.

The question for today, of course, is whether these clear and explicit prohibitions on homosexual acts can be lifted out of the context in which they were written and be applied "eternally." (And in the process, assuming they can be, should the punishment be the same as prescribed by Leviticus: death?) Virtually no conservatives in this country are so strict in their reading of this passage as to call for capital punishment for persons engaging in homosexual acts (though it has been reported—without confirmation—that some African bishops are prepared to propose this punishment). But if the Bible is the ultimate authority for moral behavior and if its moral teachings are true for all time, why observe the one forbidding homosexual acts and ignore the one requiring death for the perpetrators?

There are, of course, other cultic, ritual, or moral laws in Leviticus that have been set aside by the Christian Church as no longer binding. Menstruating women are no longer forbidden to enter the temple. Children who are found to be rebellious against their parents are no longer subject to the death penalty. The dietary laws are no longer observed by Christians. Adulterers are no longer put to death. One might even argue that the law requiring aliens to be treated as citizens (Leviticus 19:33) is not observed by most American Christians. So it is not clear why the particular prohibition against a man lying with another man is singled out for retention. Some would argue that there is a fundamental distinction between the moral laws of Leviticus and the cultic or ritual laws. But the text itself does not make this distinction, which suggests that some interpretation of the relevance of the text is already going on by contemporary interpreters. But once you let interpretation into an understanding of the Bible's authority, it is hard to say that some texts in effect interpret themselves as crystal clear and universally binding for all time while others require a more nuanced and adaptive reading not applicable for all times and places.

At this point a different argument is often appealed to by conservatives. It returns to the story of the creation of men and women in Genesis. While not in the texts themselves, the notion of the *complementarity* of the two sexes is often invoked by contemporary conservatives. Robert Gagnon, a well-known and respected conservative Biblical scholar, has argued for what he calls the "pro-complementarity" of the sexes. The Bible, he claims, reveals a "strong and uncompromising witness against all same-sex intercourse" because what is missing in homosexual behavior is the "sex complementarity of the participants." [7]

There can be no exceptions to this position (even ones in which the partners are living in a monogamous lifelong committed relationship), he claims, because "a policy with exceptions . . . flies in the face of Scripture." [8] Gagnon is aware of the distinction that some draw between core Biblical values and ones that are less important. His four criteria for core values are the pervasiveness and consistency of a particular position; the strength with which it is held by Biblical authors (measured by the intensity of the language used to describe the sinful); the more absolutely it is held; and the more it is in opposition to "broader cultural trends." [9] Gagnon does not say where these criteria are found in the Bible. In the context of his writing it appears that he has drawn them from elsewhere and is applying them to his reading of the texts. This is a procedure usually condemned by conservatives who want the text alone to determine meaning, not through the imposition of non-Biblically derived criteria of meaning. He then attacks what he calls the "gross structural incongruity" of homoerotic unions. If the latter are morally acceptable, he asks, then why not adult incest, bestiality, pederasty, and plural marriage? The complementarity assumption underlies his entire argument: sexual relations are about "merging (interlocking, fusing) with another who is structurally complementary (congruous, compatible), 'becoming one flesh' through a sexual relationship, and learning to integrate holistically with another who is neither too much like oneself, nor too much unlike *on a structural level*." And adding sex to the relationship is wrong; we know this through "a certain intuitive and instinctive sense." [10] Even if there is such a thing as a "sexual orientation" it cannot trump the intrinsic defectiveness of "too much structural sameness." As he summarizes his argument, one assumes somewhat jocularly, "It's just too weird." [11] Again, it is not clear where notions of "structural sameness," "structural incongruity," and weirdness are to be found in Scripture. They are terms as foreign to the Bible as is "homosexuality" as a sexual orientation, and they suggest the imposition of a contemporary conceptual apparatus *to* the Biblical text, not one drawn from it.

Turning to the New Testament, again everyone acknowledges that Jesus never mentioned homosexual acts. (Also there is no reference to homosexuality in the Nicaean creed, the Thirty-Nine Articles, or the *Book of Common Prayer*.) Rather, in issues of sexuality, Jesus was much more explicit about the moral wrongness of divorce. Mark (10:11) records Jesus as saying that "whoever divorces his wife and marries another commits adultery against her" and vice versa. Matthew 5:32 adds one qualifier to the absoluteness of this pronouncement: "except on ground of unchastity [or adultery]." The Episcopal Church accepted these teachings by Jesus as authoritative and absolute for most of its history and for the most part denied remarriage following divorce. At its General Convention in 1808 the Church said that it was "inconsistent with the law of God" to unite a person in marriage who has been divorced unless the other party had been guilty of adultery (employing the so-called Matthean exception).[12] But over time this canon law was modified without provoking a crisis in the Church even remotely resembling that regarding homosexual acts that now threatens to tear it apart. Revisions in the canon permitted remarriage if the cause of the divorce occurred before the first marriage took place; by 1973 the Convention removed the prohibition that no one could remarry as long as the former spouse was still living. Today all that is required for church sanctioned remarriage is that there be evidence that the first (or previous marriage) ended in a legally recognized divorce by the action of a civil court. What is significant about all this is that the clear words of Jesus prohibiting remarriage except when the first marriage was dissolved because of adultery or the statement by the General Convention that remarriage after divorce was "inconsistent with the law of God" no longer determine what the Church permits with respect to remarriage and divorce. These modifications in the historic teaching of the Church are not the object of current attack by conservatives who otherwise seem intent on adhering to the strict law of God. Instead, their target is something that neither Jesus nor the early councils of the Church ever addressed.

The New Testament sources for dealing with homosexual acts are found in Paul, not in the Gospels. The crucial texts are Romans 1:21–27, 1 Corinthians 6:9, and 1 Timothy 1:10. In Romans, Paul refers to those who, having once known God, did not honor him and became "futile in their thinking . . . and exchanged the glory of the immortal God for images resembling a mortal human." As result of their turning away from God, God

> gave them up in the lusts of their hearts to impurity, to the degrading of their bodies among themselves. . . . Their women exchanged natural intercourse for unnatural, and in the same way also the men, giving up natural intercourse with women, were consumed with passion for one another. Men committed shameless acts with men and received in their own persons the due penalty for their error.

In 1 Corinthians Paul lists a number of types of persons whose wrongdoing will keep them from inheriting the kingdom of God. Among these types are "male prostitutes" and "sodomites." And in 1 Timothy a similar "vice list" is found of the "godless and sinful, the unholy and profane," and that list also includes "sodomites."

The Greek word for "male prostitute" is *malakoi* (literally "soft ones") and the word for "sodomite" is *arsenokoitai,* which, according to Biblical scholar Robin Scroggs, is a translation of the Hebrew meaning "lying with a male" and is likely derived from Leviticus 18:22 and 20:13.[13] Biblical scholar Richard B. Hays, who supports the denial of ordination to a "practicing" homosexual, nevertheless accepts the argument of other Biblical scholars that Paul's reference to prostitutes and sodomites "presupposes and reaffirms the Holiness Code's condemnation of homosexual acts."[14] *Malakoi* does not mean "homosexuals" since no such term was found in Greek or Hebrew, but rather referred to the passive partners engaged in homosexual acts. *Arsenokoitai* are the active partners in these acts. They are male prostitutes who service men and/or women and thus are not what we would typically call homosexuals by orientation (a concept not known to Paul).[15] What is crucial here is whether Paul is assuming the continuation of the Levitical prohibitions on this kind of activity and, therefore, assuming the continuance of the holiness code for Christians. If so, he is at odds with himself because in other respects he refuses to recognize the continuing validity of the purity provisions. Food offered to idols, food shared with "gentiles," and circumcision are no longer subject to ritual prohibition given the new freedom experienced by those who have accepted Christ. There is no doubt that Paul sees homosexual acts as shameful, even disgusting, vices that ought to be given up as the newly minted Christians try to live lives worthy of their redemption. He also assumes that they are degrading because they are unnatural and what is unnatural is shameful. (But he also thought it was unseemly or in a sense unnatural for women to speak in church.)

The passage from Romans highlights the degrading and shameful dimension of homosexual acts as Paul understands them, but it also provides a theological justification for Paul's rejection of them. These acts are a sign or a consequence of human beings' rejection of the Lordship of God over all of human life. What Paul says is that God has given people up in the lusts of their heart to degrading actions *because* they have rejected him. Their rejection of God is the precipitating sin, the punishment for which was to be given up to shameful, degrading ways of behaving, among which Paul lists unnatural intercourse. (It is important to note that these acts are listed separately from Paul's long list of things "not to be done," such as covetousness, malice, envy, murder, strife, deceit, gossip, insolence, etc. It is not clear why these immoral things are not given the same weighty condemnation today as are homosexual acts which, for Paul, are simply disgusting, not essentially immoral.)

Hays argues that it is the unnaturalness and shameful quality of the consequences of the primary sin that disgraces the perpetrators. Homosexual activity provides for Paul "a particularly graphic image of the way in which human fallenness distorts God's created order." When people engage in homosexual acts "they enact an outward and visible sign of an inward and spiritual reality: the rejection of the Creator's design. They *embody* the spiritual condition of those who have 'exchanged the truth about God for a lie.' " [16] Hays also rejects any argument that suggests that what Paul thought was unnatural might, today, be seen as natural for some portion of the population. The "exchange" (of natural for unnatural passions) to which Paul refers, is a fundamental condition of the fallen world. "The fact is that Paul treats *all* homosexual activity as prima facie evidence of humanity's tragic confusion and alienation from God the Creator." [17] Regardless, in other words, of whether it is genetically based, homosexual acts are wrong because they besmirch and degrade the glory of God as reflected originally in the created order in which men's sexual relationships were designed for complementarity with women, not with other men. In this respect Hays compares homosexual acts to alcoholism: *being* an alcoholic is not a grievous sin, though refusing to seek help is morally culpable, but at the same time we do not condone the disease because it is a disfigurement of God's intention for the fulfillment of human beings. (But others would argue in response that the deleterious effects of alcoholism are empirically obvious, while the effects of homosexual activity are, for some, not deleterious at all but fulfilling, loving, and healthy.) Hays also appeals to the argument that granting moral legitimacy to homosexual acts is to succumb to our "propensity for self-deception."[18] (It is not clear why homosexual acts are any more or less self-deceptive than any other human acts. This part of Hays' argument works only if one assumes that it is unnatural [and therefore intrinsically unsatisfying] to live in homosexual relations. But to assume the unnaturalness of homosexual relations for many is to beg the question of whether it is unnatural for all people. In short, all the shameful sexual acts or passions to which Paul is referring are ones in which sex is used to undermine role expectations, and to dominate, exploit, or demean others. None of them even come close to what many people today would consider mutual, loving, consensual, and fulfilling relationships between persons of the same sex.)

The counter among Biblical scholars to the conservative argument as exemplified by Hays and Gagnon is to regard sexual practices as socially constructed, genetically determined (and thus "natural" for those with a homosexual "orientation"), and as equally capable of fidelity, commitment, love, and mutuality as are heterosexual practices. Gareth Moore, a Christian ethicist, has argued that once it became possible to separate sexual activity from reproduction (thanks to contraception, which few Anglican conservatives reject on principle), it became possible to evaluate sexual relations on the basis of what they did for the fulfillment and expression of mutual love between partners.[19] To be sure, this "relativizes" the moral dimension of sexual relations but if, as even the conservatives admit, sexual relations are for more than just reproductive purposes, then the quality of the relationships in which these sexual acts are expressed becomes the basis for evaluating their morality. If partners of the same sex have relationships characterized by all the virtues of heterosexual married relationships, then their moral quality would be the same as the latter. As Walter Wink has argued, there is no Biblical sex ethic. "The Bible knows only a love ethic, which is constantly brought to bear on whatever sexual mores are dominant in any given country, or culture, or period."[20] The Bible, according to Biblical scholar Victor Furnish, reflects nothing specifically Christian in its references to homosexual acts but instead represents a general cultural view of sexuality common at the time of Paul's writing.[21] By implication, if Furnish is right, then in a different cultural context sex might be differently evaluated. The central moral values would be those of love, not those determined by biological "structuring" as assumed in Gagnon's and at least implicitly in Hays's positions.

This leads inevitably to the question of whether some people are genetically or "naturally" fulfilled both sexually and lovingly in same sex relationships. While the evidence is not entirely in, there does seem to be a growing body of it that there is some biological/genetic basis to homosexuality that, for those who are so genetically oriented, would make it "natural." And this casts the argument into the field of "natural law" ethics, which, along with the appeal to the Bible, stands as the single most important argument against recognizing the morality of homosexual acts even in the context of loving mutual relationships. What is natural is implicit in the background of Paul's writings and was given a greater degree of prominence in the work of natural law moral theologians such as Thomas Aquinas. Perhaps the most succinct and authoritative statement of this position today is the one set forth by then Cardinal Joseph Ratzinger (now Pope Benedict XVI), writing in 1986 for the Congregation for the Doctrine of the Faith of the Roman Catholic Church. According to Ratzinger, while not immune from the influence of modern science, the Catholic view of homosexuality is not confined to what science says. He then proclaims with no nuance that the "inclination" to homosexual behavior "must be seen as an objective disorder." [22] It is not a sin to be so inclined, but it is sinful to act on that inclination given its disordering of God's creation. Conservative Anglicans would find Ratzinger's position congenial in that he only accepts Biblical interpretations that in no way contradict the Church's "living Tradition." [23] And that tradition insists that the only natural and morally appropriate use of the sexual faculty is in the marital relationship between a man and a woman and must always intend procreation (though other qualities are also valued in the relationship such as fidelity, love, and trust). Given that homosexual activity is a disorder and is "contrary to the creative wisdom of God," it cannot, by definition lead to fulfillment and happiness.[24] (No scientific evidence or personal testimony to the contrary is considered relevant here by the conservatives.) For people with the homosexual inclination the remedy of crucifying their self-indulgent passions and desires is always available. Ratzinger also adopts the "complementarity of the sexes" argument (which reflects the unity of the Creator). He accepts the reading of the Sodom story as a judgment by God against homosexual relations and the Levitical texts as justifying the exclusion from the "People of God those who behave in a homosexual fashion." [25]

It is crucial to understand that the natural law argument Ratzinger is making is not, for him, subject to historical, cultural, or contextual alteration. In a 1976 declaration, also issuing from the Sacred Congregation for the Doctrine of the Faith, came a series of propositions on sexual ethics. Given that God has implanted in creation and in the mind of every person a natural moral law, it is not possible to act morally by deviating from or compromising that law. This natural law is built into the very core of the order of nature. And the morality it dictates is "eternal, objective, and universal, whereby God orders, directs, governs the entire universe and all the ways of the human community." [26] The moral principles derived from nature are immutable, "based upon every human person's constitutive elements and essential relations—elements and relations which transcend historical contingency." [27]

This natural law argument is in some ways even more powerful than the Biblical argument because, if it is true, it is not subject to contextual or historical interpretation. I would suggest that some of the conservatives in the Anglican Communion who argue the most vociferously against the morality of homosexual relations are actually reading into the Bible principles derived (whether consciously or not) from the natural law argument. One certainly sees this in both Gagnon and Hays. What is immutably wrong transcends any attempt to relativize it by pointing to different cultural and historical contexts in which the Bible was written. Radner and Turner are actually closer to the natural law argument than they are to the Biblical argument since they both implicitly accept Ratzinger's notion that the only appropriate interpretation of the Bible is that which is determined by the traditions of the Church. And in those traditions the natural law argument has had greater valence than the Biblical one, which, as Chris Seitz has pointed out, is always subject to the machinations of Biblical scholars who operate outside the faith of the Church.

The liberal response to the natural law argument, of course, has to push that argument to its logical conclusion. It can accept that morality must, in some sense, conform to what God has created for our fulfillment as the persons God created us to be. The question is what does God intend for our fulfillment. Certainly no Christian would deny that love is the chief characteristic of relationships that God blesses with happiness and flourishing life. And love requires fidelity, mutuality, intimacy, trust, reciprocity, and commitment to the other person. If these things can be experienced in homosexual relationships, then the natural order for such persons is one that undergirds and supports homosexual forms of expressing one's love toward another. Liberals might remind conservatives of Paul's word in Galatians 5:22–23: "But the fruit of the Spirit is love, joy, peace, patience, kindness, goodness, faithfulness, gentleness and self-control. Against such things there is no law."

So where does this bring us? The Bible can be read either as subject to historical/contextual interpretation, in which case the passages used to denounce homosexual relations have, at best, an ambiguous and uncertain application to the reality of those relationships today, or it can be read in a fundamentalist absolutist way. If the Bible's meaning is subject only to Biblical literalism and the historic teachings of the Church, then there is little opening toward including homosexual relations among those behaviors that can carry the virtues of love, fidelity, and fulfillment in the eyes of God. If the traditional reading of natural law is right, there is no basis for regarding homosexual orientation as anything other than disordered. Only if natural law is subject to revision in the light of the living experience of homosexual persons can that traditional reading be altered or modified.

If one begins with an absolutist position (whether primarily based in Scripture or natural law) that cannot be changed because it is immutable, then no further debate is possible. If one begins with a position that the abiding values of Scripture and nature are deeper than the particular historical contexts and cultures in which they were first articulated, then debate can continue. And that debate would be about how communities can empower persons to live the lives most fulfilling to them in conformity with God's true intentions for the flourishing of the entire created order.

Section Six

Conclusion

Conclusion:
The Shape of the Future

"Turning and turning in the widening gyre"

The problem with writing about issues whose resolution is not yet in sight is that one must offer concluding reflections with a high degree of tentativeness. Nevertheless, I think there are some that can be made at this point in the story that are unlikely to be overturned by future events.

It seems clear, for example, that the traditionalists who are appealing to the Anglican tradition at best are highly selective in how they define that tradition and at worst are guilty of misreading and distorting it. Their exploitation of what they believe is that tradition has been revealingly laid out in a fall 2007 document addressed to TEC's House of Bishops and the Archbishop of Canterbury. It contains, I believe, a powerful and compelling understanding of what the Anglican tradition is and an intriguing proposal for how TEC and the Anglican Communion can move forward in fidelity to it. Its understanding virtually undercuts the conservatives' appeal to the Anglican tradition, and its proposal shapes the issues for the future with admirable clarity.

Entitled "The Constitutional Crisis, 2007" [1] and written by six bishops of ECUSA with legal backgrounds, the document addresses the dangers they see in the proposed Anglican Covenant. [2] What is innovative in their report is their creation of a concept that they call an "Anglican Constitution." This so-called constitution is "unwritten and unenforceable but clearly recognized and anciently respected" in the same way as is the unwritten constitution that has been in effect in Great Britain since the Magna Carta. Despite the possible misleading implications of calling it a constitution, they believe it reflects "a recognized polity, a body of canon law, a gradually developed and certain enough combination of ethos, customs, ideals, precedents, shared memory of experience, and inviolate traditions that shape the Anglican consciousness." On the basis of this Anglican constitution, the bishops argue, the idea of an Anglican covenant is "out of order" unless the constitution is first properly amended or replaced.

The bishops observe that the present debate within the Communion is being driven by two movements: the traditionalist movement wants to redefine the AC "in the name of conservative values." The bishops regard this attempt as leading to a "new rigidity in theology and structure that is patently un-Anglican and would require radical change" that would move Anglicanism toward an affiliation based on confessional compliance as determined by "monolithic juridical institutions," ones in which the Primates would become "its judicial interpreters as well as its executive and legislative bodies."

A second and conflicting movement, classical Anglicanism, accepts Anglicanism (using a phrase often deployed by conservatives) "as it was delivered," namely as "an international communion of like-minded Christian Churches united by the love of Christ for purposes of mission." This movement does not see in Anglicanism a unity founded on a single creed. It believes that whatever reforms are contemplated will take time and will occur in the "dialogue between church and society." The reforms that this second movement embraces grow out of the rediscovered importance of the Church's "baptismal theology" in which *all* the baptized are full and equal participants in all the offices of the Church by virtue of all having undergone the same baptism. The kinds of changes sought by this second movement do not require any alterations in the identity and polity of the Anglican churches and thus pose no threat to the Anglican constitution, whereas the proposed covenant would be a "fundamentally radical alteration" of it.

At the heart of classical Anglicanism and its Constitution, according to the bishops, are seven basic elements. (1) the "interlocking traditions" of comprehensiveness, the via media, and the principle of *lex orandi, lex credendi* (from prayer comes belief); (2) the three-legged stool of the authority of Scripture, Reason, and Tradition; (3) Episcopal oversight as a sign of unity within the Church; (4) baptismal bonds and community as Communion; (5) the diocese as the basic and local unit of the Church; (6) provincial autonomy; and (7) justice as the chief mission of the Church. If these are the core aspects of Anglican identity, then the core issue, according to the bishops, is not human sexuality but whether the identity of the Church as defined by these seven basic elements is to be amended or replaced.

As the Church has tried to live out the implications of the baptismal covenant (which the document clearly contrasts to the Anglican covenant idea), it has discovered the imperative to "bring the inclusiveness it implies to actual practice," such as the inclusion of children in the Eucharist, of women in the ordained ministry, and now of gay and lesbian persons in ordained ministry and in the blessing of their relationships. Anyone baptized into the Church is by that very fact eligible for all the offices and rites of the Church. This is not, the bishops insist, an imperative set by the world for the Church (as the conservatives argue) but arises from "the inexorable logic of re-forming and con-forming" its practice to what TEC considers "generative" for the Christian church. The authors recognize, however, that the specific inclusionary practices of ECUSA and the Church of Canada might not be appropriate for churches in other parts of the Communion at this time. Holding in tension both inclusionary and (for the time being) exclusionary practices regarding who is eligible for the ordained offices of the Church and the blessing of relationships is part of what has historically been lauded as Anglican comprehensiveness.

Opposition to the inclusionary actions of the Global North comes, in large part in the opinion of the authors, from resentment by previously colonized churches of the dominating wealth, power, and privilege of the colonizing powers. But the response to that resentment, according to the authors, ought not to be the placing of new powers of exclusion in the hands of the Primates. If there is a body with authority to list or "de-list" Provinces from membership in the Anglican Communion, it would be the Anglican Consultative Council, the only body on which laypersons sit alongside bishops. Even its authority, however, is severely limited. Only through a constitutional amendment, passed by Council membership and ratified by two-thirds of the provincial bodies, and with the assent of two-thirds of the Primates, can the membership list of the Communion be altered. However, the Council itself is a creature of the Communion and any move on the Council's part to remove a Province already in the Communion would be, using the legal language of the document, null and void. Ian Douglas, a professor of church missions and a member of the ACC, has argued that one result of colonization was the failure to recognize the necessity for the local adaptation of the Anglican witness in different contexts. This is part of what the Incarnational aspect of the faith requires.[3] It also coheres nicely with the argument of "The Constitutional Crisis 2007."

Using more legal reasoning, the bishops also argue that since the Anglican constitution is unwritten there would be no way to write a constitution to the conservatives' liking without starting the Communion all over again. Attempts are being made to do just that, according to the authors of the document, but in piecemeal fashion, through unprecedented and non-Anglican ideas such as alternative primatial oversight, a pastoral council appointed by the Primates to oversee problematic Primates, a Primatial Vicar reporting to the council for wayward Provinces, secret sessions of the ACC, and the authority of the ACC to expel Provinces without constitutionally mandated assent. (One could even add to that list the recent attempts by some dioceses in TEC to renounce any obligation to obey the Constitution and Canons of the Church and to replace TEC, in line with the Chapman Memo's strategy, by another body that would be "recognized" by the Anglican Communion as a Church in communion with it.) The authors insist, however, that the Episcopal Church, as a founding member of the Communion, cannot be expelled, replaced, or restricted from the privileges of full membership in it.

In making their case, the bishops point to the history of Anglicanism in which there has never been an attempt to enforce "scriptural rules based on conformity of interpretation" because Anglicanism has always accepted as "self-evident" the fact of the cultural and contextual writing and interpretation of the Bible. Augustine himself, they point out, argued that Biblical passages must be interpreted "figuratively" whenever the literal meaning fails to advance the love of God and neighbor.[4] Therefore, "all structural inferences scream out against an interpretation that finds rules in Scripture and forces us to accept them and apply them throughout the Communion." They insist that the Communion "must not allow differing approaches to Scripture to become mutually exclusive."

I would add to these observations the point that most modern Biblical scholarship, which in repeated resolutions from Lambeth Conferences, the General Conventions, and other church bodies is always commended, simply does not read the contested passages from Scripture used to condemn homosexual acts in the same way as do the conservatives. The Biblical scholarship of the conservatives, while perhaps congenial to a literalist or fundamentalist reading, is not part of the Anglican mainstream nor of Biblical scholarship as it is practiced by most Biblical scholars today.

This acceptance of variation in Biblical interpretation is not, the bishops insist, relativism, but rather an openness that "demonstrates the confidence of our faith that enables us to live with the ambiguity of human life under the rule of God." Here they appeal to the very ambiguity that the conservatives most detest.

On the issue of the via media or comprehensiveness (they treat the terms as synonymous), the bishops argue that they express the unity-in-diversity that is the "*raison d'etre* of Anglicanism." Comprehensiveness does not mean compromise but a willingness to live in dialogue with others with whom there is no theological agreement at the moment. Drawing on classical Anglicanism's grounding in the doctrine of the Incarnation, the bishops argue that Anglicanism is a "growing body of thought that is in constant dialogue with the culture within which the church finds itself incarnated." This is completely congruent with the principle of reception that is a crucial part of the Anglican tradition.

The bishops also take on the conservative attempt to redefine dioceses as "aggregates of congregations that have a like mind on certain issues." This is not how dioceses have been understood historically within Anglicanism. Dioceses are geographic areas under episcopal authority in which comprehensiveness in belief can be practiced among people with diverse views on matters not essential to the faith.

What seems to be happening from the conservative side, the authors argue, is a new kind of Donatism in which the opponents of ECUSA and Canada are looking for moral and doctrinal purity. Although the bishops do not say it, this may well explain why the revolutionary conservatives are so insistent on appealing to the purity codes of the Old Testament. They want to define the pure in belief and practice over against the contaminated and corrupted. They seem to accept the logic of the fourth century heretic Donatus that only through a ritual cleansing process of rebaptism can one who had fallen short of moral or doctrinal purity become pure enough to administer the sacraments or lead the Church. This obsession with purity in thought and morals goes hand in hand with the assertion of hierarchical authority vested in the bishops and Primates as the guardians of the boundaries that keep the pure from being infected by the impure. And all this as if the obsession with cultic purity still carries validity even after Jesus, Paul, and the early Church had argued against retaining such purity-defining boundaries (despite Paul's failure to always follow the logic of his own position).

Now whether the conservatives can accept the bishops' openness to ambiguity, comprehensiveness, the world, and less than precise and universally agreed-upon formulas for belief is one thing. But these characteristics are clearly part of the "tradition once delivered" to Anglicans. If conservatives claim to be speaking for that tradition, therefore, they are doing so in a fundamentally distorted way and are doing a disservice to the history of the tradition. In the end, the bishops express their confidence that the Anglican Communion "will stay together and muddle through in a long and respectful process to settle its ecclesiological differences." Whether their confidence is justified, of course, remains to be seen, but it is grounded in the realities of Anglican tradition and consciousness, not in the myth of a pure primitive church that must be replicated today on the basis of doctrinal and moral purity. In this respect I think the bishops' reading of Anglican tradition provides solid ground on which the Church can walk into the future without schism.

On the basis of these reflections by the six legally trained bishops, one can draw certain tentative conclusions about the conservative position. If it is not grounded in the best of modern Biblical scholarship, and if its reading of the Bible does not support the absolute condemnation of homosexual acts in any and all circumstances, then something other than Biblical "truth" is at stake for those who have identified opposition to homosexual acts as the foundation for the purity of the Church. If the obsession with homosexuality leads to the neglect of other moral issues such as economic injustice and the perpetuation of poverty, then something else must be at stake. In short, the obsessive adherence to the conviction that homosexual acts are morally abominable and ought to be the basis for who is and who is not a true Anglican must come from somewhere else because it clearly does not come from Biblical scholarship or the Anglican tradition.

I would suggest that what is at stake here, at least for many conservatives, is the fear that if the Church fails to hold on to *some* moral absolutes, moral anarchy and secular relativism will be loosed upon the world. Why they have chosen to draw their line in the sand against moral relativism around the issue of homosexuality is a question probably best left to the psychologists. (One could, for example, have chosen the treatment of the poor as the defining moral issue of our time.) One might also raise the question of why some of the conservatives are so given to vitriolic hyperbole in defending the absolutes around which they have gathered. Archbishop Akinola refers to Satan entering the Church when

Gene Robinson is elected bishop. Bishop Duncan attempts to identify the Network with the Confessing Church under Nazi persecution, expresses a belief that conservatives are slated for red martyrdom, and identifies himself with Martin Luther and the beginning of the Protestant Reformation. At the same time, the conservatives are obsessed with imposing discipline on the wayward members of the Church. Why this concentration on punishment? It is of a piece, of course, with the tendency among the conservatives to elevate the authority of the episcopal hierarchy to the virtual exclusion of the authority of the laity. Hierarchical power deployed from the top down is, for them, the ideal tool for disciplining those who have strayed from orthodoxy. Clearly there is an issue of power going on here. Ian Douglas is particularly forceful in arguing that there is a white, male, privileged class within the Episcopal Church that is fearful of losing its privileges of power as the Church increasingly opens its "higher" offices to women and racial and sexual minorities. He argues that no analysis of the current discontent is complete without some attention to the power issue.[5] I believe that Douglas's analysis is essentially correct, but I have focused in this book primarily on the *arguments* deployed by the various contestants for the soul of the Episcopal Church. I believe that, in the end, the conservatives' arguments, especially with respect to their claims to be faithful to the Anglican tradition and to Biblical scholarship, will be revealed as empty, unsubstantial, and without merit. And that fact leaves the issue of the desire to retain power in the Church by a group of mostly older male clergy and their lay partners as the only logical explanation of what is going on.

The demand for punishment of those who are challenging the power structures is of a piece with a long-standing tendency among groups that believe themselves to be under siege to insist on clear lines of purity/contamination between themselves and the corrupted others who threaten their purity. The purity codes of Leviticus, to which conservatives are attracted, were originally devised to keep the fledgling tribes of Israel, while they were gaining a foothold in the new land, from succumbing to the corruptions of their pagan neighbors. But purity codes were effectively done away with by Jesus, Paul, and the early Christians. What Jesus put in their place was a new kind of purity, the purity of heart and mind, not a purity of flesh or food. What matters for him is the *quality* of human relationships as determined by the overarching moral principles of love, mutuality, commitment, and fidelity. The conservative inclination to return to drawing new purity lines around biological characteristics that take no account of these more basic Christian principles seems odd in people who claim to live in the freedom Christ has brought them. The hatred for opposing points of view that seems to fuel much of the conservative rhetoric is no way to build a movement around traditional Christian principles such as love and compassion and a willingness to walk in the shoes of one's brothers and sisters as far as necessary to bring them the fruits of God's overpowering love and mercy. I would also venture to suggest that no Christian religious movement can sustain itself in the long run if it is built primarily on a denial of the full God-given humanity of some members of the human family. No matter how often conservatives claim that they love the persons who are homosexual, their message is one of rejection and intolerance toward them. Such a message is not compatible with the fundamental Christian virtues of love and compassion. A viable religion must be built on values that affirm and strengthen the very best in human beings, not ones that are built on fear and rejection of parts of their very being that are used to express love and affection.

The mind-set and rhetoric of the conservatives also reveals a strong apocalyptic and even Manichaean tendency. They tend to demonize the "other side" as the spawn of Satan and identify themselves with the angels of goodness. This kind of dualistic, Gnostic division between the children of light and the children of darkness was once declared a heresy by the very primitive Church to which they ostensibly cling. How such a position is consistent with the Christian understanding of the fallibility of all persons is not clear. While the conservatives rightly point out that some liberals are a little slack in acknowledging the reality and pervasiveness of sin, they do not seem to act as if sinfulness might infect their own claims to absolute truth, that their espousal of their views is immune from error. There is no room for doctrinal or moral ambiguity in the conservative position. But ambiguity has always been part of the Anglican tradition's tolerance for different articulations of the faith within the broad umbrella of Anglican comprehensiveness because ambiguity is part of the human condition. An intolerance for ambiguity suggests a closed, inflexible, and dogmatic mind to whose claims for an absolutely pristine authority no fallible, finite human being, let alone human institution, is entitled.

In particular, it is not clear how from such a dualistic position of absolute right and wrong one can enter with an open mind into dialogue with those whose positions have been deemed from the outset as morally unacceptable. What would the absolutists be willing to hear in the so-called listening process if they already know absolutely that homosexual acts are morally wrong? Could someone holding an absolutist mind-set truly hear what someone whose acts are deemed ipso facto morally abominable is saying? There is a high degree of disingenuousness going on by some conservatives in their repeated affirmations of the listening process.

There may be something in what some psychologists call the "authoritarian personality" that might apply to some of the conservatives. This is not to suggest that such a personality is psychologically or morally "wrong," but it does suggest certain correlations that seem typical of much of the conservative rhetoric as well as of its arguments. Drawing on their own studies and those of others, Canadian psychologists Bob Altemeyer and Bruce Hunsberger have outlined some of the traits of authoritarians in religion.[6] There are, they claim, "positive correlations" between authoritarianism, dogmatism, rigidity, intolerance of ambiguity, and some forms of prejudice, including that against homosexuals. Right-wing authoritarians also seem to be particularly disposed toward punishing those who violate moral standards. And they are drawn to fundamentalism, the belief that there is only one set of basic, inerrant, and absolute truths, as well as unchangeable practices of the past that ought to be binding today. Now this does not mean that all conservatives fit the authoritarian personality profile. But many of the characteristics we have been tracking in the conservative movement do seem to correlate to what Altemeyer and Hunsberger have found in the authoritarian personality. I would also argue that the power analysis suggested by Ian Douglas describes authoritarians seeking to maintain privileges that they have enjoyed and that they believe those challenging traditional views are threatening to undermine.

On the more positive side, one way in which the Anglican tradition might be invoked by contemporary "liberals" is in the time-honored practices of reception and dispersed authority. There are parts of the Communion that have been permitted to continue the practice of polygamy at least provisionally (though technically no one in the Communion can permit or deny their right to do so). Some bishops have been "permitted" to exercise a conscience clause to deny women ordination in their dioceses. Neither polygamy nor a refusal to ordain women has split the Communion. Why, then, could not the practice in some Provinces such as ECUSA and Canada of ordaining openly gay and lesbian persons and blessing their relationships be acceptable, particularly if it was a way of determining the receptivity of such practices over time? Not all Provinces would be expected to adopt this practice. It would be local in its application, recognizing as the Anglican tradition has done throughout, that the Church, through its individual churches, must be adapted to its times and places consistent with an incarnational theology without that adaptation resulting in the undermining of its core moral principles.

There may, ironically, be one area in which both progressives and conservatives can find common cause. Both, for their own reasons, reject the current cultural emphasis on individualism. Neither believes that individuals are "self-made" or that their individual "preferences" ought to be the sole or even primary basis for moral decisions.[7] Both believe in the importance of situating individual choice within the context of a community and in relation to God's intentions for the world. They clearly have different views regarding what they believe are the most important moral issues, but both condemn the reduction of all that is sacred to mere secularity. Perhaps what is needed is a willingness on both sides to discuss what ought to constitute the nature of a loving community,[8] one that holds firm to some basic moral principles, while permitting comprehensiveness in how those principles are enacted.

One of the greatest tragedies of the present conflict within the Church has been the diversion of talent, resources, energy, and time from addressing the pressing issues of social injustice around the world that have been identified by the Church in the Millennium Development Goals (MDGs). These include promoting gender equality, reducing child mortality, improving maternal health, combating HIV/AIDS, and ensuring environmental sustainability. But heading the list of the MDGs is the eradication of extreme poverty and hunger around the world. When the Church is tied up in addressing issues such as homosexuality that the conservatives have identified as core, opportunities for genuine mission in these other areas are lost. This is a tragedy not only within the Church but also for those who might be helped by a united effort from both conservative and progressive Christians to deal with poverty, racism, and economic injustice.

In the end, however, the resolution of the discontents that presently afflict the Church will, in my opinion, be decided by the implicit fourth leg of the famous three-legged stool to which Anglicanism has always referred. That fourth leg is human experience.[9] All the rules, principles, dogmas, creeds, doctrines, rulings, resolutions, and pronouncements that issue from a religious tradition mean nothing if they continually frustrate or deny the reality of human experience. African Americans knew from experience that they were not chattel, and thus slavery could not forever be sustained by the Church as long as Black persons were part of the Christian community through baptism. Women knew from experience that they were not inferior to men, and thus rejection of women from the priesthood and episcopate could not forever be justified as long as women were members of the Christian community. Gay and lesbian persons know from experience that they are not defective or incomplete human beings and are thus entitled to all the privileges available to any of the baptized within the religious community. And the experience of more and more persons, gay and straight, both within and outside the Church, is revealing that an obsession with homosexuality is going to become increasingly rare as generations change. More and more people are discovering that many of their friends and family are gay and the sky has not fallen. In particular, there is a new generation that, for the most part, is simply not obsessed with the sexual orientation of others. For them whether someone is gay or lesbian is as much a part, and of as little significance, as whether their friends are right or left handed, from the South or East, from the United States or another country. In fact, ironically, among an increasing majority of young people in America,[10] the more strident the rhetoric against homosexuals, the more Christianity is regarded as "judgmental, hypocritical and anti-gay." The rhetorical stridency against homosexuality may do more to drive people from the Church and fail to attract new members than almost anything else because it simply flies in the face of their everyday experiences. The fixation on homosexuality is, I believe, typical of an older, predominantly male generation that will soon pass from the scene. If the Church is to survive unbroken and even to flourish, it has to look to this newer more sexually mature and inclusive generation, from which its future leaders will most likely be recruited.

The present leaders of the conservative movement are also likely, if history is any guide, to preside at the splintering of their own movement. In the short run, of course, there will inevitably be some, perhaps many, individuals who leave the Episcopal Church and join or even start churches that seem to promise greater fidelity to conservative moral values. The leadership of some dioceses will try to take as many individuals in their dioceses with them. The bishops of San Joaquin, Pittsburgh, and Fort Worth are likely to be successful in taking many, if not most, of their supporters with them into other Anglican provinces or, from their point of view, ideally into an American Anglican province of some kind. This nongeographic province, should it come into existence and be recognized by the Anglican Communion, will share some basic moral values with other conservative Anglicans, but it will not be surprising if down the road, once the thrill of having cleansed themselves from the moral filth of ECUSA has begun to wear off, there will be disputes among the African and American episcopate over other issues (such as women's ordination or financial commitment to ending poverty), and over differing styles of leadership. It will be hard even for morally conservative Americans to shake the habit of ecclesial democratic decision making (no matter how much its results are decried by the conservatives) in which the laity play a major role and equally hard for some of their African and Asian counterparts to embrace a democratic polity after having practiced a much more top-down style of authority requiring deference by the laity to bishops and Primates. It is also likely that some African, Asian, and South American provinces may find themselves increasingly unsatisfied by continued alliance with the Church of England, which, despite the vacillations of the present Archbishop of Canterbury, seems headed in a more liberal direction. The negative aspects of ecclesiastical colonialism that required homage to Canterbury may finally come to the surface as the present Archbishop fails to satisfy the demands of the so-called "Global South," and even the Lambeth Conference that he convenes may prove increasingly irrelevant to those who want a purer, less complicated, and less theologically diverse Church.

It is important to remember that dioceses themselves cannot depart from the Church, only individuals can, and this fact alone will make it difficult for the departed to sustain themselves in the long run. Every time a church has split into puritan and mainstream parties, the "puritans" eventually tend to disappear from history, usually after having splintered still further as one group after enough reaches for the elusive and illusionary goal of achieving total purity, uncontaminated by the world, or after having made its peace with "secularity," opposition to which originally gave it its reason for being. This is particularly true when the splintering group is driven primarily by fear of the "different," of the "other," especially when that fear takes the form of intolerance and rejection rather than of love. The dream of purity and the attempts to achieve it only open the door to the triumph of the secular unleavened by Christian love.

As the dissatisfied depart, the Episcopal Church will, I believe, continue along the lines articulated by most of the via media groups: generally liberal, but not radical, on moral issues, more willing, since the Windsor Report, to consider the effects of its actions on the wider Communion, but at the same time no less committed to the continued inclusion of gay and lesbian persons in all aspects of the Church's life. Its biggest challenge will be to find new ways to attract and retain a younger generation for whom the issues of even the most recent past are simply no longer relevant.

If the Church is to survive, it has to be because it has something to say to each new generation, something that speaks to its experience and to its hunger for abiding principles. Love, mutuality, justice, and fidelity are values that meet the conservatives' test of permanency and the liberals' test of being abiding and deeply relevant to all human experience regardless of sexual orientation or race or gender. If the Church can keep these moral principles at the heart of its message, it has every chance to move boldly and with vitality beyond the discontents from which it presently suffers.

Timeline

1534	Henry VIII is declared the Supreme Head of the Church of England
1789	Episcopal Church in America formed
1867	First Meeting of the Lambeth Conference
1920	Lambeth Conference judges that Ordination of Deaconesses confers on them Holy Orders
1930s–1940s	East African Revival
1944	Miss Li Tim Oi ordained to the priesthood by the bishop of Hong Kong and South China
1967	General Convention of TEC votes to allow women to be eligible for election as convention deputies (to go into effect with 1970 General Convention)
1968	Anglican Consultative Council recommends that the diaconate be open to "men and women remaining in secular occupations" and that deaconesses "be declared to be within the diaconate." Also says that "the theological arguments as at present presented for and against the ordination of women to the priesthood are inconclusive" and request every province to "give careful study to the question of the ordination of women to the priesthood"
1970	General Convention recognizes women deaconesses as eligible for diaconal ordination
1972	House of Bishops endorses women's ordination "in principle"
1973	Majority of lay and clerical deputies at General Convention votes in favor of women's ordination but a parliamentary technicality means vote fails to carry
1974	July 29: Eleven women ordained to the priesthood in Philadelphia
1975	September 7: Four more women ordained in Washington, DC
1976	General Convention votes to recognize eligibility of women to serve in all three orders of ordained ministry (including episcopate) to become effective January 1, 1977, and to regularize the original ordinations of the 15 women priests irregularly ordained earlier. Convention also resolves that

"homosexual persons are children of God" and deserve pastoral care and legal protection

1976   December: Evangelical and Catholic Mission founded to provide support for Anglo-Catholics who objected to Convention's actions on women's ordination. Reorganized in 1989 as Episcopal Synod of America

1977   New York Bishop Paul Moore ordains a woman known to be a lesbian to the priesthood

1979   General Convention adopts position on inappropriateness of ordaining practicing homosexuals and forbids ordination of anyone gay, or straight, who engages in sexual relations outside of marriage

1988   Lambeth asks each Province to reassess its attitude toward gays and lesbians and passes resolution giving qualified support to polygamy in certain countries

1989   Barbara Harris consecrated as suffragan bishop of Massachusetts

1989   Bishop John Spong of the Diocese of Newark ordains an openly gay man

1995   Charges brought against Bishop Walter Righter for participating in ordination of an openly gay man

1995   American Anglican Council is formed

1995   Ekklesia Society is founded

1996   Exoneration of Bishop Walter Righter by the trial court

1997   Eighty southern bishops and archbishops meet in Kuala Lumpur, Malaysia: issue "Kuala Lumpur Statement on Human Sexuality"

       "The Virginia Report" of the Inter-Anglican Theological and Doctrinal Commission is released

       "The Eames Monitoring Group Report" on Women's Ordination is issued

1998   Lambeth adopts resolution 1.10 on sexuality

1999   Diocese of New Westminster (Canada) takes up issue of development of public rites for same sex blessings

2000   Anglican Mission in America (AMiA) begins on January 29

       January 29, Singapore: two American priests "irregularly" consecrated as missionary bishops by Archbishop Kolini of Rwanda and Moses Tay of South East Asia

       July, ECUSA General Convention: passes resolution permitting bishops who will not ordain or employ women priests a "conscience" clause

2002   Diocese of New Westminster approves same sex blessings

2003   June 7: Diocese of New Hampshire elects Gene Robinson as its new Bishop

       August: General Convention (Minneapolis) consents to the election of Gene Robinson

       October 15–16: Archbishop of Canterbury calls emergency meeting of Primates to respond to Robinson election: creates Lambeth Commission on Communion, which will issue the "Windsor Report" a year later

       November 2: Robinson consecrated in New Hampshire

2004   January 14: story in *Washington Post* revealing December 2003 Chapman Memo

       January 20: Network of Anglican Communion Dioceses and Parishes officially launched

       March 19–25: House of Bishops develops plan for delegated episcopal oversight and issues "Caring for All the Churches"

April: Council of Anglican Provinces of Africa (CAPA) refuses funding from ECUSA, calls on ECUSA to repent

May: Massachusetts approves same sex marriage, becoming the sixth jurisdiction in the world to approve same sex marriage

June: Synod of Anglican Church of Canada affirms integrity and sanctity of adult same sex relationships

October: Windsor Report is released

2005   February: Primates receive Windsor Report at Dromantine, issue Communiqué

March: House of Bishops effects moratorium on consecration of all bishops until 2006 General Convention and calls for no crossing of diocesan boundaries

June 21: "To Set Our Hope on Christ" released, responding on behalf of ECUSA to the Windsor Report

2006   June: General Convention in Columbus:

Expresses regret for straining bonds of affection from its actions in 2003

Commits to the Windsor Report and the Listening Process

Supports the development of an Anglican covenant

In resolution B033 calls upon standing committees to "exercise restraint by not consenting to the consecration of any candidate to the episcopate whose manner of life presents a challenge to the wider church and will lead to further strains on communion."

Katharine Jefferts Schori is elected Presiding Bishop

August 20: The Reverend Martyn Minns is consecrated in Nigeria for Convocation of Anglicans in North America (CANA)

September 19–22: Global South Primates issue Communiqué from Kigali, Rwanda

September 19–22: Twenty-one conservative bishops meet at Camp Allen, Texas

November 4: Jefferts Schori is consecrated in Washington, D.C.

December 17: Eight Virginia parishes announce that they are affiliating with Uganda or Nigeria. Legal disputes over property of departing parishes begin

2007   February 19: Primates' Communiqué from Dar Es Salaam, Tanzania, calls for "pastoral council" to facilitate healing and reconciliation for those unable to accept direct ministry of their bishop or presiding bishop and demands that ECUSA commit not to ordain gay persons or authorize same sex blessings

March 20: House of Bishops rejects most of Primates' Dar Es Salaam Communiqué

May 5: Nigerian Archbishop Akinola installs Bishop Minns in Virginia for CANA

September 25: House of Bishops meets in New Orleans and responds to Primates' Dar Es Salaam Communiqué

November: PB Jefferts Schori sends letters to Bishops of San Joaquin, Fort Worth, and Pittsburgh warning them not to attempt to take their dioceses out of the Episcopal Church and threatening to begin a process that could lead to their being deposed should they do so

November: trial begins in Virginia over control of property of parishes that have voted to leave the diocese

December: Diocese of San Joaquin votes to disaffiliate from the Episcopal Church

2008   March 12: House of Bishops consents to the deposition of Bishop Schofield of San Joaquin

Notes

Introduction

1. Matthai Chakko Kuruvila, *San Francisco Chronicle,* October 1, 2007.

Chapter 1

1. James Solheim, *Diversity or Disunity? Reflections on Lambeth 1998* (New York: Church Publishing Inc, 1999), 18. Solheim's is the best single study of Lambeth 1998.

2. For full texts of the resolutions from Lambeth 1998 see www.lambethconference. org.

3. Solheim, *Diversity or Disunity?* 27.

4. Miranda K. Hassett, *Anglican Communion in Crisis: How Episcopal Dissidents and their African Allies are Reshaping Anglicanism* (Princeton: Princeton University Press, 2007), 111–112.

5. Hassett, *Anglican Communion in Crisis,* 72–73.

6. Solheim, *Diversity or Disunity?* 52–53.

7. Solheim, *Diveristy or Disunity?* 62.

8. Solheim, *Diveristy or Disunity?* 65.

9. Hassett, *Anglican Communion in Crisis,* 72.

10. Stephen Bates, *A Church at War: Anglicans and Homosexuality* (London: I. B. Tauris, 2004), 137.

11. Katie Sherrod, quoted in Bates, *A Church at War,* 135.

12. Bates, *A Church at War,* 131.

13. Solheim, *Diversity or Disunity?* 59.

14. Bates, *A Church at War,* 129.

15. Bates, *A Church at War,* 192.

16. Bates, *A Church at War,* 192.

17. Bates, *A Church at War,* 192.

18. Solheim, *Diversity or Disunity?* 74, 203. (The latter comment was made by Ohio Bishop Clark Grew.)

19. Solheim, *Diversity or Disunity?* 73.

20. Solheim, *Diversity or Disunity?* 195.

21. Solheim, *Diversity or Disunity?* 210, 196.

22. Solheim, *Diversity or Disunity?* 195.

23. Hassett, *Anglican Communion in Crisis,* 79.

24. Solheim, *Diversity or Disunity?* 75.

25. Solheim, *Diversity or Disunity?* 223–24.

26. www.affirmingcatholicism.org.

27. Solheim, *Diversity or Disunity?* 90.

28. Solheim, *Diversity or Disunity?* 193.

29. Solheim, *Diversity or Disunity?* 213.

30. Solheim, *Diversity or Disunity?* 209.

31. Solheim, *Diversity or Disunity?* 220.

32. Bishop Stephen Jecko of Florida, in Solheim, *Diversity or Disunity?* 82.

33. Solheim, *Diversity or Disunity?* 124.

34. The first quote is from Bishop Rucyahana of Rwanda and the second from Bishop Broadhurst of London. Solheim, *Diversity or Disunity?* 100, 103.

35. Solheim, *Diversity or Disunity?* 117.

36. Hassett, *Anglican Communion in Crisis,* 102–104.

37. Hassett, *Anglican Communion in Crisis,* 103.

38. Hassett, *Anglican Communion in Crisis,* 66.

39. Hassett, *Anglican Communion in Crisis,* 67.

40. (Originally found at www.anglicanmissioninamerica.org, now available at www.theamia.org.)

41. Hassett, *Anglican Communion in Crisis,* 69.

42. www.anglicancommunion.org/acn/acnsarchives/acns.

43. For the full texts of resolutions from the 2000 General Convention see www.episcopalarchives.org under "The Acts of Convention."

44. www.anglicancommunion.org/communion/acc/meetings/acc12/resolutions.cfm.

45. Diocesan Web site Diocese of New Westminster, Canada, www.vancouver.anglican.ca.

46. Bates, *A Church at War,* 159.

47. www.anglicancommunion.org.

48. Michael Ingham, "Reclaiming Christian Orthodoxy," October 2003. Retrieved October 30, 2003, from www.anglicancommunion.org/acns.

49. Bates, *A Church at War,* 162.

50. Bates, *A Church at War,* 160.

51. "Pastoral Letter from the Primates of the Anglican Communion, " May 27, 2003. www.anglicancommunion.org/acns.

52. Bates, *A Church at War,* 183.

53. Martin Minns and Kendall Harmon as reported in the *Washington Times,* July 29, 2003.

54. Ian Markham, Editorial, "Episcopalians, Homosexuality and the General Convention 2006," *Reviews in Religion and Theology* 14, no. 1 (January 2007): 1.

55. Episcopal News Service (ENS), August 6, 2003. Robert Duncan, Bishop of Pittsburgh, called it a "pastoral emergency." *ABC World News Tonight,* August 6, 2003.

56. Religious News Service (RNS), August 8, 2003.

57. *Pittsburgh Post-Gazette,* August 4, 2003.

58. *New York Times,* August 6, 2003.

59. *Atlanta Journal Constitution,* John Blake, October 8, 2003.

60. John was a gay man elected to a bishopric in England but was asked by ABC Rowan Williams to resign the position. That story will be told later in the narrative.

61. London: *The Times,* August 6, 2003.

62. *New York Times,* August 6, 2003.

63. The disputes over church property will be taken up in due course.

64. *Washington Times,* August 26, 2003.

65. James Solheim, RNS, October 3, 2003.

66. E. T. Malone, Jr., ENS, October 7, 2003.

67. *New York Times,* October 5, 2003.

68. See the Web site of the Council at www.americananglican.org.

69. Bobby Ross, Associated Press, October 9, 2003.

70. Richard Ostling, *Hartford Courant,* October 9, 2003.

71. James Solheim, ENS, September 26, 2003.

72. The story of that resolution will be told below.

73. Jamie Doward, *The Guardian,* October 18, 2003.

74. Solheim, ENS, October 20, 2003.

75. Solheim, ENS, October 20, 2003.

76. CNN.com, October 23, 2003.

77. Letter issued by Bishop Griswold from the Episcopal Church Center, October 23, 2003. www.episcopalchurch.org.

78. ENS, October 28, 2003.

79. CBC.CA News, November 2, 2003.

80. CBC.CA News, November 2, 2003.

81. Laurie Goodstein, *New York Times,* November 2, 2003.

82. *New York Times,* Reuters, London, November 3, 2003.

83. www.acn-us.org.

84. Julia Duin, *Washington Times,* December 12, 2003.

85. Jan Nunley, ENS, December 18, 2003.

86. John Sorenson of Trinity Episcopal Church, Plattsburgh, NY.

Chapter 2

1. I am drawing on the work of Stephen Neill (*Anglicanism* [Baltimore: Penguin Books, 1958]), p. 37, for much of my treatment of the Church of England.

2. Neill, *Anglicanism,* 39.

3. Roland H. Bainton, *The Reformation of the Sixteenth Century* (Boston: Beacon Press, 1952), 189.

4. "Thirty-Nine Articles," in *The Oxford Dictionary of the Christian Church,* ed. F. L. Cross (London: Oxford University Press, 1958), 1349.

5. See Henry Bettenson and Chris Maunder, eds., *Documents of the Christian Church,* 3rd ed. (Oxford: Oxford University Press, 1999), 91–93.

6. Robert Bruce Mullin, *Episcopal Vision/American Reality* (New Haven: Yale University Press, 1986), 68.

7. See Edwin S. Gaustad, *Sworn on the Altar of God: A Religious Biography of Thomas Jefferson* (Grand Rapids: William B. Eerdmans, 1996), 56–57.

8. James Madison, "To the Honorable the General Assembly of the Commonwealth of Virginia. A Memorial and Remonstrance," in *The Constitution and Religion: Leading Supreme Court Cases on Church and State,* ed. Robert S. Alley (Amherst, NY: Prometheus Books, 1999), 31.

9. Thomas Bradbury Chandler, "An Appeal to the Public, in Behalf of the Church of England in America," reprinted in *Religious Issues in American History*, ed. Edwin Scott Gaustad (New York: Harper and Row, 1968), 49–57.

10. Paul Victor Marshall, *One, Catholic, and Apostolic* (New York: Church Publishing, 2004), 53–54. See especially his chapter "The Search for an American Ecclesiology."

11. For a full development of Seabury's political, ecclesiastical, and moral views, see Frank G. Kirkpatrick, "Samuel Seabury: Virtue and Christian Community in Late Eighteenth Century America," *Anglican Theological Review* LXXIV, no. 3 (Summer 1992): 317–33.

12. These quotations are taken from Seabury's "A Discourse Addressed to His Majesty's Provincial Troops" (he was serving as the chaplain to a British regiment in New York); from his "A View of the Controversy Between Great-Britain and Her Colonies," and from "Free Thoughts on the Proceedings of the Continental Congress," both of the latter pieces from *Letters of a Westchester Farmer (1774–1775),* ed. Clarence H. Vance (White Plains: Westchester County Historical Society, 1930), as found in Kirkpatrick, "Samuel Seabury: Virtue and Christian Community," 323.

13. For much of this history, I am indebted to Robert Prichard's *A History of the Episcopal Church,* rev. ed. (Harrisburg, PA: Morehouse Publishing, 1999).

14. As quoted in Marshall, *One, Catholic, and Apostolic,* 64.

15. Marshall, *One, Catholic, and Apostolic,* 66.

16. W. J. Hankey, "Canon Law," in *The Study of Anglicanism,* ed. Stephen Sykes and John Booty (London: SPCK, 1988), 207.

17. Marshall, *One, Catholic, and Apostolic,* 67.

18. Marshall, *One, Catholic, and Apostolic,* 68.

19. For a thorough review of Seabury's itinerary and struggle to get ordained see Clara O. Loveland, *The Critical Years: The Reconstitution of the Anglican Church in the United States of America: 1780–1789* (Greenwich: Seabury Press, 1956).

20. Loveland, *The Critical Years,* 106–107.

21. Loveland, *The Critical Years,* 112.

22. Loveland, *The Critical Years,* 125–26.

23. Marshall, *One, Catholic, and Apostolic,* 239–40.

24. Robert W. Prichard, *A History of the Episcopal Church* (Harrisburg: Morehouse Publishing, 1991), 95.

25. Loveland, *The Critical Years,* 189–90.

26. Loveland, *The Critical Years,* 178.

27. Loveland, *The Critical Years,* 180. This is now referred to as matters of Adiaphora.

28. Loveland, *The Critical Years,* 206–207.

29. For a somewhat fuller development of these points see Loveland, *The Critical Years,* 287–88.

Chapter 3

1. It could be argued, as I did in the previous chapter, that the Communion began when there were only two jurisdictionally separate Episcopal Churches, Scotland and the United States. But the addition of Canada makes it truly an international Communion.

2. From a letter to Archbishop of Canterbury Longley, in John Howe, *Anglicanism and the Universal Church: Highways and Hedges 1958–1984* (Toronto: Anglican Book Centre, 1990), 61.

3. Howe, *Anglicanism and the Universal Church,* 61.

4. In what follows I wili touch only on those issues relevant to the current disputes within the Communion.

5. For a good discussion of the Colenso affair see H. G. G. Herklots, *Frontiers of the Church: The Making of the Anglican Communion* (London: Ernest Benn, Ltd., 1961), 165–75.

6. Herklots, *Frontiers of the Church,* 166.

7. William Sachs, *The Transformation of Anglicanism: From State Church to Global Communion* (Cambridge: Cambridge University Press, 1993), 199.

8. Resolution 9 of Lambeth 1920 as found on www.globalsouthanglican.org.

9. H. R. McAdoo, "Authority in the Church: Spiritual Freedom and the Corporate Nature of Faith," in *Authority in the Anglican Communion: Essays Presented to Bishop John Howe,* ed. Stephen Sykes (Toronto: Anglican Book Centre, 1987), 82.

10. See *The Lambeth Conference 1948: The Encyclical Letter from the Bishops; together with Resolutions and Reports* (London: SPCK, 1948), 82–94.

11. Resolutions from Lambeth 1958. These can be found on the Web site www.lambethconference.org/resolutions.

12. See the Chapter 4: "The Uncompleted Struggle for Women's Ordination."

13. Resolution 23 on "marriage discipline" from 1968 Lambeth.

14. *Belonging Together* (London: The Anglican Communion Secretariat, 1992), 5.

15. *Belonging Together,* 6.

16. *Belonging Together,* 7.

17. *Belonging Together,* 22.

18. *Belonging Together,* 12.

19. *Belonging Together,* 19.

20. *Belonging Together,* 19–20.

21. *The Protestant Episcopal Church in the United States of America In the Court for the Trial of a Bishop, James M. Stanton, Bishop of Dallas, et al., v. The Rt. Rev. Walter C. Righter,* May 15, 1996.

22. James Solheim, *Diversity or Disunity? Reflections on Lambeth 1998* (New York: Church Publishing, 1999), 29.

23. The word "South" refers to those provinces in the AC primarily in Africa, Asia, and South America, not the southern states of the United States.

24. The Kuala Lumpur Statement on Human Sexuality—2nd Encounter in the South, 10–15 February 1997 (http://www.globalsouthanglican.org/index).

25. "The Virginia Report: The Report of the Inter-Anglican Theological and Doctrinal Commission" (London: Published for the Anglican Consultative Council by the Secretary General of the Anglican Consultative Council, 1997).

Chapter 4

1. For a brief history of these events see Michael McFarlene Marrett, *The Lambeth Conferences and Women Priests: The Historical Background of the Conferences and Their Impact on the Episcopal Church in America* (Smithtown, NY: Exposition Press, 1981).

2. Marrett, *The Lambeth Conferences and Women Priests,* 11.

3. David E. Sumner, *The Episcopal Church's History: 1945–1985* (Wilton, CT: Morehouse-Barlow, 1997), 16.

4. St. Thomas Aquinas, *The Summa Theologica,* Question XCII "The Production of Woman," Reply to Objection 1 (*Basic Writings of Saint Thomas Aquinas,* Vol. One, ed. Anton C. Pegis (New York: Random House), 880.

5. The quotation is taken from John Howe, *Anglicanism and the Universal Church: Highways and Hedges 1958–1982* (Toronto: Anglican Book Centre, 1990), 153.

6. Howe, *Anglicanism and the Universal Church,* 153–54.

7. Citations from the 1968 Lambeth Conference Report are taken from Howe, *Anglicanism and the Universal Church,* 154–55.

8. Marrett, *The Lambeth Conferences and Women Priests,* 8.

9. Howe, *Anglicanism and the Universal Church,* 155–56.

10. Howe, *Anglicanism and the Universal Church,* 157.

11. Marrett, *The Lambeth Conferences and Women Priests,* 54.

12. Marrett, *The Lambeth Conferences and Women Priests,* 56.

13. From Paul Moore's *Take A Bishop Like Me,* as quoted in Sumner, *The Episcopal Church's History: 1945–1985,* 27.

14. Sumner, *The Episcopal Church's History: 1945–1985,* 27.

15. Sumner, *The Episcopal Church's History: 1945–1985,* 23.

16. Marrett, *The Lambeth Conferences and Women Priests,* 60.

17. Marrett, *The Lambeth Conferences and Women Priests,* 60–61.

18. Marrett, *The Lambeth Conferences and Women Priests,* 61.

19. Marrett, *The Lambeth Conferences and Women Priests,* 62.

20. Sumner, *The Episcopal Church's History: 1945–1985,* 30.

21. Sumner, *The Episcopal Church's History: 1945–1985,* 29.

22. Sumner, *The Episcopal Church's History: 1945–1985,* 30.

23. Howe, *Anglicanism and the Universal Church,* 162.

24. Howe, *Anglicanism and the Universal Church,* 163.

25. From "The Eames Monitoring Group Report," www.anglicancommunion.org.

26. Mary Tanner, "The Episcopal Ministry Act of Synod in Context," in *Seeking the Truth of Change in the Church: Reception, Communion and the Ordination of Women,* ed. Paul Avis (London: T&T Clark International, 2004), 66. The Act can be found at www.cofe.anglican.org.

27. As reported by the *BBC News,* "On This Day," for February 26, 1987. (www.bbc.co.uk/onthisday.)

28. "Ordaining Women as Priests in the Church of England," www.religioustolerance.org, 1992.

29. The citation from Lambeth 1998 is found in Tanner, "The Episcopal Ministry Act of Synod in Context," 69.

30. Paul Avis, "The Episcopal Ministry Act of Synod, 1993: A 'Bearable Anomaly'?" in *Seeking the Truth of Change in the Church: Reception, Communion and the Ordination of Women,* ed. Avis, 154.

31. Avis, "The Episcopal Ministry Act of Synod, 1993: A 'Bearable Anomaly'?" 160.

32. Avis, "The Episcopal Ministry Act of Synod, 1993: A 'Bearable Anomaly'?" 161.

33. "The Eames Monitoring Group Report," paragraph 7.

34. "The Eames Monitoring Group Report," paragraph 2, citing the Lambeth 1988 resolutions.

35. "The Eames Monitoring Group Report," paragraphs 21, 23.

36. "The Eames Monitoring Group Report," paragraph 27.

37. "The Eames Monitoring Group Report," paragraph 39.

38. "The Eames Monitoring Group Report," paragraph 94 of the Grindrod Report as cited in the Monitoring Group Report.

39. "The Eames Monitoring Group Report," paragraph 49.

40. "The Eames Monitoring Group Report," paragraph 57.

Chapter 5

1. Alan Cooperman, *The Washington Post,* January 14, 2004.

2. Richard Ostling, Associated Press, January 20, 2004.

3. www.acn-us.org/about/history.html.

4. Reported in *San Antonio Express-News,* February 20, 2004.

5. Vickie Chachere, AP, February 10, 2004. Kurt Barnes, the national church's treasurer, said lower contributions were "almost not material" and the reduction was well below what was predicted last August.

6. "Caring for All the Churches," March 23, 2004.

7. See www.anglicancommunion.org/acns.

8. From www.anglicancommunion.org/commission/.

9. www.anglicancommunion.org/acns.

10. RNS, June 9, 2004.

11. *The Lambeth Commission on Communion. The Windsor Report, 2004* (London: The Anglican Communion Office, 2004), 5. (Hereafter called *Windsor Report.*)

12. *Windsor Report,* 18.

13. *Windsor Report,* 16.

14. *Windsor Report,* 73.

15. *Windsor Report,* 74.

16. *Windsor Report,* 77–78.

17. *Windsor Report,* 17.

18. *Windsor Report,* 33.

19. *Windsor Report,* 20.

20. *Windsor Report,* 22.

21. *Windsor Report,* 22.

22. *Windsor Report,* 23.

23. *Windsor Report,* 28.

24. *Windsor Report,* 28.

25. *Windsor Report,* 29.

26. *Windsor Report,* 30.

27. *Windsor Report,* 32.

28. *Windsor Report,* 33.

29. *Windsor Report,* 35.

30. *Windsor Report,* 36.

31. *Windsor Report,* 37. Emphasis mine.

32. *Windsor Report,* 37.

33. *Windsor Report,* 42.

34. *Windsor Report,* 44.

35. *Windsor Report,* 44.

36. *Windsor Report,* 46.

37. *Windsor Report,* 47.

38. *Windsor Report,* 48.

39. *Windsor Report,* 66.

40. *Windsor Report,* 67.

41. *Windsor Report,* 50.

42. *Windsor Report,* 50–51.

43. *Windsor Report,* 52.

44. *Windsor Report,* 53–54.

45. *Windsor Report,* 54.

46. *Windsor Report,* 56.

47. *Windsor Report,* 57.

48. *Windsor Report,* 57–58.

49. *Windsor Report,* 59.

50. Excerpts from Bishop Griswold's response to the Windsor Report in *Episcopal Life* (November 2004): 3.

51. Akinola's comments are taken from Ian T. Douglas and Paul F. M. Zahl, *Understanding the Windsor Report: Two Leaders in the American Church Speak Across the Divide* (With a Comprehensive Report Summary by Jan Nunley) (New York: Church Publishing, 2005), 169–70.

52. *Understanding the Windsor Report,* 57.

53. *Understanding the Windsor Report,* 75.

54. *Understanding the Windsor Report,* 51.

55. *Understanding the Windsor Report,* 25–27.

56. *Understanding the Windsor Report,* 33.

57. *Understanding the Windsor Report,* 34.

58. *Understanding the Windsor Report,* 72.

59. *Understanding the Windsor Report,* 107.

60. *Understanding the Windsor Report,* 68.

61. Much of the material on which I am drawing was made available to me by the Bishop's office of the Diocese of Connecticut. Material can also be found on its Web site www.ctdiocese.org and the Web site of the so-called Connecticut Six, www.ctsix.org.

62. Andy Newman, "Dissident Episcopal Priests Are Called Part of a Strategy," *New York Times,* April 21, 2005.

63. Letter from the Standing Committee to Bishop Smith, April 29, 2005.

64. This is a committee formed at the discretion of the Archbishop of Canterbury to hear complaints from members of the Communion.

65. http://titusonenine.classicalanglican.net. Statement by Duncan July 15, 2005.

66. "Response to Open Letter of July 27" by Bishop Smith, July 28, 2005.

67. Web site for the Diocese of Connecticut, www.ctdiocese.org/news, August 22, 2006.

68. http://www.agapepress.org.

69. The full text of the Bishop's address is found on the diocesan Web site www.ctdiocese.org/news.

70. For the full report visit the Diocesan Web site www.ctdiocese.org/news/Title_IV_Review_Committee_Decision.pdf.

Chapter 6

1. www.episcopalchurch.org.

2. Stephen Bates, *The Tablet,* March 5, 2005. It was reported that 20 of the 35 Primates held a celebratory dinner near Dromantine financed by American traditionalist Episcopalians and hosted by Archbishop of Nigeria Peter Akinola.

3. www.anglicancommunion.org/acns.

4. Appendix F of the Report of the Special Commission on the Episcopal Church and the Anglican Communion, "House of Bishops" Spring Meeting, Camp Allen, Texas, March 15, 2005. www.episcopalchurch.org.

5. www.anglicanlistening.org, or www.episcopalchurch.org/documents/ToSetOurHopeOnChrist.pdf. The authors consisted of seven theologians: The Reverend Dr. Michael Battle of the Virginia Theological Seminary; The Reverend Dr. Katherine Grieb of the Virginia Theological Seminary; The Reverend Dr. Jay Johnson of the Graduate Theological Union, Berkeley; The Reverend Dr. Mark McIntosh of Loyola University Chicago; The Right Reverend Catherine Roskam, Bishop Suffragan of New York; Dr. Timothy Sedgwick of the Virginia Theological Seminary; and Dr. Kathryn Tanner of the University of Chicago Divinity School, as well as one historian, Dr. Pamela W. Darling, an historian of General Convention legislation and Episcopal Church ministry, who prepared the Appendix, which contains the documents involved in the debates over the past four decades.

6. *To Set Our Hope on Christ,* 8.

7. *To Set Our Hope on Christ,* 9.

8. *To Set Our Hope on Christ,* 10.

9. *To Set Our Hope on Christ,* 11–12.

10. *To Set Our Hope on Christ,* 13.

11. *To Set Our Hope on Christ,* 16.

12. *To Set Our Hope on Christ,* 18–20.

13. *To Set Our Hope on Christ,* 19–20.

14. *To Set Our Hope on Christ,* 22–25.

15. *To Set Our Hope on Christ,* 24–28.

16. *To Set Our Hope on Christ,* 29.

17. *To Set Our Hope on Christ,* 32.

18. *To Set Our Hope on Christ,* 52–55.

19. *To Set Our Hope on Christ,* 56–59. The final quotations within the quote are taken from the Virginia Report.

20. For full coverage of the actions of the Convention see www.ecusa.anglican.org/53785_ENG_HTM.htm on the Convention Web site.

21. Laurie Goodstein, *New York Times,* June 24, 2006.

22. *LA Times,* June 22, 2006, Home edition, and Jonathan Petre, *London Daily Telegraph,* June 22, 2006.

23. www.anglicancommunion.org/acns.

24. Gavin White, "Collegiality and Conciliarity," in *Authority in the Anglican Communion,* ed. Stephen Sykes (Toronto: Anglican Book Centre, 1987), 213.

25. John Booty and Stephen Sykes, eds., *The Study of Anglicanism* (London: SPCK/ Fortress Press, 1988), 46.

26. Interview in *Time Magazine,* June 7, 2007 (www.time.com/time/printout/ 0,8816,1630227,00.html).

27. Stephen Bates, *A Church at War: Anglicans and Homosexuality* (London: I. B. Tauris, 2004), 145.

28. Interview with Wim Houtman, Religion Editor of a Dutch newspaper (not identified), August 19, 2006. http://www.nd.nl/htm/dossier/seksualiteit/artikelen/060819 eb.html.

29. Rowan Williams, "The Challenge and Hope of Being an Anglican Today," June 27, 2006.

30. See his interview with John Wilkins of the *National Catholic Reporter,* "Anglican Schism?" September 14, 2007.

31. Wilkins, "Anglican Schism?"

32. Alan Cooperman, *Washington Post,* June 28, 2006.

33. Sherry Day, *St. Petersburg Times,* July 8, 2006.

34. RNS, August 21, 2006.

35. They include Peter Lee, Virginia; John Lipscomb, Southwest Florida; PB Griswold, PB elect Schori, Jack Iker of Fort Worth; Duncan of Pittsburgh; Stanton of Dallas; Salmon of South Carolina; Sisk of New York; Henderson of Upper South Carolina; and Robert O'Neill of Colorado. Secretary General of the Anglican Communion Kenneth Kearon was also present.

36. news@episcopalchurch.org, September 13, 2006.

37. Mary Frances Schjonberg, ENS, September 15, 2006.

38. Schjonberg, ENS, September 15, 2006.

39. www.globalsouthanglican.org/index.php/comments/the_road_to_lambeth_ presented_at_capa/.

40. Matthew Davies, ENS, September 22, 2006.

41. Mary Frances Schjonberg, ENS, September 22, 2006.

42. Mary Frances Schjonberg and Matthew Davies, ENS, September 13, 2006.

43. news@episcopalchurch.org, September 28, 2006.

44. ENS, news@episcopalchurch.org, November 20, 2006.

45. Mary Frances Schjonberg, ENS, December 4, 2006.

46. ENS/Anglican Communion News Service, November 30, 2006.

47. Mary Frances Schjonberg, ENS, December 17, 2006.

48. Laurie Goodstein, *New York Times,* December 17 and 18, 2006.

49. www.anglicancommunion.org/commission.

50. See www.anglicancommunion.org.

51. Mary Frances Schjonberg, ENS, December 14, 2007.

52. www.anglicancommunion.org/acns.

53. Matthew Davies, ENS, February 17, 2007

54. www.anglicancommunion.org/acns.

55. ENS, February 20, 2007.

56. ENS, February 28, 2007.

57. Laurie Goodstein, *New York Times,* February 21, 2007.

58. ENS, February 23, 2007.

59. ENS, March 4, 2007.

60. There is much more on the developed views of Radner in the section on Conservatives elsewhere in the book. For their respective presentations to the House of Bishops see www.episcopalchurch.org/3577_83906_ENG_HTM.htm and www.episcopalchurch.org/3577_83881_ENG_HTM.htm.

61. House of Bishops, March 20, 2007, www.episcopalchurch.org/3577_84148_ENG_HTM.htm.

62. Conversation with Connecticut Bishop Andrew Smith, March 26, 2007.

63. Episcopal Life Online, April 30, 2007.

64. Letter from AB Akinola to PB Schori, May 2, 2007, on Web site of the Church of Nigeria www.anglican-nig.org.

65. Letter from Archbishop Peter Akinola to Archbishop Rowan Williams, May 6, 2007.

66. Episcopal Life Online, May 22, 2007. Williams's letter can be found at www.episcopalchurch.org.

67. Diocese of New Hampshire Web site, May 22, 2007. www.nhepiscopal.org.

68. Schjonberg, ENS, May 24, 2007.

69. See the Web site of CANA on which Minns's response was first posted. www.canaconvocation.org. The story is also covered by Episcopal Life Online, May 24, 2007, by Mary Frances Schjonberg. www.episcopalchurch.org.

70. www.livingchurch.org, May 22, 2007.

71. www.dohio.org.

72. Episcopal Life Online, June 1, 2007, www.episcopalchurch.org.

73. Episcopal Life Online, June 11, 2007, www.episcopalchurch.org.

74. Episcopal Life Online, June 19, 2007, www.episcopalchurch.org.

75. Episcopal Life Online, June 19, 2007, www.episcopalchurch.org.

76. Episcopal Life Online, July 20, 2007, www.episcopalchurch.org.

77. www.Kendallharmon.net/t19, posted on September 11, 2007.

78. Episcopal Life Online, June 29, 2207, www.episcopalchurch.org.

79. Ken Howard, "Speaking the Truth—with Love," August 28, 2007, www.episcopalchurch.org.

80. RNS, August 29, 2007. The candidate was not elected.

81. Episcopal Life Online, www.episcopalchurch.org. September 14, 2007.

82. "House of Bishops response 'to questions and concerns raised by our Anglican Communion partners,'" www.episcopalchurch.org/79901_90457_ENG_print.html.

83. "Pastoral Letter from the Primates of the Anglican Communion," The Primates' Meeting, May 27, 2003. www.anglicancommunion.org/acns.

84. Episcopal Life Online, September 27, 2007. www.episcopalchurch.org/81808_90504_ENG_Print.html.

85. www.acn-us.org/archive/2007/.

86. Episcopal Life Online, September 27, 2007. www.episcopalchurch.org/79901_90517_ENG_Print.html.

87. Private communication with the author from the Reverend Canon Richard T. Nolan, October 9, 2007.

88. Common Cause was founded in 2004 to connect "Anglican bodies" that "have committed to working together for 'a Biblical, missionary and united Anglicanism in North America.'" Mary Frances Schjonberg, Episcopal Life Online, September 28, 2007. www.episcopalchurch.org/79901_90545_ENG_Print.html.

89. Episcopal Life Online, September 28, 2007. www.episcopalchurch.org/79901_90545_ENG_Print.html.

90. Episcopal Life Online, October 31, 2007. www.episcopalchurch.org/79901_91480_ENG_Print.html. Jefferts Schori had previously written a letter of warning to Bishop Schofield.

91. www.episcopalchurch.org/79901_91549_ENG_Print.html.

92. "The Report of the Joint Standing Committee to the Archbishop of Canterbury on the Response of the Episcopal Church to the Questions of the Primates articulated at their meeting in Dar Es Salaam and related Pastoral Concerns," www.aco.org.

93. Private communication with the author from the Reverend Canon Richard T. Nolan, October 9, 2007.

94. Episcopal Life Online, October 8, 2007, www.episcopalchurch.org/79901_90816_ENG_Print.html.

95. Episcopal Life Online, October 15, 2007. www.episcopalchurch.org/81808_90953_ENG_Print.html.

96. For a full explanation of these principles see the summary of both national and state jurisprudence given by the California courts as found in the Court of Appeal of California, Fourth Appellate District, Division Three, Commentary on Episcopal Church Cases before the California courts. 152 Cal. App. 4th 808; 61 Cal. Rptr. 3d 845; 2007 Cal. App. LEXIS 1041. Lexus/Nexus, as of November 28, 2007.

97. Tina Eshleman, the *Richmond Times-Dispatch,* November 13, 2007.

Chapter 7

1. The phrase is from Ephraim Radner and George R. Sumner, "Introduction," *Reclaiming Faith: Essays on Orthodoxy in the Episcopal Church and the Baltimore Declaration,* ed. Radner and Sumner (Grand Rapids: William B. Eerdmans Publishing Co., 1993), 5.

2. See Russell Reno, "At the Crossroads of Dogma," in *Reclaiming Faith: Essays on Orthodoxy in the Episcopal Church and the Baltimore Declaration,* 111–12.

3. Philip Turner, "Unity, Obedience, and the Shape of Communion," in *The Fate of Communion: The Agony of Anglicanism and the Future of a Global Church,* ed. Ephraim Radner and Philip Turner (Grand Rapids: William B. Eerdmans Publishing Co., 2006), 2.

4. Ephraim Radner, "Doctrine, Destiny, and the Figure of History," *Reclaiming our Faith,* 48.

5. Christopher R. Seitz, "Repugnance and the Three-Legged Stool: Modern Use of Scripture and the Baltimore Declaration," in *Reclaiming our Faith,* 97–98.

6. Ephraim Radner, "The Scriptural Community: Authority in Anglicanism," *The Fate of Communion,* 105–106.

7. Tal Asad, "The Idea of an Anthropology of Islam," Georgetown University Center for Contemporary Arab Studies Occasional Paper Series (Washington, DC, 1986, 17) as found in Miranda Hassett, *Anglican Communion in Crisis* (Princeton: Princeton University Press, 2007), 43.

8. Philip Turner, "The End of a Church and the Triumph of Denominationalism: On How to Think About What is Happening in the Episcopal Church," *The Fate of Communion,* 20.

9. Turner, "The End of a Church and the Triumph of Denominationalism," 22.

10. Turner, "The End of a Church and the Triumph of Denominationalism," 23.

11. Philip Turner, "The Windsor Report: A Defining Moment for a Worldwide Communion," *The Fate of Communion,* 207.

12. The quote is from a document entitled *Claiming our Anglican Identity: The Case Against the Episcopal Church, USA.* It was published by the Anglican Communion Institute in 2003 and was drafted in part by Turner and Radner, and three Anglican Primates from the Global South, Drexel Gomez, Gregory Venables, and the ubiquitous Peter Akinola.

13. Radner, "Doctrine, Destiny, and the Figure of History," *Reclaiming our Faith,* 63.

14. *Claiming our Anglican Identity,* 6.

15. *First Things,* no. 155 (August/September 2005): 68.

16. See Henry Bettenson and Chris Maunder, eds., *Documents of the Christian Church,* 3rd ed. (Oxford: Oxford University Press, 1999), 91–93.

17. Ephraim Radner, "The Humiliation of Anglicanism and Christian Life," *The Fate of Communion,* 296.

18. Radner, "Conciliarity and the American Evasion of Communion," *The Fate of Communion,* 237.

19. *Claiming our Anglican Identity,* 12.

20. Philip Turner, "Diversity and Integrity," *The Fate of Communion,* 119.

21. Radner, "Doctrine, Destiny, and the Figure of History," *Reclaiming our Faith,* 80.

22. See Hassett, *Anglican Communion in Crisis,* 38.

23. John Rodgers, quoted in Hassett, *Anglican Communion in Crisis,* 37.

24. A note on evangelical Episcopalians. Religious historian Martin Marty has observed that anything anybody can say about Evangelicalism is true. (Martin Marty, "Sightings," February 4, 2008, at sightings@listhost.uchicago.edu). This cautionary note is necessary in order to decide whether some or many Episcopal conservatives can be classified as evangelicals. How many dissident Episcopalians are evangelical in the same sense that most Southern Baptists or Bible-belt Methodists are is simply not clear.

25. Hassett, *Anglican Communion in Crisis,* 52.

26. www.episcopalian.org. Accessed May 9, 2007. The Web site has changed its name to listserv.episcopalian.org. Accessed May 9, 2007.

27. www.episcopalian.org.

28. See their Web site, www.theamia.org.

29. See their Web site, www.americananglican.org/site.

30. Also on their Web site but there called "A Place to Stand: A Call to Mission."

31. www.acn-us.org/common-cause-partners/.

32. See its Web site, www.acn-us.org.

33. See Chapter 5, section "The Connecticut Story," of this book dealing with the situation in Connecticut.

34. Task Force on Property Disputes, Memorandum to House of Bishops, April 9, 2007, www.standfirminfaith.com/media/report_to_hob_4-11-07.pdf.

35. James Tonkowich, President, "About IRD," July 30, 2007. www.theird.org.

36. See Jim Naughton, "Following the Money," A Special Report from the Washington Window, Episcopal Diocese of Washington, www.edow.org, April 2006.

37. Group Watch. Institute on Religion and Democracy. Accessed on September 20, 2007, at www.rightweb.irc-online.org/groupwatch.

38. Alan Cooperman, "Conservatives Funding Opposition, Priest Says," *Washington Post,* October 24, 2003.

Chapter 8

1. H. G. G. G. Herklots, *Frontiers of the Church: The Making of the Anglican Communion* (London: Ernest Been Ltd., 1961), 115.

2. William L. Sachs, *The Transformation of Anglicanism: From State Church to Global Communion* (Cambridge: Cambridge University Press, 1993), 168.

3. Sachs, *The Transformation of Anglicanism,* 165.

4. J. F. Ade Ajayi, *Christian Missions in Nigeria 1841–1891: The Making of a New Elite* (Evanston, IL: Northwestern University Press, 1965), 107.

5. Toyin Falola, *Culture and Customs of Nigeria* (Westport, CT: Greenwood Press, 2001), 125. It is interesting that those who practice polygamy can appeal more credibly to "traditional values" than those who practice monogamy (popular among the social elite), at least in some parts of Africa. Appeal to traditional values can cut two ways.

6. Ajayi, *Christian Missions in Nigeria 1841–1891,* 105.

7. Ajayi, *Christian Missions in Nigeria 1841–1891,* 107.

8. See "The Christian Martyrs of Uganda," at www.buganda.com/martyrs.htm. Kevin Ward supports this interpretation of the story. See Ward, "Same-Sex Relations in Africa and the Debate on Homosexuality in East African Anglicanism," *Anglican Theological Review* 84, no. 1 (Winter 2002): 89. Ward also argues that in a society in which reproduction was essential to survival, homosexuality could be seen as detrimental to that survival. That reason for opposing it would, apparently, no longer be paramount today.

9. Sachs, *The Transformation of Anglicanism,* 188.

10. See the Chapter 3: "The Bishops Assembled" for a discussion of the affair.

11. See Roger W. Bowen, "Genocide in Rwanda 1994—An Anglican Perspective," in *Genocide in Rwanda. Complicity of the Churches,* ed. Carol Rittner, John K. Roth, and Wendy Whitworth (St. Paul: Aegis / Paragon House, 2004). While Bowen focuses on Rwanda, the influence of the East African Revival was more widespread than just in that country.

12. Ward, "Same-Sex Relations in Africa and the Debate on Homosexuality in East African Anglicanism," 110. Ward points out an irony arising from the Holiness or revival movement in Africa: because it put stress on one's personal experience and learning to know who one was in the presence of God, some persons came to accept themselves as gay or lesbian. He notes the coincidence of the increasing self-identification of persons who are both gay or lesbian and evangelical.

13. John Pobee, "Take Thou Authority: An African Perspective," in *Authority in the Anglican Communion,* ed. Stephen W. Sykes (Toronto: Anglican Book Centre, 1989), 198.

14. From the Web site of the Church of the Province of Uganda, July 13, 2007, "What is Anglicanism?" by Bishop Orombi. See the Web site www.firstthings.com for a full text of Orombi's paper.

15. Simon E. Chiwanga, "Beyond the Monarch/Chief: Reconsidering the Episcopacy in Africa," in *Beyond Colonial Anglicanism: The Anglican Communion in the*

Twenty-First Century, ed. Ian T. Douglas and Kwok Pui-lan (New York: Church Publishing Inc., 2001), 298–308.

16. James Solheim, *Diversity or Disunity? Reflections on Lambeth 1998* (New York: Church Publishing, Inc., 1999), 124. Though not explicitly linking his words to a tolerance for homosexuality in the West, Chiwanga's words certainly suggest that linkage would not be inappropriate.

17. Miranda Hassett, *The Anglican Communion in Crisis* (Princeton: Princeton University Press, 2007), 85.

18. Hassett, *The Anglican Communion in Crisis,* 89.

19. Hassett, *The Anglican Communion in Crisis,* 85.

20. Hassett, *The Anglican Communion in Crisis,* 86–87. Hassett notes that the issue of homosexuality is not nearly as resonant for most African Christians as it is among the bishops. This suggests that on the tribal chief model the bishops can be seen (and perhaps see themselves) as doing for the community what it is unable, unwilling, or uneducated enough to do for itself.

21. Ward, "Same-Sex Relations in Africa and the Debate on Homosexuality in East African Anglicanism," 87. Ward is a native African priest serving in Uganda.

22. Though it should be noted that while many African bishops are united on the issue of homosexuality, there is much greater acceptance of women as priests by some bishops if not by others.

23. Mary-Jane Rubenstein, "An Anglican Crisis of Comparison: Intersections of Race, Gender, and Religious Authority, with Particular Reference to the Church of Nigeria," *Journal of the American Academy of Religion* 72, no. 2 (June 2004): 341–65.

24. I owe this information to my colleague Dr. Abosede George, a Nigerian, and a member of the Department of History at Trinity College.

25. Rubenstein, "An Anglican Crisis of Comparison," 354.

26. Rubenstein, "An Anglican Crisis of Comparison," 360.

27. Elechi Amadi, *Ethics in Nigerian Culture* (Ibadan, Nigeria: Heinemann Educational Books, 1982), 73, 75.

28. Falola, *Culture and Customs of Nigeria,* 120. Ward argues, however, that in the Anglican Church of Uganda there are fewer Christian marriages today and that the churches there "have failed to convince most of their members that the ideal of Christian marriage as a life-long monogamous union is either practical or paramount." (Ward, "Same-Sex Relations in Africa and the Debate on Homosexuality in East African Anglicanism," 101, 103.) It is possible that the insistence on the Biblical "ideal" is driven by a concern over shoring up marriage and not primarily by an opposition to homosexuality, which becomes, in effect, a surrogate target for a losing battle over the issue of marriage.

29. John Howe, *Anglicanism and the Universal Church* (Toronto: Anglican Book Centre, 1990), 46.

30. John Pobee, "Newer Dioceses of the Anglican Communion—Movement and Prospect," in *The Study of Anglicanism,* ed. Stephen W. Sykes and John Booty (London: SPCK/Fortress Press, 1988), 393ff.

31. Pobee, "Newer Dioceses of the Anglican Communion—Movement and Prospect," in *The Study of Anglicanism,* ed. Sykes and Booty, 399–400.

32. Njongonkulu Ndungane, "Scripture: What Is at Issue in Anglicanism Today?" in *Beyond Colonial Anglicanism: The Anglican Communion in the Twenty-First Century,* ed. Ian T. Douglas and Kwok Pui-lan (New York: Church Publishing Inc., 2001), 237.

33. Ndungane, "Scripture: What Is at Issue in Anglicanism Today?" 239–40.

34. James Solheim, *Diversity or Disunity? Reflections on Lambeth 1998,* 144.

35. Roger W. Bowen, "Genocide in Rwanda 1994—An Anglican Perspective," in *Genocide in Rwanda. Complicity of the Churches,* ed. Carol Rittner, John K. Roth, and Wendy Whitworth (St. Paul: Aegis / Paragon House, 2004), 40.

36. Bowen, "Genocide in Rwanda 1994—An Anglican Perspective."

37. Timothy Longman, "Christian Churches and Genocide in Rwanda," paper originally prepared for Conference on Genocide, Religion, and Modernity for the United States Holocaust Memorial Museum, May 11–13, 1997. It can be accessed at http://faculty.vassar.edu/tilongma/Church&Genocide.html.

38. Cited from a new story by Marc Lacey of the *New York Times,* November 3, 2003.

39. Matthews A. Ojo, "The Anglican Crackup: The View from Lagos," *Religion in the News, 6,* no. 3 (Fall 2003), 2.

40. Editorial, *New York Times,* March 8, 2007.

41. See a remarkable and revealing interview with Akinola by Ruth Gledhill, "For God's Sake," *London Times* online. www.timesonline.co.uk.

42. RNS story by Robert Nowell, "Anglicans in Nigeria Delete References to Archbishop of Canterbury" (n.d.).

43. The interview was published under the title "Homosexual Priests: Nigerian Anglicans Will Not Succumb to Pressure from the West, Says Akinola," in *The Guardian* (Nigeria) newspaper on July 30, 2007. The reporter with whom Akinola spoke was Dickson Adeyanju. www.guardiannewsngr.com/ibru_center/article01/290707.

44. Mary-Jane Rubenstein, "Anglicans in the Postcolony: On Sex and the Limits of Communion" (unpublished paper).

45. Frederick Quinn, "Mirage in the Desert: The Myth of the 'Global South,' " Episcopal Life Online, October 26, 2007. www.episcopalchurch.org/80050_91337_ENG_Print.html.

46. Quinn, "Mirage in the Desert," Episcopal Life Online. www.episcopalchurch.org /80050_91337_ENG_Print.html.

47. From a conversation with Douglas on November 26, 2007.

48. Story by Trevor Gundy, August 28, 2007, found in Episcopal Life Online http://www.episcopalchurch.org. A follow-up story two weeks later from a synod held in the Province of Central Africa reported that Mwamba had been fired by the Archbishop of Central Africa, Bernard Malango. This report was later denied though Mwamba will step down from his position. The synod is also reported to have reaffirmed its previous position of "no" to homosexuality (though it encouraged the process of listening). See Episcopal Life Online, September 13, 2007. http://www.episcopalchurch.org.

49. African Archbishops respond to New Orleans (CAPA Primates Communiqué), October 2007. www.globalsouthanglican.org/index.php/comments/capa_primates_meeting_in_mauritius_october_2007/.

50. Jan Nunley, Episcopal Life Online, October 23, 2007, reporting on a letter Archbishop Williams sent to Bishop John Howe of Central Florida on October 14.

Chapter 9

1. John Henry Hopkins, *Bible View of Slavery* (New York: Society for the Diffusion of Political Knowledge, no. 8, 117–32), quoted in Robert Bruce Mullin, *Episcopal Vision / American Reality* (New Haven: Yale University Press, 1986), 207.

2. Hopkins, "Bible View of Slavery," in Mullin, *Episcopal Vision / American Reality,* 207.

3. Mullin, *Episcopal Vision / American Reality,* 125.

4. Mullin, *Episcopal Vision / American Reality,* 200.

5. The quotation is from Jefferson Davis, *The Rise and Fall of the Confederate Government,* in *Journals of the Protestant Episcopal Church in the Confederate States of America,* ed. William A. Clebsch (Austin: The Church Historical Society, 1962), vii.

6. Raymond W. Albright, *A History of the Protestant Episcopal Church* (New York: Macmillan, 1964), 254.

7. See Mullin, *Episcopal Vision / American Reality,* 127.

8. Mullin, *Episcopal Vision / American Reality,* 128–29.

9. Mullin, *Episcopal Vision / American Reality,* 140.

10. Thornton Stringfellow, "A Brief Examination of Scripture Testimony on the Institution of Slavery," in *The Ideology of Slavery: Proslavery Thought in the Antebellum South, 1830–1860,* ed. Drew Gilpin Faust (Baton Rouge: Louisiana State University Press, 1981), 136–167, especially 139.

11. Quoted in Elizabeth Fox-Genovese and Eugene D. Genovese, *The Mind of the Master Class: History and Faith in the Southern Slaveholders' Worldview* (Cambridge: Cambridge University Press, 2005), 502.

12. Quoted in Fox-Genovese and Genovese, *The Mind of the Master Class,* 473.

13. Quoted in Fox-Genovese and Genovese, *The Mind of the Master Class,* 498.

14. Stringfellow, "A Brief Examination of Scripture Testimony on the Institution of Slavery," 153.

15. Stringfellow, "A Brief Examination of Scripture Testimony on the Institution of Slavery," 166.

16. James Henley Thornwell, "The Rights and Duties of Masters, a Sermon Preached at the Dedication of a Church, erected in Charleston, S.C. for the Benefit and Instruction of the Coloured Population. (Charleston, S.C., 1850)," in *Issues in American Protestantism,* ed. Robert L. Ferm (Garden City, NY: Anchor Books Doubleday & Co., Inc., 1969), 189–99, especially 189.

17. Samuel Seabury, *American Slavery, Distinguished from the Slavery of English Theorists, and Justified by the Law of Nature* (New York: Mason Brothers, 1961).

18. Fox-Genovese and Genovese, *The Mind of the Master Class,* 29.

19. Fox-Genovese and Genovese, *The Mind of the Master Class,* 368.

20. Fox-Genovese and Genovese, *The Mind of the Master Class,* 109.

21. Seabury, *American Slavery, Distinguished from the Slavery of English Theorists, and Justified by the Law of Nature,* iv.

22. Seabury, *American Slavery, Distinguished from the Slavery of English Theorists, and Justified by the Law of Nature,* 161–62.

23. Seabury, *American Slavery, Distinguished from the Slavery of English Theorists, and Justified by the Law of Nature,* 85.

24. Fox-Genovese and Genovese, *The Mind of the Master Class,* 616.

25. Donald Scott, *From Office to Profession: The New England Ministry 1750–1850* (Philadelphia: University of Pennsylvania Press, 1978), 86.

26. Angelina Grimke, *An Appeal to the Christian Women of the South* (Shrewsbury, NJ: n.p., 1836), 3. For a full treatment of the Grimke sisters see Frank G. Kirkpatrick, "From Shackles to Liberation: Religion, the Grimke Sisters and Dissent," in *Women,*

Religion, and Social Change, ed. Yvonne Yazbeck Haddad and Ellison Banks Findly (Albany: State University of New York Press, 1985), 433–55.

27. Sarah Grimke, *An Epistle to the Clergy of the Southern States* (New York: n.p., 1836), 12.

28. The citation is from James Essig, *The Bonds of Wickedness: American Evangelicals Against Slavery 1770–1808* (Philadelphia: Temple University Press, 1982), 77.

29. The quotation is from evangelical preacher David Rice as found in Essig, *The Bonds of Wickedness,* 55.

30. Essig, *The Bonds of Wickedness,* 65.

31. Essig, *The Bonds of Wickedness,* 86.

Chapter 10

1. Raymond E. Brown, *The Critical Meaning of the Bible* (New York: Paulist Press, 1981), 17.

2. Brown, *The Critical Meaning of the Bible,* 18.

3. Walter Wink, "Biblical Perspectives on Homosexuality," *The Christian Century,* November 7, 1979, 1082.

4. L. William Countryman, *Dirt, Greed, and Sex* (Philadelphia: Fortress Press, 1988), 23.

5. Jerome T. Walsh, "Leviticus 18:22 and 20:13: Who is Doing What to Whom?" *Journal of Biblical Literature,* 120, no. 2 (2001): 204. Walsh also argues that the laws in Leviticus apply only to one particular kind of homosexual action: male anal intercourse, and not to male-male sexual contact in general (201).

6. Thomas Aquinas, according to John Boswell, compared homosexual acts with disgusting acts such as bestiality and eating dirt. John Boswell, *Christianity, Social Tolerance, and Homosexuality* (Chicago: University of Chicago Press, 1980), 329. Aquinas also believed that women were "defective" men, so some of his views on sexuality have already been either rejected or greatly compromised by contemporary conservatives.

7. Robert A. J. Gagnon, "Does the Bible Regard Same-Sex Intercourse as Intrinsically Sinful?" Available at http://www.robgagnon.net/ChristianSexualityArticle.htm and completed on July 19, 2003, p. 2, footnote 2.

8. Gagnon, "Does the Bible Regard Same-Sex Intercourse as Intrinsically Sinful?" 6. It is not clear what constitutes a "policy" in Gagnon's argument and whether the "policy" of communistic sharing of all goods in the earliest Christian churches ought not, in his opinion, to admit of exceptions in today's free-market economies.

9. Gagnon, "Does the Bible Regard Same-Sex Intercourse as Intrinsically Sinful?" 24–25.

10. Gagnon, "Does the Bible Regard Same-Sex Intercourse as Intrinsically Sinful?" 27.

11. Gagnon, "Does the Bible Regard Same-Sex Intercourse as Intrinsically Sinful?" 28.

12. Kenneth E. North, "Holy Matrimony, Divorce, and Remarriage," Canon Law Institute, www.canonlaw.org/article_matrimony.htm.

13. See Robin Scroggs, *The New Testament and Homosexuality* (Philadelphia: Fortress Press, 1984), 106–108.

14. Richard B. Hays, "Awaiting the Redemption of our Bodies: The Witness of Scripture Concerning Homosexuality," in *Homosexuality in the Church: Both Sides of the Debate,* ed. Jeffrey S. Siker (Louisville: Westminster John Knox Press, 1994), 7.

15. Scroggs, *The New Testament and Homosexuality,* 106–107.

16. Hays, "Awaiting the Redemption of our Bodies," 8.

17. Hays, "Awaiting the Redemption of our Bodies," 9.

18. Hays, "Awaiting the Redemption of our Bodies," 13.

19. Gareth Moore, "Sex, Sexuality, and Relationships," in *Christian Ethics: An Introduction,* ed. Bernard Hoose (London: Cassell, 1998), 224.

20. Walter Wink, "Biblical Perspectives on Homosexuality," *The Christian Century,* November 7, 1979, 1085.

21. Victor Paul Furnish, "The Bible and Homosexuality: Reading the Texts in Context," *Homosexuality in the Church: Both Sides of the Debate,* ed. Jeffrey S. Siker (Louisville: Westminster John Knox Press, 1994), 29.

22. Cardinal Joseph Ratzinger, "Letter to the Bishops of the Catholic Church on the Pastoral Care of Homosexual Persons (1986)," in *Homosexuality in the Church: Both Sides of the Debate,* ed. Jeffrey S. Siker (Louisville: Westminster John Knox Press, 1994), 39.

23. Ratzinger, "The Pastoral Care of Homosexual Persons," 40.

24. Ratzinger, "The Pastoral Care of Homosexual Persons," 42.

25. Ratzinger, "The Pastoral Care of Homosexual Persons," 40–41.

26. "The Vatican Declaration on Sexual Ethics," in *Religion for a New Generation,* ed. Jacob Needleman, A. K. Bierman, and James A. Gould, 2nd ed. (New York: Macmillan Co., 1977), 295.

27. "The Vatican Declaration on Sexual Ethics," 294.

Conclusion

1. It can be found on the Web at www.standfirminfaith.com/index.php/site/article/5918/.

2. See especially Chapters 5 and 6 for references to the proposed Covenant.

3. Conversation with Professor Douglas, November 26, 2007.

4. See Augustine, *De Doctrina Christiana* (1.84–85 [XXXV–XXXVI]).

5. Conversation with Professor Douglas, November 26, 2007.

6. See Bob Altemeyer and Bruce Hunsberger, "Authoritarianism, Religious Fundamentalism, Quest, and Prejudice," Research Report, *The International Journal for the Psychology of Religion* 2, no. 2 (1992): 113–22. I am indebted to James W. Jones for suggesting these sources to me.

7. To avoid linguistic confusion, I use the word "progressive" rather than "liberal" in this context because liberalism is often associated with granting individual choice the highest possible moral value.

8. For a further development of the notion of community in a Christian context, see Frank G. Kirkpatrick, *The Ethics of Community* (Oxford: Blackwell Publishers Ltd., 2001), and *Together Bound: God, History and the Religious Community* (New York: Oxford University Press, 1994).

9. Some would argue that experience is implicit in the "reason" leg as articulated by Richard Hooker. Reason grasps the laws by which God structures the world as well as

when our experience in the particular contexts in which we live in the world ought to be in conformity with those laws. Reason adapted to those experiential contexts confirms experience, and experience is "rational" when it is in harmony with divine law as grasped by reason.

10. Adele Banks, "Study: Young People See Christians as Judgmental, Anti-Gay," RNS, October 9, 2007.

Bibliography

Alexander, J. Neil. *This Far by Grace: A Bishop's Journey Through Questions of Homosexuality*. Cambridge: Cowley, 2003.

Allbright, Raymond W. *A History of the Protestant Episcopal Church*. New York: Macmillan Co., 1964.

Anglican Communion Institute. *Communion and Discipline: A Submission to the Lambeth Commission by the Anglican Communion Institute*. Colorado Springs: The Anglican Communion Institute, 2004.

Anglican Consultative Council. *For the Sake of the Kingdom*. London: Anglican Consultative Council, 1986.

Anglican Consultative Council. *Inter-Anglican Theological and Doctrinal Commission: Belonging Together*. London: Anglican Consultative Council, 1993.

Anglican Consultative Council. *The Virginia Report: The Report of the Inter-Anglican Theological and Doctrinal Commission*. London: Anglican Consultative Council, 1997.

Avis, Paul, ed. *Seeking the Truth of Change in the Church: Reception, Communion and the Ordination of Women*. London: T&T Clark International, 2004.

Bates, Stephen. *A Church at War: Anglicans and Homosexuality*. London: I. B. Tauris, 2004.

Bennett, Joyce M. *Hasten Slowly: The First Legal Ordination of Women Priests*. London: Little London Associates Publishing, 1991.

Booty, John. *The Episcopal Church in Crisis*. Cambridge: Cowley Publications, 1988.

Boswell, John. *Christianity, Social Tolerance, and Homosexuality*. Chicago: University of Chicago Press, 1980.

Brown, Raymond E. *The Critical Meaning of the Bible*. New York: Paulist Press, 1981.

Brown, Terry. *Other Voices, Other Worlds: The Global Church Speaks Out on Homosexuality*. New York: Church Publishing, 2006.

Carnley, Peter. "Review of the Work of the Archbishop of Canterbury's Panel of Reference." May 2007. Retrieved May 8, 2007, from www.episcopalchurch.org.

Clebsch, William, ed. *Journals of the Protestant Episcopal Church in the Confederate States of America.* Austin: The Church Historical Society, 1962.

Countryman, L. William. *Dirt, Greed, and Sex.* Philadelphia: Fortress Press, 1988.

Decision of the Title IV Review Committee of the Protestant Episcopal Church in the United States of America, in the matter of the Verified Charges against the Right Reverend Andrew D. Smith, Bishop of the Diocese of Connecticut, April 11, 2007.

Douglas, Ian. *Beyond Colonial Anglicanism: The Anglican Communion in the Twenty-First Century.* New York: Church Publishing, 2001.

Douglas, Ian, and Paul Zahl. *Understanding the Windsor Report.* New York: Church Publishing, 2005.

Dowell, Susan, and Jane Williams. *Bread, Wine and Women.* London: Virago Press, 1994.

Emerson, Michael O. *Divided by Faith: Evangelical Religion and the Problem of Race in America.* New York: Oxford University Press, 2000.

Essig, James. *The Bonds of Wickedness: American Evangelicals Against Slavery 1770–1808.* Philadelphia: Temple University Press, 1982.

Faust, Drew Gilpin. *The Ideology of Slavery: Proslavery Thought in the Antebellum South, 1830–1860.* Baton Rouge: Louisiana State University Press, 1981.

Fox-Genovese, Elizabeth Fox, and Eugene D. Genovese. *The Mind of the Master Class History and Faith in the Southern Slaveholders' Worldview.* New York: Cambridge University Press, 2005.

Furnish, Victor Paul. "The Bible and Homosexuality: Reading the Texts in Context." In *Homosexuality in the Church,* edited by Jeffrey Siker. Louisville: Westminster John Knox, 1994.

Gagnon, Robert A. J. "Does the Bible Regard Same-Sex Intercourse as Intrinsically Sinful? An Evaluation of Mark Powell's Essay in *Faithful Conversation* (Sections I–III). (On author's Web site: www.robgagnon.net).

Gagnon, Robert A. J. "Review Essay" on *Faithful Conversations: Christian Perspectives on Homosexuality,* edited by James M. Childs, Jr. (Minneapolis: Fortress Press, 2003). (On author's Web site: www.robgagnon.net/ChristianSexualityArticle.htm.)

Gomez, Drexel, and Maurice Sinclair. *To Mend the Net: Anglican Faith and Order in a Renewed Mission.* Carrollton, TX: Ekklesia Society, 2001.

Grimke, Angelina. *An Appeal to the Christian Women of the South.* New York: New York Antislavery Society, 1836.

Grimke, Sarah. *An Epistle to the Clergy of the Southern States.* New York: n.p., 1836.

Harris, Barbara, Suzanne R. Hiatt, Rose Wu, and Mabel Katahweire. *Women's Ordination in the Episcopal Church: Twenty-Five Years Later.* EDS Occasional Papers. Cambridge, MA: Episcopal Divinity School, 2000.

Harris, Mark. *The Challenge of Change: The Anglican Communion in the Post-Modern Era.* New York: Church Publishing, 1998.

Hassett, Miranda K. *Anglican Communion in Crisis: How Episcopal Dissidents and Their African Allies are Reshaping Anglicanism.* Princeton: Princeton University Press, 2007.

Hays, Richard B. "Awaiting the Redemption of Our Bodies: The Witness of Scripture Concerning Homosexuality." In *Homosexuality in the Church: Both Sides of the Debate,* edited by Jeffrey Siker. Louisville: Westminster John Knox, 1994.

Hein, David, and Gardiner H. Shattuck Jr. *The Episcopalians.* Westport: Praeger, 2004.

Herklots, H. G. G. *Frontiers of the Church: The Making of the Anglican Communion.* London: Ernest Benn Ltd., 1961.

Hoose, Bernard, ed. *Christian Ethics: An Introduction*. London: Cassell, 1998.

House of Bishops of the General Synod of the Church of England. *Issues in Human Sexuality*. Harrisburg: Morehouse Publishing, 1991.

Howe, John. *Anglicanism and the Universal Church: Highways and Hedges 1958–1984*. Toronto: Anglican Book Centre, 1990.

Ingham, Michael. "Reclaiming Christian Orthodoxy." Retrieved October 25, 2003, from www.anglicancommunion.org/acns (ANS 10/30/03).

Kave, Bruce. *Reinventing Anglicanism: A Vision of Confidence, Community and Engagement in Anglican Christianity*. New York: Church Publishing, 2004.

Kirkpatrick, Frank. "From Shackles to Liberation: Religion, the Grimke Sisters and Dissent." In *Women, Religion, and Social Change*, edited by Yvonne Yazbeck Haddad and Ellison Banks Findly. Albany: State University of New York, 1985, 433–455.

Kirkpatrick, Frank. "Samuel Seabury: Virtue and Christian Community in Late Eighteenth Century America." *Anglican Theological Review* LXXIV, no. 3 (Summer 1992): 317–333.

Kirkpatrick, Frank. *Together Bound: God, History, and the Religious Community*. New York: Oxford University Press, 1994.

Kirkpatrick, Frank. *The Ethics of Community*. Oxford: Blackwell Publishers Ltd., 2001.

Kirkpatrick, Frank. "The Anglican Crackup." *Religion in the News* 6, no. 3 (Fall 2003).

Kirkpatrick, Frank. "Maybe the Center Holds After All." *Religion in the News* 9, no. 2 (Fall 2006).

Konolige, Kit and Frederica. *The Power of Their Glory: America's Ruling Class: The Episcopalians*. New York: Wyden Books, 1978.

Lambeth Commission on Communion. *The Windsor Report*. London: Anglican Communion Office, 2004.

Lambeth Conference 1948: The Encyclical Letter from the Bishops; together with Resolutions and Reports. London: SPCK, 1948.

Lewis, Harold T. *Yet with a Steady Beat: The African American Struggle for Recognition in the Episcopal Church*. Valley Forge: Trinity Press International, 1996.

Linzey, Andrew, and Richard Corker. *Gays and the Future of Anglicanism*. Ropley, U.K.: O Books, John Hunt Publishing, 2005.

Locke, David. *The Episcopal Church (Hippocrene Great Religions of the World)*. New York: Hippocrene Books, 1991.

Loveland, Clara O. *The Critical Years: The Reconstitution of the Anglican Church in the United States of America: 1780–1789*. Greenwich: Seabury Press, 1956.

MacMullen, Ramsay. *Voting About God in Early Church Councils*. New Haven: Yale University Press, 2006.

Malherbe, Abraham J. *Social Aspects of Early Christianity*. Baton Rouge: Louisiana State University Press, 1977.

Manross, William Wilson. *A History of the American Episcopal Church*. New York: Morehouse Publishing Co., 1935.

Marrett, Michael McFarlene. *The Lambeth Conferences and Women Priests: The Historical Background of the Conferences and Their Impact on the Episcopal Church in America*. Smithtown, NY: Exposition Press, 1981.

Marshall, Paul Victor. *One, Catholic, and Apostolic*. New York: Church Publishing, 2004.

Marx, Herbert L., ed. *Religions in America*. New York: H. W. Wilson Co., 1977.

McGeary, Laura, John Martin, and James Rosenthal, eds. *A Transforming Vision: Suffering and Glory in God's World*. London: Church House Publications, 1993.

Moore, Gareth. "Sex, Sexuality, and Relationships." In *Christian Ethics: An Introduction,* edited by Bernard Hoose. London: Cassell, 1998.

Mullin, Robert Bruce. *Episcopal Vision/American Reality.* New Haven: Yale University Press, 1986.

Neill, Stephen. *Anglicanism.* Baltimore: Penguin Books, 1960.

North, Kenneth E. "Holy Matrimony, Divorce, and Remarriage." Canon Law Institute. www.canonlaw.org/article_matrimony.htm (n.d.).

O'Donovan, Oliver, et al. "The Current Crisis in the Anglican Communion—What are the Ecclesiological Issues Involved?" www.anglicancommunion.org.

Prichard, Robert W. *A History of the Episcopal Church.* Harrisburg: Morehouse Publishing, 1991.

Primates of the Anglican Communion and the Anglican Consultative Council. *A Transforming Vision: Suffering and Glory in God's World: Cape Town 1993.* London: Church House Publishing, 1993.

Protestant Episcopal Church in the United States of America. "In the Court for the Trial of a Bishop: Stanton et al. vs. Righter." May 15, 1996. Available at www.andromeda. rutgers.edu/~lcrew.

Radner, Ephraim, and George R. Sumner. *Reclaiming Faith: Essays on Orthodoxy in the Episcopal Church and the Baltimore Declaration.* Grand Rapids: Wm. B. Eerdmans, 1993.

Radner, Ephraim, and Philip Turner. *The Fate of Communion: The Agony of Anglicanism and the Future of a Global Church.* Grand Rapids: Wm. B. Eerdmans, 2007.

Ratzinger, Cardinal Joseph. "Letter to the Bishops of the Catholic Church on The Pastoral Care of Homosexual Persons." In *Homosexuality in the Church,* edited by Jeffrey Siker. Louisville: Westminster John Knox, 1994.

Rubenstein, Mary-Jane. "An Anglican Crisis of Comparison: Intersections of Race, Gender, and Religious Authority, with Particular Reference to the Church of Nigeria." *Journal of the American Academy of Religion* 72, no. 2 (June 2004): 341–365.

Rubenstein, Mary-Jane. "Anglicans in the Postcolony: On Sex and the Limits of Communion." Unpublished paper. October 2007.

Sachs, William. *The Transformation of Anglicanism from State Church to Global Communion.* Cambridge: Cambridge University Press, 1993.

Scroggs, Robin. *The New Testament and Homosexuality.* Philadelphia: Fortress Press, 1983.

Seabury, Samuel. *American Slavery, Distinguished from the Slavery of English Theorists, and Justified by the Law of Nature.* New York: Mason Brothers, 1961.

Scott, Donald. *From Office to Profession: The New England Ministry 1750–1850.* Philadelphia: University of Pennsylvania Press, 1978.

Seitz, Christopher. "Biblical Authority in the Late Twentieth Century: The Baltimore Declaration, Scripture-Reason-Tradition and the Canonical Approach." In *Word Without End: the Old Testament as Abiding Theological Witness.* Grand Rapids: Eerdmans, 1998.

Shattuck, Gardiner H. *Episcopalians and Race: Civil War to Civil Rights.* Lexington: University Press of Kentucky, 2000.

Siker, Jeffrey, ed. *Homosexuality in the Church.* Louisville: Westminster John Knox, 1994.

Smith, H. Shelton. *In His Image, But . . .* Durham, NC: Duke University Press, 1972.

Stringfellow, Thornton. "A Brief Examination of Scripture Testimony on the Institution of Slavery." In *The Ideology of Slavery: Proslavery Thought in the Antebellum South, 1830–1860,* edited by Drew Gilpin Faust. Baton Rouge: Louisiana State University Press, 1981, 136–167.

Sumner, David E. *The Episcopal Church's History 1945–1985.* Wilton, CT: Morehouse-Barlow, 1987.

Sykes, Stephen W. *Authority in the Anglican Communion.* Toronto: Anglican Book Centre, 1987.

Sykes, Stephen, and John Booty, eds. *The Study of Anglicanism.* Minneapolis, MN: Fortress Press, 1988.

Taylor, J. Glen. "Homosexuality: Before and Beyond the Soundbytes," "The Bible and Homosexuality," "Blessing Same-Sex Unions?" Three brochures issued by Professor Taylor of Wycliffe College, University of Toronto (n.d.).

Temple, Gray. *Gay Unions in the Light of Scripture, Tradition and Reason.* New York: Church Publishing, 2004.

Thornwell, James Henley. "The Rights and Duties of Masters, a Sermon Preached at the Dedication of a Church, erected in Charleston, S.C. for the Benefit and Instruction of the Coloured Population. (Charleston, S.C., 1850)." In *Issues in American Protestantism,* edited by Robert L. Ferm. Garden City, NY: Anchor Books Doubleday & Co., Inc., 1969.

"The Vatican Declaration on Sexual Ethics." In *Religion for a New Generation,* edited by Jacob Needleman, A. K. Bierman, and James A. Gould, 2nd ed. New York: Macmillan Co., 1977.

Walls, Andrew. *The Cross-cultural Process in Christian History: Studies in the Transmission and Appropriation of Faith.* Maryknoll, NY: Orbis Books, 2002.

Walsh, Jerome. "Leviticus 18:22 and 20:13: Who is Doing What To Whom?" *Journal of Biblical Literature* 120, no. 2 (2001).

Will, George. "Anglicans' Undoing." *Washington Post,* October 15, 2003.

Williams, Rowan. *The Truce of God.* Grand Rapids: Eerdmans, 2005.

Windsor Report 2004: Lambeth Commission on Communion. Anglican Communion Office.

Wink, Walter. "Biblical Perspectives on Homosexuality." *The Christian Century,* November 7, 1979.

Wood, Forrest G. *The Arrogance of Faith: Christianity and Race in America From the Colonial Era to the Twentieth Century.* New York: A. A. Knopf, 1990.

Wright, J. Robert, ed. *Quadrilateral at One Hundred: Essays on the Centenary of the Chicago-Lambeth Quadrilateral 1886/88–1986/88.* Cincinnati: Forward Movement, 1988.

Index

About the Author

FRANK G. KIRKPATRICK is Ellsworth Morton Tracy Lecturer and Professor of Religion, Trinity College. He has published five books, *Community: A Trinity of Models; Together Bound: God, History, and the Religious Community; The Ethics of Community; A Moral Ontology for a Theistic Ethic: Gathering the Nations in Love and Justice;* and *John Macmurray: Community Beyond Political Philosophy.* He has also published a general textbook in the field of ethics, *Living Issues in Ethics* with Richard Nolan, numerous articles in scholarly journals as well as op-ed pieces, and topical analyses of current religious events.